# PUBLIC MORALITY, CIVIC VIRTUE, AND THE PROBLEM OF MODERN LIBERALISM

# Public Morality, Civic Virtue, and the Problem of Modern Liberalism

*Edited by*

T. William Boxx
*and*
Gary M. Quinlivan

**WILLIAM B. EERDMANS PUBLISHING COMPANY**
**GRAND RAPIDS, MICHIGAN / CAMBRIDGE, U.K.**

© 2000 Wm. B. Eerdmans Publishing Co.
255 Jefferson Ave. S.E., Grand Rapids, Michigan 49503 /
P.O. Box 163, Cambridge CB3 9PU U.K.

Printed in the United States of America

05 04 03 02 01 00      7 6 5 4 3 2 1


**Library of Congress Cataloging-in-Publication Data**

Public morality, civic virtue, and the problem of modern liberalism /
edited by T. William Boxx and Gary Quinlivan.
     p.   cm.
  Includes index.
  ISBN 0-8028-4754-4 (pbk. : alk. paper)
  1. Liberalism — Moral and ethical aspects. 2. Civil society.
I. Boxx, T. William, 1953-
II. Quinlivan, Gary M., 1952-

JC574 .P83 2000
301 — dc21
                                   99-088895

Dedicated to

Winnie Palmer

*Mulieri bonae ac sapienti*

# Contents

CONTENTS

# Acknowledgments

This collection of essays, except for one essay, is based on papers presented at a conference on "Public Morality, Civic Virtue, and the Problem of Modern Liberalism" held at Saint Vincent College on April 15 – 17, 1999. The one other essay was a paper presented at the annual Civitas Forum on Principles and Policies for Public Life held at Saint Vincent College on October 21, 1998 and previously published by the editors in *Foundations of American Civilization*. These conferences were sponsored by the College's Center for Economic and Policy Education. Since its founding in 1991, the Center has examined not only economic issues but the moral-cultural and political aspects of contemporary society.

There are many individuals and organizations that made this book possible to whom we owe our appreciation. We especially thank members of the Center's staff including Rosey Doelling, program coordinator, for handling all the activities necessary for a conference attended by close to 1,000 people, and Andrew Herr, fellow in economics and policy, for helping with various facets of the conference. We also thank the administration of Saint Vincent College for its support and appreciate the efforts of several members of its staff: Rev. Martin R. Bartel, O.S.B., president, for his welcoming message that initiated the conference; Don Orlando, Saint Vincent College's director of public relations, for handling the conference advertisements; Br. Norman Hipps, O.S.B., provost, for his time and advice; and Barbara Edwards, academic dean, for her general support. In addition, we wish to thank Fr. Thomas Devereux, O.S.B., director of special events; and Joseph F. Reilly, director of Saint Vincent Theatre and instructor of film, for technical assistance with the Walter

# ACKNOWLEDGMENTS

Berns lecture. We offer a special thank you to Ronald J. Pestritto, assistant professor of political science at the University of Dallas, formerly of Saint Vincent College, for moderating the conference sessions. Our gratitude is also extended to the following Saint Vincent College students who volunteered their time and efforts to ensure the success of the conference: Ryan Beiser, Jaime Crawford, Cecilia Dickson, Brian Dodson, Pete Evans, Bill Helzlsouer, Tomas Kersis, Richard Kessler, Tony Kovalchick, Robert McBride, Jennifer Miele, Siddhartha Namasivayam, Troy Ovitsky, Joseph Polka, Nicholas Racculia, Amy Rustic, and Karen Simmons.

We thank our indexer, Sandra S. Quinlivan, M.A., and Richard Kessler, the Center's summer 1999 intern for his computer expertise and the formatting of this book. We thank the contributors to our book for their conscientious work and good will. Any errors remaining are, of course, the fault of the editors. In addition, we offer a special thanks to our reviewers for their comments on the back cover of this book: William A. Galston, Director, Institute for Philosophy and Public Policy, University of Maryland; Robert P. George, McCormick Professor of Jurisprudence, Princeton University; Gertrude Himmelfarb, Professor Emerita of History, Graduate School of the City University of New York; and Harvey C. Mansfield, Professor of Government, Harvard University. Our appreciation is also extended to our publisher, William B. Eerdmans, Jr.

We are grateful to the following donors that made the conference and this book possible: Aequus Institute, Earhart Foundation, Intercollegiate Studies Institute, Inc., the JM Foundation, Massey Charitable Trust, and Philip M. McKenna Foundation.

Finally, we give thanks for Saint Benedict and the heritage of Benedictine education which preserved classical learning and culture and helped lay the foundations of Western civilization.

# Preface

This book is a reflection upon the fundamental principles, institutions, and norms of American and Western society in light of the growing apprehension about moral decline, civic strife, and basic incivility. In recent years these concerns have prompted increasing questions about the philosophical foundations of America's political and social order and, more pointedly, liberalism's culpability for these circumstances. In particular, how is the virtue and moral character upon which our liberal democratic society depends and which seems in short supply, to be rejuvenated and sustained?

The term "liberalism" refers to the principles and conditions of the free society as distinct from the more narrow, although not unrelated, politics of contemporary American life in which those known as "liberals" compete with their "conservative" opponents. Liberalism is the paradigmatic political philosophy of the West, a philosophy based on human freedom and equality and the natural rights of individuals that government exists to protect. The American founders drew upon these philosophical principles in declaring their independence from Britain and establishing our constitutional order.

But the liberal tradition does not encompass all of America's social heritage. There is an older tradition, one which particularly characterized America's origins and historical development — and that is religion or what is often referred to as the Judeo-Christian tradition. Biblical religion and church-based social life contributed profoundly to the moral character and vitality of American society and, indeed, played no inconsiderable role in shaping the political life of the developing country. Historically, the

American government, although a liberal constitutional order, encouraged general religion and moral education while avoiding sectarian and doctrinal entanglements, thus presupposing the necessity of moral-cultural tradition.

The relationship between virtue and politics in liberal philosophy is a strained one. Liberalism seeks to give maximum freedom to individuals to live their lives as they see fit without undue interference by either government or other institutions of society. Yet, it is observed, liberalism needs character- or virtue-forming influences that by definition require some level of social authority over individual conduct to be effective. Thus, it would seem to many that a liberal political order needs to somehow find peace with social institutions and practices based on belief and moral tradition without abandoning its principles of freedom and equality of all individuals. That conundrum is at the heart of the most contentious political and social disagreements of our times; and the particular issues involved will not be resolved without an accommodation at the philosophical level — that is, between liberty and moral-cultural tradition.

The free society was a great advance in human affairs allowing for the kind of human flourishing not seen before. But freedom is only meaningful within a context of personal and civic responsibility and social order. Without virtue, freedom becomes license and self interest narrowly defined, so that a generally-held sense of the common good and civic unity is lost, and in the long run, self-government itself becomes tenuous. Thus we are led to ask, how can liberal political philosophy be shown to revitalize virtue and order, or should we look to the moral-cultural tradition or both; and how are these distinct but overlapping spheres of society to relate?

We enter a new American century with many questions, perhaps, it must be admitted, not all of which will be resolvable. We will no doubt have to continue to live with a degree of ambiguity as the price of human freedom. But it might be hoped that reasonable people of good will can more readily agree that public morality and civic virtue are essential characteristics of the free society and that the institutions and practices of public life, as well as private, cannot be indifferent to their encouragement.

The authors of this book are all formidable scholars who have thought deeply about these things. From their own philosophical and disciplinary perspectives and with varying approaches to liberal philosophy and social order, their works serve to further a national dialogue on behalf of a free and responsible society, which is the goal of this book.

# 1. *The Cultivation of Citizenship*

## WALTER BERNS

"Happy families are all alike; every unhappy family is unhappy in its own way."

So begins Tolstoy's novel *Anna Karenina*. The American story begins in 1776 when we, nominally as "one people," declared our independence and our right to constitute a government, but at the same time, in the same document, recognized each individual's right to pursue happiness, which is to say, to be happy, or unhappy, in his own way.

From this it might appear that we came together only in order to live apart, as if, having constituted the society, we were thenceforth free to think only of ourselves. A foolish opinion, no doubt, but Alexis de Tocqueville thought that modern democracies would have to contend with it and with the habits it engenders. He gave it a name, individualism. "Individualism," he wrote, "disposes each member of the community to sever himself from the mass of his fellows and to draw apart with his family and his friends, so that after he has thus formed a little circle of his own, he willingly leaves society at large to itself." Leaves society to itself and leaves it to take care of itself; an individualist is the opposite of a citizen. Individualists come with the democratic territory (so to speak) and, as the title assigned me suggests, citizenship has to be cultivated. It is, presumably, a product of education.

Aristotle, the first political scientist, emphasized the political importance of education, its character (or what is taught) depending on the sort of regime being established (whether a monarchy, theocracy, aristocracy, or democracy). But our democratic or republican Constitution

1

says nothing whatever about education, nor was the subject so much as raised in the Constitutional Convention. George Mason, a delegate from the state of Virginia, came closest when he said that "no government can be maintained unless the manners be made consonant to it." And, with that in mind, he proposed that Congress be empowered "to enact sumptuary laws," that is, laws inhibiting sumptuous display by restricting extravagance in food, dress, furniture, and the like. Sumptuous display would be appropriate for aristocracies, but inappropriate for a democratic republic. But nothing came of Mason's proposal, perhaps because the other delegates thought sumptuary laws had no place in a Constitution intended to "secure the blessings of liberty." Or perhaps they thought education to be the business of the states. Whatever their reasons, the Framers of the Constitution made no provision for the education of citizens; they may even have thought they had devised a plan that made it unnecessary.

That, at least, is the implication of the argument made by Publius (Alexander Hamilton) in *Federalist* 9. It used to be thought (and Aristotle had a lot to do with this) that republics especially had to cultivate the moral qualities required of citizens, but, according to Hamilton, "the petty republics of Greece and Rome" could not serve as models for America. Flourishing for a time, he said, they were soon overwhelmed by "tempestuous waves of sedition and party rage." So much was this the case that, "if it had been found impracticable to have devised models of a more perfect structure, the enlightened friends to liberty would have been obliged to abandon the cause of [republican] government as indefensible."

This "more perfect structure," which was unknown or imperfectly known by the ancients, was the work of an improved "science of politics," and made known to our Founders by the 18th century French political philosopher, the "celebrated Montesquieu." It consisted of certain institutional arrangements: "the regular distribution of power into distinct departments; the introduction of balances and checks; the institution of courts composed of judges holding their offices during good behavior; the representation of the people in the legislature by deputies of their own election [and] the "*enlargement of the orbit* within which such systems are to revolve." As Hamilton said, these are the means by which "the excellences of republican government may be retained and its imperfections lessoned or avoided."

It was left to John Adams to state the principle of this system. "The best republics will be virtuous," he said, "but we may hazard a conjecture that the virtues have been the effect of the well ordered constitution rather than the cause." He went on to suggest that, "by setting one rogue to watch another," a republic could exist even among highwaymen, the knaves themselves being "made honest men by the struggle."[1]

Montesquieu might very well be credited with having delineated the elements of this "more perfect structure."[2] But he is also known as having taught that politics depends on morals/manners (*moeurs* in the French), and *moeurs,* in turn, depend on the education of the sentiments. Thus, it is not surprising the Framers' focus on institutional arrangements — by which one rogue was to watch another, or, as James Madison put it in *Federalist* 51, "ambition [was] to counteract ambition" — did not lead Adams and the other Americans at the time to ignore the importance of civic or moral education. This was especially true of Thomas Jefferson.

Jefferson was, as he claimed to be, "Father of the University of Virginia," and in that capacity he proposed that students, especially the law students, be taught John Locke's treatises and Algernon Sidney's discourses on government, as well as other works expounding "the general principles of liberty and the rights of man, in nature and society."[3] His purpose, of course, was to secure republican government in America by ensuring that students be thoroughly schooled in its first principles. But he had to know that a grasp of these principles does not entail or necessarily promote a love of country, even a country founded on those principles.[4] After all, Karl

---

[1] John Adams, *Defence of the Constitutions*, in *The Life and Works of John Adams*, ed. Charles Frances Adams (Boston, Little, Brown, 1851), vol. 6, p. 219.

[2] Montesquieu, *The Spirit of the Laws*, vol 1, book 11, ch. 6.

[3] Jefferson, "From the Minutes of the Board of Visitors, University of Virginia, 1822–1825," in *Writings* (Library of America, ed., 1984), p. 479.

[4] Aristotle made this point in his discussion of virtue. As he put it (*Nicomachean Ethics*, Book II, iv, 6), "the mass of mankind, instead of doing virtuous acts, have recourse to discussing virtue, and fancy that they are pursuing philosophy and that this will make them good men. In so doing they act like invalids who listen carefully to what the doctor says, but entirely neglect to carry out his prescriptions." Anyone who believes that students can be persuaded to act properly by taking a course in ethics would do well to reflect on this statement.

Marx, who, to say the least, was no friend of republican government, probably had a better understanding of Locke's treatises and Sidney' discourses than did any of the professors employed to teach them at the University of Virginia.

Inculcation of citizenship or a love of country, like moral education generally, takes place at an earlier age, which is why Jefferson also proposed that the young — boys and girls alike, and without regard to "wealth, birth, or other accidental condition or circumstances" — be educated at public expense. A liberal education in "reading, writing, and common arithmatick," he said, followed by the reading of "Graecian, Roman, English, and American history," would render them "worthy to receive, and able to guard the sacred deposit of the rights and liberties of their fellow citizens."

He further proposed that the elementary schools, these schools for citizenship, be established and controlled locally. Let every county in Virginia be divided into "hundreds" or, as he later put it, "wards," then explain to the people therein the purpose of the schools, have them build "a log school-house" and defray the costs of instruction. Better, he said, that this be done by "the parents within each ward" than by the county or the state (to say nothing of the national government). Where every man shares in the direction of his ward-republic, and participates in the government of affairs, "not merely at an election one day in the year, but every day; when there shall not be a man in the State who will not be a member of some one of its councils, great or small, he will let the heart be torn out of his body sooner than his power be wrested from him by a Caesar or a Bonapart."

Jefferson's point was that by giving parents the ultimate responsibility for the civic education of their children, they will themselves be made better citizens, and republican government will be the beneficiary. "Divide the counties into wards," he said. "Begin them for the single purpose [of educating the young]; they will soon show for what others they are the best instruments."[5] In short, political participation at the local level contributes to an education in republican citizenship.

Well before Jefferson, the political philosophers — not only Plato and Aristotle but even John Locke — thought it necessary to address the question of how the young should be educated. And however different their prescriptions, they agreed that a moral education informed by

---

[5] Jefferson, Letter to Joseph C. Cabell, Feb. 2, 1816, in *Writings*, pp. 1380–81.

philosophy should not be an education in philosophy, or political theory. Which is to say, they agreed that moral education was less a matter of theory than of practice or habituation, a forming of character rather than a training of the intellect, and that this had to be done not in the university but at an early age.

Locke said this could best be done in the home, and the Founders were surely aware of the importance — the *political* importance — of what is taught in the home. This led them to emphasize, something Locke neglected to mention, the importance of educating young women. In this, they anticipated Tocqueville who, in his masterpiece, *Democracy in America*, said, "no free government ever existed without moral/manners [*moeurs*], and morals/manners are the work of women."[6]

That the Founders were of the same mind on the role of women in a republic is made clear in a speech by Supreme Court Justice James Wilson. Wilson was one of only six men to sign both the Declaration of Independence and the Constitution; he was also a key figure in the drafting of the Constitution and in its ratification by his state of Pennsylvania, and the principal author of this state's constitution, and, reputedly, the most learned and profound legal scholar of his generation. I mention these biographical details by way of suggesting that, on law and related matters, Wilson can be said to speak for the Founders.

In 1790–91, he delivered a series of lectures on the law at what was to become the University of Pennsylvania, delivered before an audience that included President George Washington, Vice President John Adams, and a "galaxy of other republican worthies, some of them with their ladies at their sides." In the course of these lectures, he asked — after acknowledging that the laws were made by men — what are laws without manners, and how can manners be formed except by a "proper education." Providing that education, he went on, is the job of women. Speaking directly to the ladies present, he said: "You have, indeed, heard much of publick government and publick law, but these things were not made for themselves; they were made for something better; and of that something better, you form the better part — I mean society — mean domestick

---

[6] Alexis de Tocqueville, *Democracy in America*, vol.1, p. 304; vol 2, p. 198 (Vintage Classics ed.)

5

society; there the lovely and accomplished woman shines with superior lustre."[7]

According to Noah Webster — and I shall have more to say about him presently — women were to be educated because of their influence, not only in the home, but in "controlling the manners of the nation." He put it this way:

> Women, once abandoned, may be instrumental in corrupting society, but such is the delicacy of the sex and such the restraints which custom imposes upon them that they are generally the last to be corrupted. . . . A fondness for the company and conversation of ladies of character may be considered a young man's best security against the attractions of a dissipated life. . . . For this reason, society requires that females should be well educated and extend their influence as far as possible over the other sex.[8]

Webster was the editor of our first dictionary, and also an essayist, teacher, educator — in a way, our first educator — and the author of spellers, grammars, and other books for the young, including, in 1785, a book of readings, renamed in 1787, even as the Constitution was being written, *An American Selection of Lessons in Reading and Speaking*. This Reader went through 77 editions in the half century following its first publication, educating, or helping to educate, several generations of young Americans. One can get some sense of the influence he intended to have on these students, as well as some sense of how seriously our early educators took the task of citizenship education, from the epigraph he put on the title page, a quote from the pen of the French republican revolutionist, Count Mirabeau: "Begin with the infant in the cradle; let the first word he lisps be Washington."

His Reader is essentially a collection of edifying stories and speeches (with instructions for reading aloud); stories of the Revolutionary War, famous American orations and state papers, including the Declaration of

---

[7] *The Works of James Wilson*, ed. Robert Green McCloskey (Cambridge: The Belknap Press of Harvard University Press, 1967), vol. 1, p. 86.
[8] Noah Webster, "On the Education of Youth in America," in Frederick Rudolph, *Essays on Education in the Early Republic* (Cambridge: Harvard University Press, 1965), p.69.

Independence and Washington's farewell order to the army, as well as extracts from the works of certain famous authors, Swift, Pope, Johnson, and Shakespeare (Shakespeare's made more edifying for the young by careful editing), and Joseph Addison's play, *Cato*.

Written in 1713 and set in the waning days of the Roman republic, this play tells the story of the legendary patriot, Cato the Younger, who has withdrawn to Utica, a city on the north coast of Africa, in order to rally what is left of Rome's republican Senate against the encroaching power of Julius Caesar. Although written by an Englishman, *Cato* was a favorite during the colonial period, and it became still more popular with the approach of the war with England, Caesar reminding Americans of George III, or vice versa. Its central theme is honor, which may explain its appeal for Washington. Not only did he see it performed more than once and, like those legendary patriots Patrick Henry and Nathan Hale, quote lines from it on appropriate occasions, but, to rally their spirits, he encouraged his troops to stage a performance of it at Valley Forge during the miserable winter of 1778.[9]

No modern American general, not even Douglas MacArthur, would hazard its performance, or anything like it, for his troops. Equally significant is the fact that Webster chose to reproduce parts of it in his Reader. It is an example of the dramatic and didactic poetry, employed by the Founders to shape the morals and passions of their young countrymen. Its language is too stilted for modern audiences, and its moralizing too overt, but generations of American schoolchildren read it. So too, were succeeding generations taught to read, write, and speak, and in the process taught to love their country, from McGuffey's *Readers*, with their stories of Washington and other American heroes.

William H. McGuffey was a Presbyterian clergyman and, from 1845 to his death in 1875, a professor of moral philosophy at the University of Virginia. His *Readers* were both the most popular and, in the public schools, the most widely read of schoolbooks. Originally published in four volumes, with the third and last edition coming in 1879, after his death, they were to sell more than 120 million copies in the years 1836 through

---

[9] On this, and on the general subject of the political education of the young, see Lorraine Smith Pangle and Thomas L. Pangle, *The Learning of Liberty: The Educational Ideas of the American Founders*, 1993.

1920. The principal historian of American education estimates that half the schoolchildren of America "drew their inspiration and formulated their codes of morals and conduct from this remarkable series of Readers." The following dialogue is printed in a lesson entitled "The Young Witness" in McGuffey's Fourth Reader, second edition, and I reprint it here because it is typical of the sort of things young Americans used to read.[10] It goes as follows:

- "Did you ever take an oath?" inquired the judge.
- The little girl stepped back with a look of horror; and the red blood rose and spread in the blush all over her face and neck, as she answered,"No, sir." She thought he intended to ask if she had ever used profane language.
- "I do not mean that," said the judge, who saw her mistake; "I mean were you ever a witness?"
- "No, sir; I was never in court before," was the answer.
- He handed her the Bible open. "Do you know this book, my daughter?"
- She looked at it and answered, "Yes, sir; it is the Bible."
- "Do you ever read in it?" he asked.
- "Yes, sir; every evening."
- "Can you tell me what the Bible is?" inquired the judge.
- "It is the word of the great God," she answered.
- "Well," said the judge, "place your hand upon this Bible, and listen to what I say"; and he repeated slowly and solemnly the following oath: "Do you swear that in the evidence which you shall give in this case, you will tell the truth, and nothing but the truth; and that you will ask God to help you?"
- "I do," she replied.
- "Now," said the judge, "you have been sworn as a witness; will you tell me what will befall you if you do not tell the truth?"
- "I shall be shut up in the state prison," answered the child.

---

[10] I confess that this dialogue caught my fancy because I happened upon it during the impeachment trial of President Bill Clinton.

– "Anything else?" asked the judge.

– "I shall never go to heaven," she replied.

– "How do you know this?" asked the judge again.

– The child took the Bible, turned rapidly to the chapter containing the commandments, and, pointing to the one which reads, "Thou shalt not bear false witness against thy neighbor," said, "I learned that before I could read."

So much for McGuffey and the sort of lessons young Americans were expected to read by way of preparing them to be citizens. But it is worth repeating that citizenship education, like moral education generally, begins as an education of the imagination, which takes place when we are young. As I indicated earlier, we become moral not by thinking about morality or endlessly talking of our need of it, not even by taking a course in ethics, but by performing, repeatedly performing, moral actions. And the actions we imitate are those of persons we respect or admire: our parents (who, as we say, must set good examples) and our heroes, whom we read about in books. They serve as models for us. And it makes a great difference whether the young fancy themselves a Cato, Washington, Jefferson, or Lincoln, rather than an Elvis Presley or some of the rock stars who followed him.

I say the education of citizens begins at an early age, but it obviously cannot end there; it begins there because a person must be disposed to love his country before he can be expected to defend it; and it cannot end there because he must understand its principles in order to meet the arguments arrayed against them. In general, as someone has said, at each stage of learning, "the pre-existing bond of attachment to country must be deepened by the learning appropriate to that stage."

Children can be told, and can come to believe, that democracy is the best form of government, but only at a later stage can they learn to weigh its disadvantages and weaknesses (as well as its advantages and strengths) with those of the other forms of government. For this purpose they can, when older, study Tocqueville's *Democracy in America*, where they will learn the reasons why, all things considered, democracy on the American model is better than any of the available alternatives. They should also be required to study history — Jefferson prescribed "Graecian, Roman,

9

English, and American history" — and, I would add, American biographies. By studying the biographies of the men who founded this republic (and of those who defended it or, as in Lincoln's case, saved it), students can come to appreciate their greatness and the greatness of their achievement.

Cultivating citizenship is not high on our agenda today, perhaps because we think we can get along without it. For example, we don't require military service; we leave that to volunteers whom — except in the case of the Marine Corps — we recruit by promising a vocational training that will lead to higher paying jobs in the private sector. We live in a self-governing democracy, but in fact we are not expected to govern; we leave that to our representatives. We are asked to pledge allegiance to the flag of the United States and to the republic for which it stands, but, thanks to the Supreme Court, we have a constitutional right to burn the flag in order to show our contempt for it and for the republic for which it stands.[11] This decision deserves an extended commentary.

The majority opinion in the case was written by Justice Brennan, and was much praised by those quasi-official bodies, the American Civil Liberties Union and the editors of *The New York Times*. Brennan's argument takes the form of a syllogism: the flag stands for the republic, the republic stands for freedom of expression, therefore the flag stands for freedom of expression.

Now, of course, the First Amendment protects freedom of speech, not expression (and there is a difference); and, while I do not mean to belittle the importance of freedom of speech — it is an essential feature of republican government — I think it important to understand that the flag stands for *everything* the country stands for, and therefore, Brennan's understanding of it is partial or incomplete. As such, it cannot explain why, for a conspicuous example, the Marines on Iwo Jima, where some 6,000 of them died fighting for their country, raised it on Mount Suribachi, in fact (as we know from the famous photograph, and especially from the Marine Corps Memorial in the Arlington National Cemetery), struggled to raise it on the only staff available to them, a piece of battlefield pipe. Nor can it explain why it was thought appropriate to drape the flag over the body of the Marine sergeant killed in the bombing, last August, of our

[11] *Texas* v. *Johnson.* 491 U.S. 397 (1989); *United States* v. *Eichman*, 496 U.S. 310 (1990).

10

embassy in Nairobi, Kenya, or why the embassy staff — I'm quoting the Marine Corps report — "stood erect and silent as the flag-draped body was removed from the rubble and placed in a waiting vehicle." The fact is, the flag is used to express what is in the hearts and minds of American citizens on such occasions. The Chief Justice said as much when, in his dissent in the 1989 flag-burning case, he spoke of "the deep awe and respect for our flag felt by virtually all of us." We are, as the Chief Justice suggests, emotionally attached to it.

For it is our emotions, or our sentiments, more than our rational faculties, that are triggered by the sight of the flag, not when it is used (or abused) for commercial purposes, but when it is waved and flown on the Fourth of July, and displayed at the various war memorials on the mall in Washington or, for that matter, in towns and cities around the country, and on the battlefields at Bull Run, Antietam, and Gettysburg, and at the cemeteries where those who fought and died are buried, not only at Arlington and Gettysburg, but in the far-away places we sometimes visit, among them, Manila in the Philippines, Cambridge in England, Chateau-Thierry in the north of France, and, perhaps most famously (since the film, *Saving Private Ryan*), above Omaha Beach in Normandy. The sight of it, especially in these places, evokes memories of past battles and of those who fought them, and to whom we are indebted. They served our country and were the better for it; by honoring them, as we do, we pay a service of our own and are the better for it. I can make this point with an analogy: not every American can be a Lincoln, but all Americans are made better by reading his words and coming to love him.

To the end that we remember him, and by remembering, come to love him, the government authorized the building of the Lincoln Memorial. It was intended as a means of cultivating citizenship; and no one, I think, not even the most zealous of our civil libertarians, would argue that we are free to express ourselves by spraying its walls with graffiti. There is something about the Memorial that forbids its desecration, and because it, too, causes us to remember, the same ought to be true of the flag. In fact, it is true of the flag, insofar as no patriotic citizen would ever think of burning it.

This country has had its share of summer soldiers and sunshine patriots (a phrase coined by Tom Paine in 1776). For example, the "draft dodgers" who, in 1863, paid the commutation fee that exempted them from

11

military service or, during the Vietnam years as well as in the 1860s, fled to Canada (or, in one notorious case, to Oxford in England) in order to avoid it. But they were few in number compared with the millions of citizens who, over the course of our history, have willingly put their lives at risk for the country. We know little about them save for that fact, and that they must have wanted the country to endure. (Why else would they have fought for it?) But to know that they wanted the country to endure is to know something of importance about them: that they felt themselves obligated to their forebears and their posterity, the forebears because, from them, they had inherited a country worth fighting and dying for, this "inestimable jewel," as Lincoln referred to it,[12] and the posterity because, being related to them, by nationality if not by blood, they were anxious that they, too, might enjoy its benefits.

It seems almost naive to speak of these things at a time when Americans are told in their schools that there is nothing special about their country and, therefore, no good reason to admire the men who founded it; and told by the Supreme Court that the flag stands for freedom of speech, meaning any kind of speech, or freedom of opinion, meaning any opinion, and any speech and any opinion because none is better or truer than any other.

But this nation was not founded on an opinion. The men who declared our independence said, "We hold these truths to be self-evident," and in support of this declaration they pledged their lives, their fortunes, and their sacred honor. Had they known what we are alleged to know, they might have said, "In our opinion, all men are endowed by their Creator with certain unalienable rights." But who would pledge his life, his fortune, and his sacred honor in support of an opinion, knowing it to be merely an opinion? Would Americans have fought for the Union — and 359,528 of them died fighting for it in the Civil War — if they had been taught that the Union was founded on nothing but an opinion concerning human nature and the rights affixed to it? Not likely; but fight they did, and for that we honor them.

[12] Lincoln, Speech to the 166th Ohio Regiment, August 22, 1864. *Speeches and Writings,* The Library of America ed., vol.2, p. 624.

Because of them, and the patriotic citizens who followed them, this country has endured, and with it has endured what Lincoln rightly called "the last best hope of earth."

## 2.  *Religion and American Democracy*

### JEAN BETHKE ELSHTAIN

Alexis de Tocqueville didn't miss much during his tour of America, a mission that yielded his nineteenth century masterwork, *Democracy in America*. Although he failed to pick up the often extraordinary energies of American evangelism — his reaction to what he considered such frenzy being the following: "From time to time strange sects arise which endeavor to strike out extraordinary paths to eternal happiness. Religious insanity is very common in the United States" — he did see how thoroughly religion and politics were saturated with one another. American democracy from the beginning was premised on the enactment of projects that were a complex intermingling of religious and political imperatives. The majority of Americans were religious seekers and believers who saw in communal liberty the freedom to be religious rather than freedom from religion. It is, therefore, not surprising that such a huge chunk of American juridical life has been devoted to sorting out the often inaptly named church-state debate. In a less churched society this would be a far less salient issue.

But what does our profession of belief — some 95 percent of Americans claim belief in God and fully 70 percent membership in a church, synagogue, or mosque — really mean? How does it play itself out on the ground, so to speak? Here a bit of backdrop is helpful in order that we might better situate and explore the vagaries of the present moment.

The West is perhaps unique in this regard, namely, that it has never been hospitable to theocracy, a fusion of, or non-distinction between, the political and the religious. Religion is not only established in theocracies, it dominates politics as in contemporary fundamentalist Islamic states in which mullahs also run the government. There were often close alliances

14

in the history of the West between throne and altar, to be sure. But this isn't the same thing. In other words, a differentiation between politics and religion was sown in Western culture from the very early on, quite pointedly so with the coming of Christianity. Christians asked: what has Christ to do with Caesar? The answer varied widely. Too, the Church, and the synagogue before it and ongoingly, embodied an alternative politics, having its own understandings of community membership, authority, rule, and the nature of the kingdom. The central distinction marked in medieval papal doctrine was that between *regnum* and *sacerdotium*, roughly marking the sword of earthly kingdoms and the spiritual kingdom respectively. The two got all tangled up with one another, to be sure, but they were nonetheless distinct. The spiritual sword was held to be superior because it gestured beyond the immediate realm to the eternal, but the secular sword had its own dignity; its own autonomy and purposes. It could, however, be called to account by the sacred realm, by those who wielded the spiritual sword in behalf of the city of God on earthly pilgrimage. The nations were under judgment and not wholly autonomous in all things.

The post-medieval history of the West is a story of various comings-together and, finally, definitively, teasing apart of church and state. But religion and politics are something else. These simply cannot be separated. Too much of the same territory is claimed by each. Consider the American democracy, then. We begin from the beginning with no establishment of religion but with the free exercise of religion. Bear in mind as well that the views of a few of the great Founders of this republic were somewhat anomalous, Jefferson first and foremost who famously claimed that it mattered not whether his neighbor believed in no God or twenty gods: it neither picked his pocket nor broke his leg. The vast majority of Americans, then and now, were not nearly so agnostic about their neighbor's beliefs.

It is utterly unsurprising, then, that when Tocqueville toured America in the Jacksonian era, he wrote of the ways in which religion in the United States, by which he primarily meant Christianity in its various incarnations including Catholicism, both generated and made use of democratic instincts; religion helped to shape the mores, the habits of the heart. Tocqueville further observed that settled beliefs about God and human nature were indispensable in the conduct of daily life — you simply couldn't function if you woke up every morning and had to determine what truths would guide you over the next twenty-four hours — and that, in general, when a people's religion is destroyed, it enervates and prepares them, not for liberation but for bondage.

This is, of course, an extraordinarily complex story and an often bewildering one, especially for foreign observers. So let's add a few more Tocquevillian bits. Remember that, for Tocqueville, America embodied a coming age of democracy and equality. One could not understand the great movement toward equality without understanding the Christian insistence that all are equal in the eyes of God. This equality, enacted politically, brings great benefits but it also opens the door to certain dangerous tendencies. Democratic egalitarianism tends to isolate people from one another as we all, as competing individuals, go in quest of the "same" thing. We become strivers and isolate ourselves one from the other. Here religion is vital as a chastening influence as it inspires contrary urges by drawing people into community and away from narrow materialism. Religion, in Tocqueville's words, helps to "purify, control, and restrain that excessive and exclusive taste for well-being human beings acquire in an age of equality."

Religion contributes to the maintenance of a democratic republic by directing the mores and helping, thereby, to regulate political life. Tocqueville insisted that the ideas of Christianity and liberty are so completely intermingled that if you tried to sever religion from democracy in America you would wind up destroying democracy. Democracy needs the sort of transcendent justification that religion helps to provide; thus, the eighteenth century philosophers were wrong about the weakening of religion. "It is tiresome," notes Tocqueville ironically, "that the facts do not fit their theory at all." For, surprisingly, the separation of church and state in America had led to an astonishingly religious atmosphere. By diminishing the official power of religion, Americans had enhanced its social strength. Perhaps, deep down, Americans understood that religion feeds hope and is thus attached to a constitutive principle of human nature. Amidst the flux and tumult of a rambunctious democratic politics, religion shaped and mediated the passions. Were the day to come when those passions got unleashed upon the world unrestrained, then we would arrive at an unhappy moment indeed, a dreary world of democratic despotism.

For there were at least two great dangers threatening the existence of religion (and indirectly, democracy) according to Tocqueville, namely, schism and indifference. Schism pits us against one another in suspicion and enmity; indifference invites us not to care about one another at all.

Were Tocqueville around today, I believe he would point to both and he would worry that we are in danger of losing that generous concern for others that religion, in institutionally robust forms, not "spirituality" in vaporous individualist forms, promotes. As well, operating from some common moral basis which does not require doctrinal leveling but does demand searching for certain core norms we share, helps people learn how to compromise because they agree on so many important things. If we slide into a world of schism, a world in which differences become the occasion for isolation, we lose authentic pluralism which requires institutional bases from which to operate. It is pluralism that gives us the space to be both American and Protestant, Catholic, Jew, Muslim, on and on. Absent robust and vibrant faith and civic institutions, we are thrown back on our own devices; we lose the strength that membership provides; we forget that we can know a good in common that we cannot know alone. Should we arrive at this Tocquevillian impasse, we would find that individuals, striving to stand up-right in the winds blowing from centers of governmental or economic power now operating minus that chastening influence from other vital sources, would soon be flattened. People would grow apart and become strangers one to another. We might still have kin, but we would no longer have a country in the sense of a polity of which we were essential parts.

This is where a form of dogmatic skepticism, corrosive of all belief, enters. Tocqueville knew that people would always question and challenge. But what happens if there is nothing but skepticism of a dogmatic sort that is unable to sustain any beliefs. Don't you think Tocqueville would see that we Americans at the end of this century might be in this danger zone as well? In our desire to be sophisticated; in our determination to be nobody's fools, we may well and truly be undermining our ability to believe and to affirm anything at all save the ephemeral ground of our own subjective experience.

So where are we at this point? What do we see when we look around? Whose America? Which religion? First, we see a smorgasbord religiosity whose primary aim seems to be to make me feel good about God but god forbid that this should place any demands on us. Second, as a corollary, we see what might be called a hollowing out or de-institutionalization of religion in many quarters, a loss of institutional robustness. This creates a real problem as faith absent strong institutions cannot be sustained over

17

time: religious life becomes all fission and fragment absent framing rules and doctrines and underlying beliefs: here we stand.

A de-institutionalized, feel-good religiosity cannot carry out the tasks of formation Tocqueville found so central in forging a sturdy, decent, self-governing American character. If religion is just another voluntary association, it isn't religion any more in a strong sense. This puts us in danger of losing the connection between freedom and truth. For freedom isn't just me maximizing my preferences, as some who favor market models hold, but is tethered to truth as a part of our very being, our inner constitution. Freedom, rightly understood, which is always a chastened notion of freedom, frees us for solidarity with others. An authentic view of freedom — understood in and through the prism of relationality, of brotherhood and sisterhood — must challenge misguided views that undermine authentic freedom. But without certain formative institutions we cannot sustain freedom in the authentic sense. We enter a danger zone in which our differences, which should be great blessings, become instead destructive divisions. Our great religious traditions offer hope and solace, the promise of a community of the faithful. One's internet chat room isn't quite the same thing.

I want to be careful here because I would not want to leave the impression that I believe religion performs certain useful functions and that is its ultimate and most defensible aim and purpose. No, instead the aim of religion is to bear us toward the truth; to direct our very beings toward a conformity with true freedom as relationality, as communion, grounded always in the dignity of persons. Religion opens us to the God in whose likeness we were created. In the words of the great St. Augustine, "Thou hast made us to thyself and our hearts are restless til they rest in Thee." And this restlessness — "everybody's got a hungry heart" sings Bruce Springsteen — channeled and made ever fresh through religious belief, helps us to face and to try to make whole a wounded world. But this mission of religion may be blocked, oddly enough in the name of religious freedom or tolerance.

Let me explain what I mean. In a recent book by the distinguished sociologist, Alan Wolfe, *One Nation After All*, Wolfe details what he calls modern religious tolerance under a discussion entitled "Morality Writ Small."[1] Wolfe's middle-class respondents — and the vast majority of

---

[1] Alan Wolfe, *One Nation After All*, (USA Penguin, 1995).

Americans are middle-class and understand themselves through this lens — see religion as a private matter to be discussed only reluctantly. This already departs in quite dramatic ways from a deeper, richer understanding of what tolerance is or what it requires, for one thing, and, for another, it suggests that many of our fellow citizens have come to believe that to endorse a properly secular state which has no established ties to any religious institution means one is obliged to support a secularized society in which religion is reduced to a purely private role. Not so. Yet this is precisely what so many of the respondents in this important book seem to be saying they want. So much for William Lloyd Garrison, Dorothy Day, Martin Luther King, and a small army of other great citizens who didn't embrace this nicety!

Now Professor Wolfe describes his respondents as trying to be welcoming to all faiths. His Mrs. Tompkins — one of the people interviewed in the book — thinks that one way to ease the rough edges off religious conviction is to refuse to accept any particular "dogma whole" as if the doctrines or teachings of various faith communities were arbitrary impositions rather than worked out and complex teachings that took shape over centuries. Instead, she continues, one should just "live with the concept of God as you perceive it." Is this not a form of terminal subjectivism? If it's all up to you, a community of belief is lost and we slide into indifference.

But something even more troubling seems to be going on. There is a deep undercurrent of fearfulness running just beneath the surface of the words of so many of the middle-class Americans in Professor Wolfe's book. They seem to have struck a tacit bargain with themselves that goes like this: If I am quiet about what I believe and everybody else is quiet about what he or she believes, then nobody will interfere with the rights of anybody else. But this is precisely what real believers, whether political or religious or both, cannot do: keep quiet. Whether believers in Martin Luther King's beloved community or in ending the war in Vietnam on justice grounds derived from religious conviction or in opposing the current abortion regime for similar reasons. To tell political and religious believers to shut up for they will interfere with my rights by definition simply by speaking out is an intolerant idea. It is, in effect, to tell folks that they cannot really believe what they believe or be who they are. Don't ask; don't tell.

What fears underwrite this attitude? One, surely, is of religious intolerance, even religious warfare, though, of course, if you were to do a body count the murderous anti-religious ideologies of the twentieth century would win that prize hands down. But the fear now seems to extend to public expression itself. Professor Wolfe claims that his respondents are disturbed when religion is taken out of the private realm. But a private religion is no religion at all. One must have the public expression of faith for it to be faith. And public expression isn't forcing anything on anybody. But, to those interviewed for *One Nation After All*, that in and of itself — public expression — seems to cross a line because you are supposed to keep quiet about what you believe most strongly. If you do not, it may require of me that I actually enter into an act of discernment — what do I think about what you are claiming? — and that many Americans do not want to do.

There are, of course, certain virtues here imbedded: don't rush to judgment; live and let live. But I want to focus on the vices. Although Wolfe describes the demand for privatization as a tolerant one flowing from a desire to be "inclusive" and "nonabsolutist," I wonder. Many of his respondents do seem quite absolutist — about everybody shutting up. Consider the remarks of Jody Fields, used as an example of tolerance and laissez-faire. "If you are a Hindu and you grew up being a Hindu, keep it to yourself. Don't impose your religion, and don't make me feel bad because I do this and you do this." Surely this isn't tolerance at all but extraordinary intolerance of religious pluralism: if one changes Hindu to Jew in the comment, that becomes stunningly clear. So when we are told that "keep it to yourself" presages a "period of increasingly religious pluralism," I would say, "hardly." Telling a Hindu to hide being a Hindu is scarcely a picture of robust pluralism.

Now some respondents in *One Nation After All* do seem to be authentic religious pluralists, more generous in their attitudes. Here, for example, is Cathy Ryan, perturbed because Christmas carols can't be sung anymore in the public schools of her town at Christmas time because Muslims may get upset. Her response: "Well, excuse me, but let's teach Muslim songs too — don't wipe out all culture, add to it. Do Hanukkah songs. Let's find out what a dreidel represents. let's find out what Muslims do." This is real tolerance, I would submit, of a sort that encourages the public expression and representation of differences with the view that we are all enriched through the process. As Pope John Paul II always tells us: "Be Not Afraid!" Cathy Ryan is open to robust pluralism. And one might argue that it is in America that such forms of trans-nationality, as the great proponent and critic of early twentieth century progressivism, Randolph Bourne, called it, have found and continue to find multiple forms of relatively benign expression.

Legal scholar Michael McConnell, in a paper on "Believers as Equal Citizens," reminds us of several different versions of Jewish emancipation historically. One expected Jews to disappear as a distinctive group once they were given their civil rights. Under the terms of Jewish emancipation in France, for example, Jews were expected to give up civil aspects of Talmudic law; to disavow any political implications of their faith; to abandon altogether the use of Yiddish; and to relinquish their semi-autonomous communal institutions. This by contrast to American pluralism. Writes McConnell:

> The great public feast given in 1789 in Philadelphia, then the nation's capital, to celebrate ratification of the Constitution included a fitting symbol of this new pluralistic philosophy: the feast included a special table where the food conformed to Jewish dietary laws. This was a fitting symbol because it included Jewish Americans in the celebration without requiring that they sacrifice their distinctiveness as Jews. By contrast, in France Napoleon summoned the leaders of the Jewish community to a 'Great Sanhedrin,' where he insisted that the Jewish law be modified to enable the Jewish people to be integrated into the French nation. In a gesture no less revealing than the kosher table in Philadelphia, Napoleon's Minister of the Interior scheduled the first session to be held on Saturday. Here we see three alternatives. Under the *ancien regime*, Jews would be excluded from the celebration, for they could not be citizens. Under the secular state, Jews would be welcome to attend, but they would be expected to eat the same food that other citizens eat. If they want to keep kosher, they should do it at home, in private, at their own expense. Under the pluralist vision, multiple tables are provided to ensure that for Protestants, it is a Protestant country, for Catholics a Catholic country, [for Muslims, a Muslim country], and the Jew, if he [or she] pleases, may establish in it his [or her] New Jerusalem.[2]

So let us not worry so much about conflict or difference that we deny pluralism its forms of public expression — the only way, really, that we have of learning about the gifts others have to offer. There is a

---

[2] Unpublished manuscript.

difference between "keep it to yourself" and tolerance. In the words of Stephen Carter: "Tolerance is not simply a willingness to listen to what others have to say. It is also a resistance to the quick use of state power... to force dissenters and the different to conform."[3] If we don't allow religious dissenters to display their beliefs as public moral critics, in their own voices, then it is we who are intolerant.

Now let us draw politics and religion together one more time. Political commentator, E. J. Dionne, has written that Americans are fed up with politics and many among us just want politics to go away.[4] The majority of middle-class Americans in *One Nation After All* also seem to want real religious conviction to go away, too, especially in light of their distrust of "organized religion," as if there was any other kind. I want to suggest that contemporary distrust of organized politics and organized religion go hand-in-hand. Both involve public expression; collectivities of persons involved in a shared enterprise; rules and convictions; and sometimes hard-hitting encounters. That we seem not to have the stomach for either suggests our capacity for democracy itself is growing ever more anemic. A distaste for conflict is a distaste for politics. The great Frederick Douglass once remarked that you cannot have rain without occasional thunder and lightning. Yet that is what so many of us seem to want: spring showers, lovely gardens, but no thunderstorms. Need I note that life doesn't work like that and that no complex democratic politics can survive if we go underground with what we care about most deeply. To me this suggests that we are not doing a very good job of social and political and, yes, religious formation: preparing people for a world in which there are disagreements and there are decisions to be made and one cannot always tell the Hindus to keep it to themselves.

This draws us, at last, to certain basic questions. Who are we anyhow? In what does the good of human beings consist? How can we come to recognize, to honor, and to cultivate that good in wisdom and in truth? In two of the great American director, John Ford's, great films, a shocked outsider puts fundamental questions. Consider "My Darling Clementine" when Henry Fonda as Wyatt Earp, who has given up his badge and left Dodge City with his brothers to try to create a new life, enters a town for a shave and finds people fleeing in horror and screaming as a

---

[3] *The Dissent of the Governed* (Cambridge: Harvard University Press, 1998).
[4] E.J. Dionne, *Why Americans Hate Politics* (New York: Simon and Schuster, 1991).

drunk shooter lays waste to the place and law enforcement officials flinch and throw down their badges because they aren't getting paid enough for such really dangerous duty. "What kind of a town is this?" queries Fonda in amazement.

In the opening of "Who Shot Liberty Valence?," Jimmy Stewart, as lawyer, Rance Stoddard, is riding in a coach into Shinbone to start a new life in the West when the stagecoach is robbed and the local villain — Liberty Valence who takes all sorts of liberties until those who struggle to create a settled civil society, to build churches and schools and political institutions, triumph — steels a broach off a lady's garment although she pleads, please take everything else, but not that, it was a gift from my late husband, and Stewart, who doesn't carry a gun and is surrounded by armed desperadoes, cries out: "What kind of a man are you?" An aim of religion is to help us, with God's help, to ask and struggle to answer those questions: What kind of a place is this? What kind of people are we?

# 3. *The Moral Foundations of Liberal Democracy*

## DANIEL J. MAHONEY

This chapter addresses the question of "the moral foundations of democracy." One natural way of doing so, especially for an American writing for an American audience, is to examine the moral resources of the American Founding. And, of course, any cursory examination of the Declaration of Independence, the Constitution, or the statesmanship of Lincoln, for example, makes clear that this republic is endowed with rich moral and civic resources. Such constitutive American premises as the idea that "all men are created equal," that legitimate government rests upon the consent of the governed, and that individuals are endowed by the Creator with inalienable rights that frame and limit the exercise of popular sovereignty, readily come to mind. Lincoln powerfully illuminated the moral possibilities inherent in the Declaration's affirmation of human equality, the ways in which the fact of human equality gives rise to a moral obligation to respect the rights and dignity of others. I would not be the first commentator to point out that, with Lincoln, equality becomes the *telos* of a republican regime, a moral and political *proposition* to be ever more closely approximated. Lincoln's propositional view of equality resembles one of Immanuel Kant's "ideas of reason" such as "perpetual peace" that regulate and guide human conduct toward the ever fuller realization of the abstract "idea."

But even in Lincoln's highly moralized understanding of democracy, with its striking similarities to Kant's categorical imperative ("as I would not be a slave so I would not be a master," Lincoln wrote in a personal note

24

of 1858 explicating his understanding of democracy), there is much formality and hence *indetermination*. Our natural rights republic, like all modern liberal regimes, is rich with moral content but that content is defined in a remarkably formal or *tautological* way. Human beings are rights-bearing individuals and hence worthy of respect. This is the unchallenged faith of modern democracy. We speak endlessly about human rights but have difficulty saying very much about the nature of man, of this human being whose dignity we must respect. This equivocation or indetermination is not a result of a later departure from a more substantial or determinate liberalism present at the origins of liberal modernity or in the American founding. As the French political philosopher Pierre Manent has pointed out in *The City of Man*, the entire modern natural rights tradition defines man in a tautology: man is the "X" with rights.[1] But the history of modern political philosophy is, as Manent also demonstrates, the story of the "desubstantialization of man."[2] Of course, it is well known that the architects of the modern liberal state wanted to construct a political order that was not dependent upon contentious ideas about "the good life" that inevitably give rise to civic and sectarian strife. But, more radically, they were committed to the view that human dignity could be realized only when its horizon was thoroughly "terrestialized." If human beings were to live with dignity in this world, they must come to terms with their merely "human condition," and jettison the pretense to know the goods of their "nature."

Now, it is undoubtedly true that earlier forms of liberal political theory, not to mention the moral philosophy of Immanuel Kant, did not hesitate to make serious moral demands on liberal citizens. John Locke, perhaps the single most important architect of modern Anglo-American constitutionalism, believed that rational liberty (which begins with the indetermination of human nature and the myriad ways in which we make ourselves, even in our moral constitution) needs to be supported by inherited forms of moral understanding, rooted in prejudice or public opinion (Locke's so-called "law of reputation"). The American Founders generally agreed, whatever their differences, that republican government had certain prerequisites that were dependent upon traditions and habits

[1] Pierre Manent, *The City of Man*, translated by Marc A. LePain (Princeton, New Jersey: Princeton University Press, 1998), pp. 126–129.
[2] Ibid., especially Chapter IV, "The Hidden Man," pp. 111–155.

that antedated the theory and practice of representative government (a good example of this can be found in George Washington's discussion of the salutary civic effects of religious belief in his "Farewell Address"). And Tocqueville, about whom we'll hear more later, famously suggested that "the spirit of liberty" needed to be accompanied by "the spirit of religion," even if democratic religion is forced to adjust itself to the circumstances and exigencies of a democratic age.

All this said, it is difficult to contest the fact that liberalism, in practice, inevitably erodes the "moral capital" or inheritance which is essential to its well-being. Tocqueville, the sober friend of American democracy, is the best guide to the fruits of democracy's essential indetermination. He insisted that democracy needs an "art" of liberty to check its egalitarian "nature." In his view, the nature of democracy inexorably erodes the moral contents of pre-democratic intellectual and spiritual life, and even threatens the essential humanity of democratic man. (Tocqueville, with his concerns about the "enervation" of democratic man, anticipated, although in an infinitely more responsible way, Nietzsche's critique of the "last man.")

Contemporary moral and political theory, in both its respectable Anglo-American liberal outposts and in its continental Kantian ones, champions this indetermination as the true ground of human freedom and responsibility. In this understanding of the moral foundations of democracy, indebted to Kant but shorn of his demanding morality, the emphasis is placed on the self-determining or autonomous character of moral choice. Human beings are worthy of respect because they are capable of moral agency. But this agency is emptied of any content other than the act of willing or choosing itself. The French political theorist Luc Ferry goes as far as to insist that the foundation of human dignity is rooted in man's *nothingness*, in his transcendence of all natural or divine determination. Kant's categorical imperative to treat others as ends in themselves is still reflected in contemporary liberalism's emphasis on toleration and mutual respect and understanding. But as Pierre Manent has pointed out in an impressive reflection "On Modern Individualism," modern humanism becomes, in practice, a rather indulgent form of humanitarianism. "Kant's rigorous understanding of respect for others, then, becomes displaced by a sentimental version that grounds itself in compassion."[3] Manent proceeds to point out that compassion is by its very nature egalitarian and open to demagogic manipulation. It contributes to the "pantheistic" tendencies within democracy powerfully diagnosed by Tocqueville, by undermining the natural human capacity to distinguish between the highest and lowest in man and between human beings and that which is above and below them. Compassion does not even discriminate between the suffering of human beings and animals as the politicized "compassion" of the growing animal rights movement makes abundantly clear every day.[4]

In the next section of my paper, I wish to draw out, with the help of Pierre Manent, Tocqueville, and Aurel Kolnai, the implications of this democratic indetermination for the liberty and dignity of man. I will then briefly examine the analyses of two thinkers from the East of Europe, the Russian writer and Nobel Laureate Aleksandr Solzhenitsyn and the Polish Pope John Paul II. Solzhenitsyn and John Paul II have both radically challenged the claim that atheistic or anthropocentric humanism is the true foundation of democratic liberty. In their struggle against the communist or ideological "lie" they appealed to permanent Truths about the nature of man, society and even the constitution of "Being." They insist that the appeal to Truth was not merely a weapon in the battle against totalitarianism but an essential element in the proper understanding and exercise of human freedom itself. In that sense, they remain dissidents, even after the fall of communism, and are worthy of our continuing attention and respect.

## The Tocquevillean Analysis

The real human beings who inhabit our modern democracies are much more than atomistic individuals. They live within families, they belong to churches, and by the tens of millions practice the "art of (voluntary) association" lauded by Tocqueville in *Democracy in America*. It is also no doubt the case that critics of liberal democracy on both the left and right tend to romanticize the "communitarian" alternatives to liberal individualism and have obscured the "inequality and wretchedness" that

---

[3] Pierre Manent, "On Modern Individualism" in *Modern Liberty and Its Discontents*, edited and translated by Daniel J. Mahoney and Paul Seaton, with an introduction by Daniel J. Mahoney (Lanham, MD: Rowman & Littlefield, 1998), p. 157.
[4] Ibid., p. 157.

marked the communal life of pre-democratic societies. Tocqueville did not hesitate to claim in his 1836 essay on "France Before and After the Revolution" that the democratic understanding of liberty, which rooted liberty not in inherited privileges or natural human differences but rather in universal and imprescriptible rights, was the true because just notion of liberty.[5] But he also understood that this true but abstract understanding of liberty increasingly undermines the moral contents of human life. In premodern European societies, these had been effectively embodied in corporate entities such as the nobility, the church, the guilds, and communal self-government. For all the injustice and wretchedness of "aristocratic" society, there was a constant mechanism of mutual and overlapping *influences* that guaranteed the solidity of the social tie. In contrast, the theoretical goal of a democratic society is something like the establishment of a civilized state of nature, where the self-determining actions of individuals are held together through the nexus of commerce and culture. Montesquieu had famously argued in the second of the two chapters on the English constitution in *The Spirit of the Laws* (Book 19, Chapter 27) that the English were more "conféderés que concitoyens" — more "allies than fellow citizens."[6] Tocqueville was less sanguine than Montesquieu about the civic and moral consequences of democratic individualism. He had less confidence than his great predecessor that a civilized state of nature was finally compatible with the preservation of the full range of human excellence, or even of the integrity of the human soul. In Tocqueville's view, democracy undermines salutary *natural* as well as conventional inequalities. It promotes a dogma of individual self-sufficiency, of the freedom and equality of individuals, which is both false and finally too weighty for the overwhelmed individual to bear. It therefore makes possible new forms of majority tyranny and intellectual and spiritual conformity. Pierre Manent has lucidly described Tocqueville's fears about the effects of "the democratic dogma" upon the nature of man:

> Democracy strives to prevent — or at least weaken as far as possible — any influence from an individual, even based on reason or virtue, that subjects the

---

[5] "État Social et Politique de la France Avant et Depuis 1789" in *Tocqueville: De la Démocratie en Amérique, Souvenirs, L'Ancien Régime et la Révolution* (Paris: Éditions Robert Laffont/Bouquins, 1986), p. 943.

[6] See the discussion of this passage in Pierre Manent, *An Intellectual History of Liberalism*, translated by Rebecca Balinski (Princeton, NJ: Princeton University Press, 1995), p. 61.

weakest to the naturally better endowed. This done, it supposes that any man at all can fulfill his nature without the help of these influences, which, in any case, are accidental and provisional at most. Democracy tends to impose a real equality of men that it does not uphold in theory. For all that, it tends to stultify human nature. Democracy embodies nature in a way that puts nature in danger.[7]

Tocqueville, of course, did not give up on democracy because it tended to give way to "a narrow individualism where all public virtues" and indeed many private ones "were smothered."[8] He knew that in the new democratic dispensation nothing was permanently fixed and that there could be no possible return to the hierarchies and corporate ties that structured the social life of all the "old regimes." As he wrote in the preface to *The Old Regime and the Revolution*, "Humanity is driven by an unknown force which we can hope to moderate, but not to defeat, which sometimes gently urges and sometimes shoves us towards the destruction of the aristocracy."[9] The new society that emerges from this process of destruction is afflicted by certain "natural vices," among them a debilitating passion for material gratification, to be sure, but even more dangerously by an individualism which increasingly isolates the individual within his narrow circle of family and friends. In Tocqueville's chilling description, democracy "freezes" human relations, and thereby makes possible a despotism that "takes away from citizens all common feelings, all common needs, all need for communication, all occasions for common action."[10]

Democratic individualism is conducive to despotism precisely because it shares with despotism an animus against mutual human influence and hence against action within common public space. Although Tocqueville does not use the Aristotelian vocabulary, it is clear that for him the human being is by nature a social and political animal, at least in the sense that our humanity has a chance of developing itself only where the intellectual and moral virtues of some are capable of influencing or moving others. Political liberty serves the indispensable purpose of reminding men that they are

---

[7] Pierre Manent, *Tocqueville and the Nature of Democracy*, translated by John Waggoner (Lanham, MD: Rowman & Littlefield, 1996), p. 79.
[8] Alexis de Tocqueville, "Preface" to *The Old Regime and the Revolution*, Vol. 1., translated by Alan S. Kahan (Chicago, IL: University of Chicago, 1998), p. 87.
[9] Ibid., p. 87.
[10] Ibid., p. 87.

much more than individuals. Freedom creates a public space where individuals become familiar with each other, where they "join together through the need to communicate with one another, persuade each other and satisfy each other in the conduct of their common affairs."[11] The exercise of responsibility in public life mitigates the vices of individualism and excessive love of material well-being that are natural to the democratic social state. The cultivation and sustenance of the political character of human life is at the heart of Tocqueville's "art of liberty." Tocqueville goes so far as to state that political liberty alone "creates the light which allows one to see and judge human vices and virtues."[12] One cannot confront the full truth about human nature outside a framework of political liberty.

Tocqueville's "liberalism," we have seen, finally has little in common with the natural rights liberalism of Thomas Hobbes and John Locke. Tocqueville never questioned the desirability of democratic liberties or rights themselves. But he does make clear that the effort to sustain a society based upon the dogma of the self-sufficient *individual* is bound to fail. It is bound to fail because it does not do justice to the nature of man or the requirements of genuine social life. Tocqueville appreciated, in the words of the Hungarian-born moral and political philosopher Aurel Kolnai, that the well-being of the liberal democratic order is dependent upon "pre-liberal traditions" that are "ideally negated and condemned by the very conception of man's unlimited self-sovereignty."[13] Tocqueville expressed concerns about the maintenance of these pre-or extra-liberal traditions and habits precisely because the democratic notion of popular sovereignty or consent does not limit itself to the political realm. The dogma of popular sovereignty "regulates the greater part of human actions"[14] and thus transforms family life, religion and other inherited institutions in ever more "democratic" directions. Tocqueville was certainly no speculative philosopher but he had already observed what Kolnai states in more explicitly philosophical language:

---

[11] Ibid., p. 88.

[12] Ibid., p. 88 (translation corrected).

[13] Aurel Kolnai, "Privilege and Liberty" in Kolnai, *Privilege and Liberty and Other Essays in Political Philosophy*, edited and with an introduction by Daniel J. Mahoney (Lanham, MD: Lexington Books, 1999) p. 38.

[14] Tocqueville, *Democracy in America*, vol. 1, part 2, chapter 10.

the liberal-democratic social order reposes on axioms, conventions, traditions and habits (whether they be expressly held or tacitly respected) which transcend the liberal-democratic framework itself and impose certain 'material' or 'objective' limits on both individual liberty and popular sovereignty, thus helping to maintain a kind of accord among the multiple individual 'wills'; between the free citizenship of the individual on the one hand, and the 'General Will,' as monistically embodied in state-power, on the other.[15]

## "Liberty Under God"

Aurel Kolnai remains little known outside of selected academic circles. A convert to Catholicism and a student of Husserl, he wrote penetrating criticisms of moral subjectivism and a first rate analysis of "the utopian mind." In his remarkable 1949 essay "Privilege and Liberty" Kolnai defended a conservative conception of liberty that he called "liberty under God" because it recognizes that freedom cannot be a guarantee of itself. Kolnai writes:

> no organization of freedom *qua* freedom can in itself constitute a guarantee of freedom; . . . civic liberty is rather a precious fruit than a foundation or a mainspring of Civilization; or in other words again, that the freedom and self-government of man, both individual and corporate, must be grounded in some other principle than the specious 'evidence' of an unlimited validity of the subjective human *placet* or *fiat*, of the ego's *bon plaisir* or *sic volo*, of one's 'right' to 'do what one likes' subject to the 'identical right of others.'[16]

In asserting the dependence of liberty upon Civilization and in challenging the identification of liberty with *fiat* or will, Kolnai gives philosophical depth to Tocqueville's intuition. He also anticipates Solzhenitsyn's and John Paul II's critique of atheistic humanitarianism by rooting liberty properly understood in a natural order of things within which human beings "participate" but which they do not make. Kolnai argued that individualism ultimately has its origins in a philosophical error that ignores "the basic truth that *response*, not *fiat*, is the prime gesture of the human person."[17] When human beings "participate" in reality they

[15] Kolnai, Ibid., p. 38.
[16] Ibid, p. 39.
[17] Ibid, p. 26.

31

affirm their loyalty to "Being, Forms and Limits" that structure our choices and overcome "the prideful illusion of human omnipotence."[18] Kolnai argues more controversially that the inequalities, hierarchies, and "privileges" present even in a democratic society remind human beings of the reality of intrinsic superiorities and hence of the limits of the human will. The conservative democrat or constitutionalist who rejects the self-sovereignty of man, who understands that liberty is always "liberty under God," does not as a result deny the common humanity of human beings or ignore the injustice of narrowly plutocratic and oligarchic social arrangements. But he refuses acquiescence in an ideology of the "common man." For Kolnai, this egalitarian ideology is indistinguishable from "an aesthetical craving for a symmetrical pattern of figures of the same size, as an undertaking destined to achieve the god-like omnipotence of man and a gigantic attempt to uproot wholly man's allegiance to God."[19]

Perhaps Aurel Kolnai's most profound contribution to political philosophy is his articulation of the "indetermination" characteristic of the modern liberal notion of the "common good." He identifies the radical egalitarianism inherent in an indeterminate or content-less view of the common good. If there is no "Entity and Law above man," one inevitably takes one's bearings from the equality of human subjectivities, every one of which is a "sovereign determinant of the good."[20] A totalitarian or "identitarian" concept of liberty haunts the democratic one from the beginning: in such a conception,

> anarchy cannot be averted except by the actual sameness and fusion of human thoughts and volitions *as such*; unity, no longer a function of the convergency of minds towards a transcendent Cause, Measure and End, becomes a self-contained *theme* of society; whoever questions the evidence of the 'self-evident' or fails to fit in with the 'typical' constitution of 'needs' places himself (virtually at least, but perhaps with massive consequences) outside the bounds of recognized humanity.[21]

The totalitarian conception of the "general will" is the political expression of the pantheism or loss of individual distinctiveness which

[18] Ibid, pp. 26–27.
[19] Ibid, p. 50.
[20] Ibid p. 29.
[21] Ibid, pp. 29–30.

Tocqueville claimed "seduced the mind in democratic ages" and threatened "the true nature of man's greatness."[22] The totalitarian or collectivistic conception of liberty is a logical consequence of individualism, of a subjectivism that defines "liberty in terms of human power unrestrained and omnipotent."[23] Kolnai's philosophical analysis provides an impressive link between Tocqueville's description of democratic individualism and Solzhenitsyn's and Pope John Paul II's insistence upon the essential link between liberty and the search for transcendent truth and thus the limits of all anthropocentric or man-centered humanism.

## Solzhenitsyn and John Paul II — "The View from the East"

Aleksandr Solzhenitsyn is not a figure from whom Americans think they can learn much about democracy. The author of *The Gulag Archipelago*, to the extent that he is still thought about at all, is recognized as a major player in the battle against communism, but one with little relevance to the contemporary concerns of the established democracies of the West or the emerging postcommunist regimes of the East. For many years, his political views have been stereotyped as those of, at best, a romantic "Slavophile" and, at worst, an illiberal theocrat, imperialist and even anti-semite. The fact that there is no basis for these charges has not deterred their ready dissemination in political, journalistic and scholarly circles. Solzhenitsyn's widely misinterpreted Harvard Address of 1978, "A World Split Apart," confirmed the worst suspicions of his critics and solidified the consensus about his anti-democratic views.

The Harvard Address, to be sure, did raise fundamental questions about the adequacy of the modern principle that "governments are meant to serve man and that man lives in order to be free and pursue happiness."[24] Solzhenitsyn argued that such a principle necessarily leads to an erosion of public spiritedness and civic courage and "to an engrossment in everyday life."[25] He criticized our contemporary one-sided emphasis on individual

---

[22] Tocqueville, *Democracy in America*, Vol. II, part 1, chapter 7.

[23] Kolnai, *op cit.*, p. 32.

[24] See Aleksandr I. Solzhenitsyn, "A World Split Apart," in Ronald Berman, ed., *Solzhenitsyn at Harvard: The Address, Twelve Early Responses, Six Later Reflections* (Washington, DC: Ethics and Public Policy Center, 1980), p. 6. Hereafter cited as *SH* in notes.

[25] *SH*, p. 19.

rights and suggested that a society "organized legalistically has . . . shown its inability to defend itself against the corrosion of evil."[26] In recent years, he has provided a more nuanced judgment without in any way modifying his fundamental judgment about the limits of a legalistic understanding of freedom. In a speech delivered at the International Academy of Philosophy in Liechtenstein in September of 1993, on the eve of his return to his native Russia, Solzhenitsyn stated that "the West cannot . . . lose sight of its own values, its historically unique stability of civic life under the rule of law — a hard won stability which grants independence and space to every private citizen."[27] The experience of the post-communist slide into a new form of lawlessness, the widespread identification in "democratic" Russia of freedom with nihilistic self-assertion and the power of the strong to do what they will, undoubtedly played some role in strengthening Solzhenitsyn's appreciation of the absolute indispensability of the rule of law. In the Liechtenstein Address, he emphasizes his own "vulnerability" in criticizing the West since in his homeland the "moral axes" of freedom "have fallen into even greater disuse than in the West."[28] But it should be remembered that in the Harvard Address, Solzhenitsyn had already stressed that "a society without any objective legal scale is a terrible one indeed"[29] and that the final volume of his great indictment of communist totalitarianism, *The Gulag Archipelago*, concludes with a forceful chapter entitled "There is No Law."

I would like to suggest that Solzhenitsyn's *ultimate* concern in 1978 was not with politics in the narrow sense of the term but rather with the decline in the spiritual integrity of all modern societies, which despite their grave political differences are indebted to common philosophical principles. Solzhenitsyn's real target was never constitutional government or institutions of self-government (he has been an indefatigable advocate of local self-government and a critic of "oligarchy" in the new Russia) but rather the dimunition of "man's sense of responsibility to God and society."[30]

---

[26] *SH*, p. 9.
[27] Solzhenitsyn, "Address to the International Academy of Philosophy," in *The Russian Question at the End of the Twentieth Century* (New York: Farrar, Straus and Giroux, 1995), p. 125.
[28] Ibid., p. 115.
[29] *SH*, p. 8.
[30] *SH*, p. 17.

Solzhenitsyn believes that United States and other Western democracies are torn between two competing concepts of liberty. The traditional understanding of "liberty under God," the belief that "all human rights were granted on the ground that man is God's creature"[31] has gradually been displaced by a new view that "could be called rationalistic humanism or humanistic autonomy: the proclaimed and practiced autonomy of man from any higher force above him. It could also be called anthropocentricity, with man seen as the center of all."[32]

Solzhenitsyn appreciates that rationalistic humanism, the animating impulse of modern consciousness, was an understandable and perhaps inevitable response to the theocratic propensities of the Middle Ages. He states, in no uncertain terms, that in the Middle Ages, the physical nature of man was "cursed" and subject to "despotic repression" in the name of the spiritual authority.[33] His alternative to "the calamity of an autonomous, irreligious humanistic consciousness"[34] is not a romantic communal or theocratic society but rather a free one where individual rights are limited by "the moral heritage of Christian centuries with their great reserves of mercy and sacrifice."[35]

Like Aurel Kolnai, Solzhenitsyn is convinced that secular humanitarianism is vulnerable to radicalization and self-destruction in the name of more consistent forms of humanistic self-assertion. The most consistent currents of humanism, such as Marxism, emphasize thoroughgoing materialism, atheism, and sociological determinism. The problem for Solzhenitsyn is not liberty or humanism *per se* but a humanism that has "lost its Christian heritage"[36] and, as a result, is vulnerable to ever renewed assaults from the intellectual left.

I have already suggested that Solzhenitsyn has no fundamental objection to the ideals of constitutional government or to the institutions of political liberty. Far from it. He believes that the political problem in Russia today does not stem from excessive democracy, but rather from the absence of anything resembling real accountability on the part of the political class. Not only is there "no legal framework for creating local self-

---

[31] *SH*, p. 17.
[32] *SH*, p. 16.
[33] *SH*, p. 16.
[34] *SH*, p. 19.
[35] *SH*, p. 17.
[36] *SH*, p. 18.

government" but "the fate of the country is now decided by a stable oligarchy of 150 to 200 people, which includes the nimbler members of the old Communist system's top and middle ranks, plus the nouveaux riches." The new oligarchs "exhibit no higher goals of serving the country and the people"[37] and, with a few exceptions, identify freedom with their self-aggrandizement.

For Solzhenitsyn, the situation in post-communist Russia reveals the effects of a radical individualism where human beings are emancipated from the requirements of conscience or from humility before "a Supreme Complete Entity" that restrains human passions and irresponsibility. Western social commentators, journalists, social scientists and politicians alike, speak about "civil society" as if it is a merely sociological construct which can be resuscitated at will through governmental design or through the opening of economic markets. But the market, and civil society in general, depends upon legal structures and, even more importantly, on a developed sense of self-restraint and moral obligation. In Solzhenitsyn's view, post-communist nihilism is the bastard child of communism. Communism, in truth, is not an antidote to democratic individualism but rather its inhuman intensification and radicalization. It is infinitely more individualistic than liberalism because it does not merely erode or weaken but actively attempts to destroy the intermediate associations that embody the moral capital of civilized society. It eliminates the political and social space where human community and individual virtues are nourished. In his latest works, Solzhenitsyn spends much time considering the prospects for education, the church, and local self-government in Russia because these are the seedbeds for a reconstituted civil society. "We must build a *moral* Russia or none at all,"[38] he writes plaintively at the conclusion of *The Russian Question at the End of the Twentieth Century* (1994). But Solzhenitsyn knows that while politics depends upon moral criteria it is not reducible to them. As he states in his 1993 Liechtenstein Address:

> Moral criteria applicable to the behavior of individuals, families and small circles certainly cannot be transferred on a one-to-one basis to the behavior of states and politicians; there is no exact equivalence, as the scale, the

---

[37] These quotations are drawn from Solzhenitsyn, "What Kind of Democracy is This?" *New York Times*, 7 January 1997.
[38] *The Russian Question*, p. 108.

momentum and the tasks of governmental structures introduce a certain deformation.[39]

Nonetheless, whether addressing the destruction of civil society in his homeland or the more subtle degradation of personal and public life in the prosperous, commercial West, Solzhenitsyn appeals to the same imperative of "freely accepted and serene self-restraint."[40] Only "the golden key"[41] of voluntary self-limitation, rooted in respect for conscience and in a sense of religious responsibility can rescue modern man from "the calamity of an autonomous, irreligious humanistic consciousness." Solzhenitsyn has never expressed nostalgia for a premodern Russian or western past. Instead, he recognizes the practical need to move beyond the philosophical and moral presuppositions of modernity. This advance toward the "next anthropological stage"[42] does not entail a rejection of modern Progress ("which cannot be stopped by anyone or anything") but an active effort to direct "its might toward the perpetration of good."[43]

Pope John Paul II is in full agreement with Aurel Kolnai and Solzhenitsyn in rejecting the "self-sovereignty" of democratic man. They agree, as Solzhenitsyn formulated it in his Harvard Address, that if "man were born only to be happy, he would not be born to die."[44] Modern rationalism does not do justice to the spiritual destiny of man. Nor does it adequately comprehend what John Paul II called in his 1995 United Nations address, "the moral structure of freedom."[45] No Roman Pontiff has done more to reconcile the Catholic Church to "rights talk" or to the essential link between human dignity and the respect for basic human rights. The whole world knows the Polish Pope's crucial role in inspiring Solidarity and undermining communism in Poland and throughout the eastern bloc. But while accommodating himself to the demands of constitutional democracy and (somewhat more grudgingly) to the requirements of a market economy, John Paul II firmly rejects the identification of freedom with moral

---

[39] Ibid., pp. 114–115.
[40] *SH*, p. 19.
[41] *The Russian Question*, p. 125.
[42] *SH*, p. 20.
[43] *The Russian Question*, p. 120.
[44] *SH*, p. 19.
[45] See John Paul II's address of October 5, 1995 to the U. N. General Assembly, "The Fabric of Relations Among Peoples," *Origins*, October 19, 1995, p. 297.

autonomy and the "license to do whatever we like." The Pope repeatedly stresses that freedom needs to be "ordered to the truth."[46] It is important to note that the Pope does not identify the ordering of freedom to truth with clerical authoritarianism in any form. In fact, he has been quite critical of extreme conservative elements within the Polish Catholic Church who would like the Church to have a veto power over the public settlement of vexing social and moral issues. What John Paul II seems to have in mind is the cultivation of an ethos or public philosophy (granting the ambiguity of that term) that recognizes that freedom is inseparable from "the truth about the human person — a truth universally knowable through the moral law written on the hearts of all."[47]

In his encyclical *Evangelium Vitae*, John Paul II connects a utilitarian understanding of human liberty to the degradation of human life in a "culture of death" increasingly accepting of abortion and even euthanasia and infanticide. *Fides et Ratio*, John Paul's most "philosophical" encyclical, addresses the crisis of reason and the threat posed by historicism, in particular, to the integrity of faith and reason. The papal confrontation with historicism is of particular importance since historicism, in its diverse forms, poses the most radical challenge to the idea of a sempiternal human nature rooted in a natural (and ultimately supernatural) order of things. Of course, John Paul II is neither a statesman nor a political theorist. But he is an unusually philosophically astute Pontiff whose reflections on the "structure of freedom," at least, are broadly congruent with the best political and philosophical reflection on the meaning of "liberty under God."

## Conclusion

For the past two generations, it has not been uncommon for political theorists to speak of "the crisis of our time" or of "the crisis of liberal democracy." It should not be surprising that émigré political philosophers such as Leo Strauss or Hannah Arendt, in particular, readily resorted to the language of "crisis." Having witnessed the institutional and spiritual fragility of liberal democracy in Weimar Germany and the rise of virulent communist and national socialist despotisms in Europe, they had a palpable

---

[46] Ibid., p. 297.
[47] Ibid., p. 298.

sense of democracy's limits. But they also witnessed the inability of so-called liberals to give a rational defense of liberty and their resulting vulnerability to the totalitarian temptation. If twentieth century discussions of the "crisis of democracy" are often tied to a direct experience of a contingent European social crisis, they also reflect a deeper intellectual understanding and intuition of the moral crisis that is consubstantial with liberal democracy itself.

We have seen that this crisis is tied to the essential indetermination that marks the democratic conception of man and the common good. Some of the thinkers surveyed in this paper have a perhaps excessive confidence in the possibility of a post-modern reconciliation of rights and duties, of the "natural moral law" and the modern emphasis on subjectivity and rights. I, for one, do not share the expectation that modern man is about to embark on the movement toward a new "anthropological state" or is particularly receptive to a "civilization of love" marked by "solidarity" and an openness to divine truth.[48] Rather, it is to be expected that the two notions of liberty, that we have discussed, the "self-sovereignty" of man and "liberty under God," will continue to compete for the loyalty of democratic citizens and for the souls of individual men and women. This division is what is ultimately at stake in our "culture wars." Decisions about whether to proceed with new gene-altering bio technologies or how to respond to the increasing prospects for human cloning will bring this choice home in increasingly dramatic ways.

The prominent Polish dissident turned Warsaw newspaper editor Adam Michnik suggests in his new book *Letters from Freedom* that the "moral absolutes" appealed to by such anti-totalitarian heroes as Solzhenitsyn, Václav Havel and Pope John Paul II in their struggle against communism are no longer appropriate in a working democracy where the issues are not black and white but "gray." Michnik is certainly right to emphasize the crucial role that modest virtues — such as civility and mutual respect — play in the successful operation of democracy. He is also right to insist that no political partisan has a monopoly on the truth. But he is wrong to believe that human liberty is thinkable without serious and sustained attention to the ends which structure our human nature and ennoble our freedom.

---

[48] On John Paul II's idea of the "civilization of love," see Ibid., p. 299.

# 4. Fleeing the Universal: The Problem of Relativism

## GILBERT MEILAENDER

Anyone who, being generally unfit for truly useful work, has taught ethics for the last several decades in a college or university in this country is likely to have had an experience something like the following: You assign to your students some fairly difficult, though undeniably important, piece of reading — say, a book like Michael Walzer's *Just and Unjust Wars*. And you also assign these students to write a short paper dealing with some part of the book's argument. On the whole, students do this with diligence. They may find the book hard, they may get lost at some places in the argument, but they really try to do what you have asked. They work hard to get clear on the argument. They sort through its complications. They develop, as fairly as they can, Walzer's position on whatever question they are examining. And then, somewhere near the end of this rather careful treatment of Walzer's thought, a student writes, almost in so many words: "Of course, it's only his opinion."

Relativism — or, more accurately, subjectivism — is in our blood, in the air we breathe. Truth is truth for me, or truth for you — grounded only, finally, in our subjective choices and agreements. Or truth for us — relative and limited in validity to the communities to which we belong or the groups with which we identify. But there is no universal reason by which to transcend the divide that separates these individuals or groups. How we have come to this point may be hard to say. To some degree, of course, moral relativism is a perennial possibility, and its appearance requires no special explanation. Yet, there are features of our moral landscape that make it especially unsurprising. In part, this is, I think, because politics — in particular, a certain conception of liberal politics — so dominates our understanding of ethics. When we insert "values" into the curriculum we are not really hopeful that we may together learn something about "the good life" for human beings. What we have in mind is a kind of balancing of forces, different views pitted against each other. The anthology of "pro" and "con" readings perfectly illustrates our vision. And in a world where "ethics" becomes the balancing of forces, the best way to advance an ethical position may not, finally, be with argument — but with the maximum force. To think that through may be to understand a good bit about American colleges and universities today.

## Flight From God

Just as important a contributing factor in the rise of the kind of implicit subjectivism with which so many students come to college may be the displacement of religious faith from its culturally privileged position. At least for Jewish and Christian belief, God is the author of that single story into which each of our personal stories can be placed. Without God, we have no reason to suppose there is any single story that unites us. Instead, we have only different classes, races, sexes, and cultures — and a never-ending struggle among them to see which will most shape and determine our identity. This is the world we call multicultural.[1] If there is no single story within which we must understand ourselves in order to be authentically human, we are, in a sense, free — free to form our own opinions without constraint.

Such freedom is quite alluring. Indeed, we should, I believe, think of relativism not chiefly as an epistemological but as a moral problem. That is, the issue is not primarily what can be established as knowable or true, as if argument might come to an end. Nor need we deny that our knowing must always begin from some particular place, even when we hold that, having begun there, it may open up into a vision of the universally human. Relativism as a moral problem has to do more with our desire for independence. The universal constrains us, and so we flee from it.

---

[1] For an exposition of this claim, see Robert W. Jenson, "How the World Lost Its Story," *First Things* (October, 1993), pp. 19–24.

I want to be careful with this claim, even though it makes sense to me; for I know that it can easily have about it a pop psychology air — which condescendingly refuses to take disagreement seriously by offering amateur analysis of those with whom one disagrees. I am strengthened to have the courage of my convictions, however, by the remarkable concluding chapter of Thomas Nagel's recent book, *The Last Word*.[2] Nagel presents a sustained argument against subjectivism and relativism in several spheres of knowledge. He argues that there must be such a thing as universal reason that is valid independently of anyone's particular point of view, and he thinks that a healthy public discourse depends on the possibility of such universal reason.

Nevertheless, in the concluding chapter, instructively titled "Evolutionary Naturalism and the Fear of Religion," he pauses to ponder the sources of resistance to the kind of view for which he has argued. And he suggests that his view, which sees a sort of fit "between the deepest truths of nature and the deepest layers of the human mind," makes many people today uneasy. "I believe," he writes, that "this is one manifestation of a fear of religion which has large and often pernicious consequences for modern intellectual life." If religious belief of, say, a Jewish or Christian sort is true, then we are not creators of our world. We are neither independent nor autonomous. We are, in fact, constrained. Our reasoning, then, ought to try to follow the grain of the universe, to acknowledge truth that exists independently of our decisions.[3] That is exactly what we fear. Nagel writes:

> I speak from experience, being strongly subject to this fear myself: I want atheism to be true and am made uneasy by the fact that some of the most intelligent and well-informed people I know are religious believers. It isn't just that I don't believe in God and, naturally, hope that I'm right in my

[2] New York and Oxford: Oxford University Press, 1997.
[3] I realize, of course, that it is possible to argue that the relation to God actually liberates us from submission to any universally binding morality. Thus, for example, one might argue, as Kierkegaard is sometimes thought to have done in *Fear and Trembling*, that the freedom of God requires that we acknowledge his authority to command what he will when he will — and that we interpose no system of universally binding rules between ourselves and God. I think this is only a partially accurate reading of *Fear and Trembling*, and it is, in any case, a very different kind of concern about universal morality, a concern that is not likely to give rise to subjectivism but, rather, to that dreaded "heteronomy."

belief. It's that I hope there is no God! I don't want there to be a God; I don't want the universe to be like that.

We might recall the similar complaint brought against the gods by Orual in C.S. Lewis's haunting novel, *Till We Have Faces*: "That there should be gods at all, there's our misery and bitter wrong. There's no room for you and us in the same world."[4] And again, anyone who has taught ethics for long enough will not be surprised to find this passionate belief in one's own autonomy alive and well even in those who simultaneously think of themselves as religious believers. Each of us is eager to assert our particular identity, our angle of vision on the cosmos. We are not eager to see the world as resistant to our projects and desires. All the noble existentialist language notwithstanding, we would not so much mind a world in which the greatest virtue was authenticity — being true to oneself, accepting without bad faith the burden of choice and bearing it nobly.

Nevertheless, we must do justice to the moral case *for* relativism. Against claims of universal truth we might simply assert the particularity of our own identity. There is a case to be made for saying that too singleminded an emphasis on universal moral obligations may lose sight of an important aspect of our humanity. We cannot and should not try to live our lives as if we were simply the disinterested ideal observers of whom moral philosophers have sometimes spoken — people who would try to view even their own lives from the standpoint of an external observer. If we act as though we might be anyone, we will be no one in particular. So, if we are not careful, anti-relativist claims may be destructive of the particularities of individual identity and may fail to appreciate the proper place of freedom. Your life or mine is not just an instance of human life, but is ineluctably and eternally yours or mine and no one else's. This is an old issue in the history of Western thought and perhaps the crucial problem in moral philosophy at least since Kant. An assertion of universal truth seems to undercut our freedom, but an emphasis on freedom appears to subvert the claims of reason and land us in some form of subjectivism.

It is, then, a moral issue that I want to ponder. Once we give up the subjectivist attempt to envision a world entirely malleable to our choices,

[4] C.S. Lewis, *Till We Have Faces: A Myth Retold* (Grand Rapids, MI: Eerdmans, 1956), p. 291.

once we accept that the created world — being what it is — may resist our projects and desires, what shall we make of particular identity? Does a non-subjectivist and non-relativist morality, while attempting to deliver us from partiality, lose the richness of our particular identities? Or is the attempt to ground moral decisions in our own individual choices or communal constructs finally, in Augustine's terms, "living a lie"?

## Particular Identity and Universal Truth

I will focus this issue by examining in some detail the thought of just one contemporary thinker whose work is, I believe, a rich resource for reflection on the tension between particular identity and universal truth: the political theorist Michael Walzer. There are relativist moments in his thought, which he, or so it seems to me, simultaneously embraces and draws back from. There is an emphasis on individuals and their commitments, but those individuals are situated within particular communities and not simply within any universal human community. His work provides, therefore, a rich resource for reflection upon the degree to which our moral judgments can or cannot transcend the communities in which we are located.

Many themes intersect in Walzer's work, but here we should note the depth of his commitment to particularity: to a pluralistic world of particular communities and, finally, to the individuals who form such communities. This commitment is not without its tensions. For all his emphasis upon communities and shared moral life, his understanding of morality is grounded in something still more particular and arbitrary: the consent of individuals. Indeed, one might wonder whether communities do not become so important in his thinking because they offer the individual a kind of deliverance — escape from the restricted world of the self and into a larger arena in which to flourish. That is, relativism delivers him from subjectivism. In any event, I will look first at his case against universal moral claims and his location of moral argument within the life of communities.

Stories occupy an important place in Walzer's writing. In the two books that are his most ambitious undertakings — *Just and Unjust Wars* and *Spheres of Justice* — the arguments are sprinkled with historical illustrations.[5] These vignettes do far more than provide illustrative material to flesh out the bare bones of a theory. Their presence is important to the kind of theory Walzer himself offers, as he makes clear in *Just and Unjust Wars*.

When we want to argue about warfare, we need not start *de novo*. Instead, Walzer writes, we find near at hand "a more or less systematic moral doctrine." This doesn't mean that we agree about the issues being argued. It means only that we "acknowledge the same problems, talk the same language." The historical illustrations are not, therefore, illustrations of an argument that could, if necessary, get along perfectly well without them. They are the conversation of our culture about war, a conversation and an argument into which Walzer seeks to initiate the reader.

Within the history of this conversation much has been learned, some moves have gradually been ruled out, but the conversation never simply ends. It is important to see this, lest we misunderstand the reasons for beginning here. Indeed, Walzer himself may not always be as clear about this as one might wish. Thus, for example, he writes: "I am not going to expound morality from the ground up. Were I to begin with the foundations, I would probably never get beyond them; in any case, I am by no means sure what the foundations are. The substructure of the ethical world is a matter of deep and apparently unending controversy." But surely this cannot be the reason for beginning with stories that already presume a shared world of moral argument. For disputes within this *shared* world — i.e., the disputes captured in Walzer's historical illustrations — are every bit as unending and frustrating. In fact, it is exactly their frustrating quality that may tempt us to seek what Walzer eschews — a theory comprehending our own and any other moral world, a theory for anyone anywhere.

Ambiguity is also present in the more sustained argument of *Interpretation and Social Criticism,*[6] where Walzer rejects theories of morality that seek a ground or starting point outside a moral world already shared. He turns from such potentially universal moralities to morality as interpretation of a world within which we stand, a moral world already

---

[5] *Just and Unjust Wars: A Moral Argument with Historical Illustrations* (Basic Books, 1977); *Spheres of Justice: A Defense of Pluralism and Equality* (Basic Books, 1983).
[6] Harvard University Press, 1987.

shared. He turns, that is, to relativism of a sort. Why begin there? In some moments Walzer seems to suggest that we have no alternative.

> Morality, in other words, is something we have to argue about. The argument implies common possession, but common possession does not imply agreement. There is a body of tradition, a body of moral knowledge, and there is this group of sages arguing. There isn't anything else.

This alone will hardly suffice, however, if only because Walzer himself grants that there *is* something else — a "minimal and universal moral code." Examples include prohibitions of "murder, deception, betrayal, gross cruelty." He grants the existence of such a minimal moral code (a bottom tier in the moral life) but seems to doubt its usefulness. The minimal code is grounded in *nature* rather than *history*. It will serve our needs only to the extent that we can think of ourselves as belonging to no particular group (or, what comes to pretty much the same thing for him, as belonging simply to humanity). Since Walzer believes it is very difficult indeed to think of ourselves in such a way, he suggests that there can be (almost) no universal moral appeals; for the whole of humanity has only the most minimal shared history and no overarching story of stories.

Moreover, the simple fact that our thinking must of necessity begin from somewhere does not in itself mean that this thinking cannot open up into what is universal. Hence, even if we were drawn to Walzer's grounding of morality in particular narratives, further argument would be needed. Sometimes he suggests that appeals to particular shared histories are strategically wiser than more universal appeals to human nature; that is, they are more likely to be persuasive. Yet his own examples from the Hebrew prophets cut the other way: Jonah has more success when making universal appeals to the Ninevites than Amos does when speaking as an Israelite to fellow Israelites. And more generally, intra-family quarrels are notoriously bitter and terrible; the shared story does not seem to make amicable resolution any more likely.

In other places Walzer suggests a second reason. He argues that those who make universal appeals grounded in claims about human nature may be unwilling simply to continue the conversation/argument indefinitely. Instead, like those who step across the line dividing just war from crusade, they may turn to manipulation, compulsion, conversion, and conquest. This is an interesting suggestion, well worth pondering; for Walzer is turning the table on those who argue that people with ethnocentric or parochial viewpoints are unlikely to be able to appreciate or sympathize with the outsider. With considerable insight he notes that this may be untrue. Those who love their own particular history may be most likely to sense the way in which others, in turn, love theirs. By contrast, those who think they see a truth that applies to all human beings past, present, and future are more likely to want to impose that vision through conversation or conquest. Surely there is something to this argument, but perhaps not as much as Walzer supposes. One might surmise that temptations to conquest can arise within either sort of view.

Even though Walzer often sounds skeptical of our ability to know much about human nature as such, his description of that "minimal and universal moral code" suggests that we can in fact transcend our historical location to some degree. In a wonderful discussion of Rawls — even if a discussion that Walzer himself admits to be in part caricature — he imagines a gathering of strangers from different moral cultures meeting in some neutral space. He grants that they could arrive at minimal principles of cooperation, just as one can design a hotel room suitable for anyone from anywhere to live in for a time. But there is no reason, Walzer argues, for us to suppose that these principles of cooperation, arrived at in the pressure of such a moment, should constitute a "universally valuable arrangement" or "a way of life." Nor is there any reason these strangers should want to bring back to their own culture the principles arrived at there any more than they or we would call a hotel room, however rationally constructed and nicely appointed, "home." This is due not to any epistemological defect but to our love of home and our unwillingness to allow our own way of life to become simply an instance of a universally shared way.

The metaphor is a nice one, and I am not inclined to argue with Walzer's claim that almost all people do want something more than such a hotel room or minimal principles of cooperation. They do want a home, "a dense moral culture within which they can feel some sense of belonging." They want to be able to locate themselves within a history, a narrative that gives significance to their life. This amounts, though, only to saying that we need to be more than free spirits who transcend every time and place and share a "thin" moral world available to such transcendent spirits. We need also to be bodies within a particular location. But are we not both? And the very fact that many who leave the home that provided them with a sense of belonging and, having learned to make their way in a different world, find it difficult to return, suggests that they may not want to leave behind everything learned elsewhere. The experience of Camus as described by Walzer in *The Company of Critics*[7] is, in fact, only an extreme example of our common problem: to be both "apart and united." That formula points to what must be called a two-tier theory of morality, embracing both the impulse toward universally shared moral understanding and the rich diversity of different ways of life.

Finally, we should note that it may not be easy to combine the social emphasis in more recent Walzer writings with the emphasis on consent theory in his early work, *Obligations*.[8] If we want to know what are our obligations, we must, he says, look to the commitments we have made. "One does not acquire any real obligations . . . simply by being born or by submitting to socialization within a particular group." This grounding of obligation in consent gives rise to a tension Walzer never fully escapes. Individuals must be saved from the fate to which consent theory has consigned them, and "belonging" provides the needed salvation. To avoid subjectivism we turn to relativism. Hence, the importance of public participation in Walzer's thought. The single individual with whom he begins must get beyond that restricted world of self, must become public-spirited rather than self-concerned. Perhaps a philosophy that begins in individual consent must always make a little too much of the narratives these selves tell.

To see this is, however, to begin to discern the real heart of Walzer's critique of universal moralities. The narrative that finally counts is the history of one's consent. This explains why he can make little sense of a "human community" or duties to humanity. For how could we commit ourselves to a group as unorganized as humanity? What would it mean to belong, if belonging is always grounded in our commitment? In *Interpretation and Social Criticism* universal moralities seem to be *epistemologically* deficient. But Walzer's real objection is a *moral* one.

---

[7] Basic Books, 1988
[8] Simon & Schuster, 1970.

Smaller rather than larger groups are to be morally preferred because in them one's consent is less likely to be tacit or presumed and more likely to be explicit. They make it easier to believe that we are bowing to no external authority but only to a decision in the making of which we ourselves have been significant participants. Once again we have run up against a moral issue. I began earlier with the suggestion that relativism involves a flight from the universal — which, precisely because it is universal, constrains each of us. But Walzer seems to turn to relativism largely for more positive reasons — to preserve identities shaped in particular communities, communities to which we might plausibly think of ourselves as having chosen to belong. To this moral claim in Walzer's social criticism I therefore now turn.

## In Defense of Particularity

It is worth recalling that Walzer's first book was about the Marian exiles, a study of the Puritans as revolutionary modernizers.[9] Of those exiles he wrote: "There is hardly a word in their letters or tracts to suggest nostalgia or sorrow for England." Such a sentence might also describe what, in his later work, Walzer calls a disconnected critic. To trace just one strand of his early work on the Puritans will be a way into thinking about the moral issues at stake here.

The Marian exiles were Protestants, many of them clergymen, who fled England during the reign of the Catholic Queen Mary. Walzer depicts at least some of them as outsiders in two ways, double exiles — first from England and, then, from the less radical of their fellow exiles. Certainly they could speak the language of the England to which they mailed back letters and tracts, but they saw their cause as distinct. In the terms of *Interpretation and Social Criticism*, they thought of themselves as more like Jonah than Amos.

These saints-in-exile no longer thought of themselves fully as members of that order in England. They thought of their prophetic role in Calvinist terms as a public office to which God had called them. This could, of course, only be the status of an outsider, one no longer "connected" to the old order. "In the old political order, the saint was a stranger. It was appropriate, then, that he be the creation of an intellectual

---

[9] *The Revolution of the Saints* (Harvard University Press, 1965).

in exile." The old world was, according to the saints, deeply entrenched in Satan's control. Believing this, these saints-in-exile found themselves having "virtually no social connections or sympathies for it." Ties of personal loyalty or friendship could not be important; what counted was the impersonal loyalty shared by those with similar divine callings. And lacking any real sense of connection with the older England they criticized, they felt little need for "limits" in their criticism of it (or, later, in their war upon it). "In a sense," Walzer writes, "radicalism was the politics of exile, of men who had abandoned 'father and fatherland' to enlist in Calvin's army. This was an army capable of making war ruthlessly, because it had nothing but contempt for the world within which it moved." Thinking of themselves as divine instruments and standing apart from the society they criticized, the saints inaugurated a movement that ended in a (partially successful) conquest and conversion. The aim was universal; they would have refashioned the world had they been able.

Walzer is drawn to these Puritan saints because of their public-spiritedness, a quality to which he is deeply committed, but he is also dissatisfied with them as social critics for reasons only fully developed in more recent writings. That Walzer himself sees unifying threads within his thought should be clear from the introductory chapter of *The Company of Critics*, a chapter that explicitly names "the radical divinity students and the dissident divines of the Reformation period" as among the first examples of alienated, unattached social critics. But note: the lack of attachment here is moral, not epistemological. After all, the Puritan radicals may have appealed to a special truth, but they still shared a common language and tradition with the old order. What they wanted to assert was not unintelligible to the society they had left; it was simply dangerous. In saying that their lack of connection was not epistemological but moral I mean to capture something of what it means to be a disconnected critic in Walzer's sense. Their failing was that they did not love that which they criticized and sought to change. They were unable to be apart *and* united. This is the same issue depicted sensitively in the central chapter on Camus in *The Company of Critics*. The difficulty facing Camus was a formidable one: how to direct his social criticism to Europeans who were no longer simply colonizers of Algeria but residents there, people for whom acquiescence to the demands of the Algerian National Liberation Front might well mean destruction.

The problem with universal principles in such circumstances is not that they cannot be understood, nor is it even that they will always fail to prick the consciences of those to whom they are addressed. The problem, rather, is that such principles alone will seem to be all spirit and no body. They will not recognize the absolute centrality of particular ties of love in human life. The universal and detached critic who can bloodlessly articulate them in such circumstances — who can be apart and not united — has failed morally. "Intimate criticism is a common feature of our private lives; it has its own (implicit) rules. We don't criticize our children, for example, in front of other people, but only when we are alone with them. The social critic has the same impulse, especially when his own people are confronted by hostile forces." Camus was unwilling to violate the implicit rules of intimate criticism, and anyone reading Walzer's chapter must, I think, feel his own sympathy and, indeed, approval. He quotes Camus: "We could have used moralists less joyfully resigned to their country's misfortune."

Walzer's description of Silone's social criticism seems an apt description of the sort he himself favors:

> The principles of morality are permanent but they are also local. They reflect the needs and hopes of particular people with faces and proper names, occupations, and places of residence, customs and belief. One reaches mankind only through serious engagement with such people — though it seems to me that Silone is in no great hurry to reach mankind.

This we might call a defense of relativism, though surely not anything like the unsophisticated student's subjectivism with which I began. Walzer admires the public-spiritedness of political radicals to whom so much of his work has attended. But they believe too much in a universal moral truth that commits them to remaking particular people and communities — to reshaping particular identities in the name of some universal, and presumably more rational, ideal. Their criticism fails because it does not embody love for what is given. Contrary to what one might have supposed about Walzer, a man of the left, his view is grounded in an essentially conservative appreciation for what is given in particular communities. The case against universal reason is not exactly an epistemological one.

51

Defenders of the social order and its critics can understand each other. The case against universal reason is a moral one: it subverts particular identity.

## From Particular to Universal

This is as appealing a defense of particularity as I know, seeming almost to make benign the muted and thoughtful relativism in which it is necessarily grounded. But I do not think we should stop with it. The impulse toward detachment and a moral criticism claiming universal applicability is an impulse that Walzer labels Platonic, Stoic, and Christian. Against it he sets the connected criticism of the Hebrew prophets. Although other nations might learn from the message of the prophets, that will not happen by transposing the content of their message to a different social setting but by "reiterating" in a way appropriate to one's own society the kind of criticism the prophets practiced. "Each nation can have its own prophecy, just as it has its own history, its own deliverance, its own quarrel with God." But Walzer has very little interest in any attempt to join these particular stories, to find in them some common narrative thread that might make them a single story. Like Silone, he is in no hurry to reach mankind. And yet one wonders whether he ought not be just a little more interested, if his claim that each nation can have "its own quarrel with God" is to be taken monotheistically, if it is the one God with whom they all quarrel in their particular histories.

In a chapter on Buber in *The Company of Critics*, Walzer discusses the "reiterative" quality of Buber's thought. But then in a footnote he suggests that Buber sometimes goes too far, as, for example, in writing that "we need . . . the ability to put ourselves in the place of the other . . . the stranger, and to make his soul ours." This language, Walzer claims, "suggests a good deal more than we need to do (or can do). Morality requires that we recognize, not that we possess, the soul of the stranger." Perhaps 'possess' presses Buber's metaphor too far, but, surely, 'recognize' calls for considerably less than Buber had in mind. Walzer will draw back from any suggestion that we should identify our cause with that of a stranger, assuming a shared story that transcends the boundaries that divide us. He seems to think, perhaps rightly, that the density of particularity would then be diminished or endangered.

What might happen, though, if Walzer were to break free of the vestiges of consent theory in his thought and stop bracketing God as decisively as he does in almost all his work? To say "this is my people, my community" may mean something rather different if it means "the people given me" rather than "the people to whom I have given myself." To say "the people given me" would ground the particular attachment in what always transcends it — toward which one moves, without obliterating that from which one moves. Walzer is quite right to reject the notion that, having designed a universally functional hotel room, we ought to use it as a model for transforming our home. But perhaps the movement can be in the other direction — from the old and much beloved home to that same home enlarged and improved in ways that enhance rather than destroy its distinctiveness while, at the same time, making place for others to visit and, perhaps, to stay.

I began, you will recall, with Thomas Nagel's suggestion that fear of religion — or, perhaps more accurately, of God — underlay our contemporary resistance to the possibility of universal moral truth and our preference for the assertion of our particular identities. I have now tried, at length, to use the thought of Michael Walzer to depict as alluring and thoughtful a relativism, a defense of particular moral vision(s), as I know. But, thoughtful as it is, it suggests, to me at least, that Nagel has seen something important.

We could try to ground our deliverance from the tyranny of universal moral principle simply in human freedom itself, but then we end with a subjectivism that knows only "opinions," for which "ethics" can finally be no more than balancing the force of one opinion against the force of another — and may the strongest force win. Ethics becomes politics, not conversation but conquest, and we are all too familiar with it in the academy today. To escape an ethic grounded only in consent and choice we might try to connect morality more firmly to particular communities — settling, really, for relativism as a way of taming subjectivism. And there is no doubt that we must stand somewhere in particular, rather than nowhere or anywhere, when we begin to think about moral matters. But we will find, I suspect, that the moral life requires not only connection but also detachment — that we be not only united but apart. We do not belong to the whole extent of our being to any earthly community; in our freedom we rise above them. We reach toward the universal.

What we need is an understanding of our humanity that recognizes both our "locatedness" and our "freedom." As bodies, located creatures, we live lives that are peculiarly ours, that are more than applications of a universally shared morality. As free spirits, we transcend our communities in order to explore and affirm that tier of moral principle which is not just ours but is universally shared. But that freedom must itself encounter a limit if it is to be creative rather than destructive. The limit — which both locates us and calls us out of location — is God. It is a fearful thing to be located, and, understandably, we often resist it, asserting our subjectivity. It is equally fearful to be called out from location into freedom, and we often resist that, falling back into the particular identities that secure our person. But if we are to be delivered from both our subjectivist emphasis on choice and our relativist claims about social construction of moral truth, if neither of these can say all that needs to be said about morality, then we may need to find a way to come to terms with our fear of God.

# 5. *Liberalism and Virtue*

## DOUGLAS J. DEN UYL*

"Virtue is never such a sufferer, by being contested, as by being betrayed. My fear is not so much from its witty antagonists, who give it exercise, and put it on its defense, as from its tender nurses, who are apt to overlay it, and kill it with excess of care and cherishing." (Shaftesbury, *An Essay on the Freedom of Wit and Humor*)

Recent events in Washington and elsewhere have made the subject of morality and moral education omnipresent. This appears to be a time of the greatest need for moral education, yet it is equally true that there is confusion as to how to go about it. Part of the problem is that the cause of the present state of immorality or amorality is itself the subject of much debate. Everything from "liberalism" to birth control has been blamed for moral decline. Though the possible causes of the problem are diverse, that something must be done by way of correction is pronounced almost with one voice. No one doubts the need. Indeed to express such a doubt would be to expose oneself to incredulous ridicule. And because of that, many are scrambling to give advise on what should be done to improve the moral character of the nation.

What follows is not exactly a dissenting voice, but it is one that is quite outside the patterns of debate on this issue. Moral education, we would hold, is not a proper object of public concern, if by "public" concern

* I would like to thank Ruth Abbey, Douglas B. Rasmussen, and Chandran Kukathas for many helpful and critical comments on this paper. For the same reason, I would like to thank the Fellows and Spring 1999 Visiting Scholars at Liberty Fund for their discussion of this paper in one of its early drafts.

one means political concern. Moreover, that moral education is not a proper object of politics is, and rightly so, the essence of liberalism. Unlike other political doctrines or philosophies, liberalism is especially keen on keeping politics and morality distinct. Indeed, the essential *uniqueness* of liberalism as a political theory is its divestment of morality from politics. Politics is not suited "to make men moral."[1]

Although this thesis does not seem entirely new and would seem to play right into the hands of critics of liberalism, it is not a thesis born out of a posture of moral skepticism or moral minimalism, as much of liberalism traditionally is. Indeed, the view that liberalism is necessarily connected to moral minimalism or skepticism is to accept what is being rejected here.[2] Liberal minimalists must be included among those who accept that the promotion of moral conduct is a legitimate function of politics and a necessary part of any political theory. In this one very important respect, many minimalists or skeptics are very much like their critics. They differ from them only with respect to the *degree* or *level* of morality to be made the subject of political action. By contrast, we posit the claim about the distinctiveness of politics and morality from the standpoint of a *robust* moral framework and claim further that the political posture of liberalism is consistent with, indeed presupposes, that robustness.

Since our approach is not generally manifested in the actual doctrines of some well-known liberals, our case is conceptual rather than one derived primarily from historical examples. As we have noted elsewhere, the possible frameworks within which to consider the theoretical relationship between morality and politics could be represented as follows:[3]

---

[1] See, for example, Robert P. George, *Making Men Moral* (Oxford: Clarendon Press, 1993). "Liberalism" as we understand it is primarily of the classical variety with an emphasis on so called "negative" liberty. More contemporary forms of liberalism (which emphasize "positive" liberty) may be more amenable to "making men moral." In mentioning this, our point is not necessarily to condemn contemporary forms of liberalism, but rather to take up the harder challenge of combining an ethics of self-perfection with a politics of negative liberty.

[2] A representative case might be, for example, H.L.A. Hart's discussion of their separation in his debate with Lon Fuller over morality in the law. The problem is that Hart opts for amorality and Fuller, though in some respects closer to the position taken here, seems to be moving on the path of their conjunction. See section three below for a working out of this issue.

[3] Liberty and Nature: An Aristotelian Defense of Liberal Order, (with Douglas B. Rasmussen), La Salle, Illinois: 1991, p. 222–223.

| | |
|---|---|
| Ancient Ethics<br>Ancient Politics<br>(Plato and Aristotle) | Ancient Ethics<br>Modern Politics<br>(Spinoza) |
| Modern Ethics<br>Ancient Politics<br>(Rousseau ?) | Modern Ethics<br>Modern Politics<br>(Locke, Kant, Mill) |

Ancient ethical theory is characterized by the centrality of virtue and the idea that the central problem of moral life is to understand the good and to achieve it. It often speaks in the language of "flourishing" or "self-perfection." Ancient political theory would have the promotion of virtue or the promotion of the good as its central goal. Modern ethical theory, by contrast, is defined in terms of the relationships or obligations one has to others. Modern political theory, therefore, is concerned with the scope of individual liberty, because what our obligations are have something to do with the nature and scope of the liberties we shall enjoy.

Liberals have typically fallen into the bottom right hand quadrant of this scheme. Our approach, by contrast, is to give an account of liberal politics from the base of ancient ethics or to fit ourselves within the top right hand quadrant. We believe that not only can liberalism find a home in that quadrant, but also that it is most suited to that quadrant and is less defensible elsewhere. One can see, therefore, that there would be little historical precedent for our position. Nevertheless, our position is not entirely without such precedent.

## I

There is, we believe, at least one historical figure who fully understood what must be a central feature of liberalism — Spinoza. Spinoza understood not only that the scope of morality was wider and deeper than the scope of politics, but also that politics was not suited to the production of virtue. He understands these principles from a framework that includes a very robust ethics, that is, an ethics that does not reduce moral excellence to some form of social cooperation, as most liberal theorists do. The notion

57

that morality transcends the political is a part of Spinoza's political theory. We find, for example, statements like the following from the *Tractatus theologico-politicus*:

> Simplicity and integrity of spirit are not inspired in men by the command of laws or by public authority, and it is quite impossible to make anyone blessed by force or legal enactments; the means required are pious and brotherly counsel, a good upbringing, and, above all, a judgment that is free and independent. (TTP VII)

In the *Tractutus politicus* also Spinoza makes similar remarks:

> Those who believe that a people, or men divided over public business, can be induced to live by reason's dictate alone, are dreaming of the poets' golden age. . . . For freedom or strength of mind is a private virtue; the virtue of a state is stability. (TP I, 5-6)

The theoretical basis for making the foregoing statements is found in the TTP where we are told that the objects of human desire fall into three categories: knowledge of primary causes, control of the passions, and security and physical well being (*sano corpore*). The objects of desire also seem to be ranked by Spinoza with the highest being the first mentioned, to the lowest being the third. Politics is only applicable to the last category.

> The direct means to the first two goods, their proximate and efficient causes if you like, are contained in human nature itself; so that their attainment largely depends on our own unaided power, i.e., on the laws of human nature alone. . . . But the means to security and [conservation of the body (*corpus conservandum*)] lie mainly in things outside us. Accordingly, these goods are called gifts of fortune. . . . Still, human guidance and vigilance can do a great deal to help men live in safety and avoid injury. . . and the surest means to this end, and the means prescribed by reason and experience, is to form a society with definite laws. . . . (TTP III)

Political life is concerned with security and physical well being. It is not concerned with ethical matters as described in the first two goods. Keeping in mind what Spinoza calls "fortune" in the above passage, he tells us later in the TTP that, "the happiness and peace of the man who cultivates his natural understanding depends mainly on his own inherent virtue . . . and

58

not on the control of fortune."(TTP IV) Indeed, politics seems so far removed from moral perfection that at one point Spinoza tells us that "a man can be free in any kind of state; for, of course, a man is free in so far as he is guided by reason."(note 33 to TTP XVI)

The foregoing attitude towards the political is illustrated as well when we come to the issue of God and religion. In chapter four of the TTP Spinoza distinguishes human from divine law and tells us that they have a different aim. Divine law is the love of God which stems neither from fear or the "love of anyhing else we desire to enjoy" but from knowledge which is "self-validating and self-evident." In this chapter of the TTP Spinoza is trying to show that belief in historical narratives is not necessary for our supreme good, but he is at the same time demonstrating that fears and rewards do little for that end as well. Consequently,

> Actions whose only claim to goodness is the fact that they are prescribed by convention, or that they symbolize some good, can do nothing to perfect our understanding, but are simply empty forms, and no part of conduct which is the product or fruit of understanding and sound sense. (TTP IV)

Sacred rights, we are told in chapter five, have nothing to do with divine law and "consequently nothing to [do with] blessedness and virtue." Sacred rights are, in effect, political forms for Spinoza, so this is equivalent to saying that politics has nothing to do with virtue or moral excellence.

The typical liberal procedure was not to distinguish politics from morality, but rather to define the morally good in ways consistent with liberal politics. This often had the consequence of reducing morality to versions of cooperation. Notice that Spinoza does not make this move. Matters of security and physical well being are really not matters of substantive morality, because they are so far removed from a state of moral excellence or blessedness. It is not that "peace and commodious living" as Spinoza elsewhere refers to them, are unconnected to the human good. Rather, securing the conditions for their fulfillment may have little to do with qualities of character one might associate with moral excellence. The reasons are that the forms of conduct required to secure the conditions of peace — for example, refraining from injuring others or tolerating differences among non-threatening neighbors — do not require any special forms of excellence on the part of acting agents and are thus available to any and everyone. More importantly, the basic conditions for peace and commodious living do not require any qualities of character at all, since they can be, for the most part, coerced by law. They also do nothing to further develop our natures as rational beings. To refrain from injuring someone or to seek to be cooperative with them are valuable interpersonal modes of conduct, but they demand at most a modestly developed moral sentiment.

Traditional liberals, other than Spinoza, have followed their intellectual forefathers in the belief that political theory must concern itself with the moral character of the community. Since they were liberals who sought minimal state involvement in people's lives, the realm of morality would itself have to be minimized, if there was to be a substantial congruence between morality and politics. As we have argued elsewhere, this emphasis upon liberty within a traditional framework of joining politics and morality provides strong tendencies in liberalism to reduce morality to rights.[4] Rights respecting conduct, tolerance, open mindedness, and other such "liberal virtues" implied by an ethic of cooperation, thus came to be identified with the *whole* of morality.[5] In the face of such pressure, the "liberal" (meaning one who believes the state should be restricted to protecting people's rights) desirous of a more robust ethics must expand the realm of rights, thus allowing more state direction and guidance into the lives of its citizens.

Of course, this latter sort of welfare state liberal who may be moved by considerations of human dignity or benevolence that extend well beyond an ethics of cooperation does not necessarily argue, for example, that re-distributive actions by the state encourage the virtue of charity. Nor, for that matter, does the classical liberal necessarily claim that charity has no connection with morality because it cannot be enforced as a right by the state. But the welfare state liberal would insist that morality requires the redistribution, while the classical liberal would claim that morality does not — acts of charity being moral but supererogatory. Both see the problem as being one of getting the right fit between politics and morality. The notion that politics has, or should have, little or no connection with the promotion of morality is not considered. The result of not distinguishing morality from

---

[4] *Liberalism Defended* (with Douglas B. Rasmussen) (Cheltenham, UK, and Northampton, MA, 1997), Ch. 2, 9–7ff.
[5] Hobbes' list of "natural laws" in *Leviathan* is a source of instruction in the ethics of cooperation.

politics as we would suggest results in what might be called the dilemma of liberalism — it tends to either impoverish morality or trivialize rights. It does the former when it relegates moral excellence to the supererogatory. It does the latter when it inflates the language of rights to cover every conceivable human good.

At first, the distinction between the usual way of conceiving of classical liberalism and our position of keeping politics out of morality looks like it is merely a semantic matter. Politics should concern itself in some way with the promotion of cooperative conduct for the sake of peace and order. The typical classical liberal wishes to call such conduct "moral" whereas we do not, but the actual political agenda is the same. So far as it goes, this observation is true, but as we are arguing here, all is not political. The adverse consequences have to do precisely with our topic of moral education as well as the pathologies that have developed within liberalism because of its ambiguities with respect to the moral and the political. Before examining some of these pathologies, however, we need to look briefly at the basics of our proposal for distinguishing morality from politics through our theory of metanormativity.[6]

## II

Traditionally rights have been the language through which liberalism is spoken. The language of rights addresses a problem that is definitive of liberalism and its conception of politics. It is the problem of how to both recognize and provide for plurality in human pursuits and also simultaneously give one's social order a sense of moral legitimacy. Moral legitimacy would seem to require a certain uniformity of principles and conduct. Since people have diverse interests, values, and conceptions of the good, uniformity would apparently come at the expense of liberty and diversity. Liberal political theory, then, must address the issue of pluralism, and this means more than acknowledging the existence of many *views* of the human good. It means realizing that the human good is in fact plural and complex, not monistic and simple.

This realization creates a problem. We call it "liberalism's problem." "Liberalism's problem" may be expressed by the following questions: How

---

[6] I shall often speak in this paper in terms of "our" or "we." This is not an affectation. The approach to liberalism taken in this paper is one I have developed in conjunction with Douglas Rasmussen. It is, therefore, "our" doctrine and not simply my own.

do we find a standard which is concerned with the creation, interpretation, and evaluation of a political/legal context that will *in principle* not require that the human flourishing of *any* person or group be preferred to others? How do we make possible relationships among humans, each of whom has a unique form of human flourishing, ethically compossible? That is to say, how do we allow for the possibility that individuals might flourish in different ways (in different communities and cultures) without creating inherent moral conflict?[7]

Liberal rights theorists have tended to drift in the direction of solving liberalism's problem by upholding the primacy of the right over the good and viewing rights as totally independent of any consideration of human goods, consequences, circumstances, values, goals, or interests. Rights so conceived have been generally construed as expressions of an impersonalist moral theory — one where the principle of universalizability is paramount. However, an impersonalist approach grounded in the principle of universalizability will not suffice as a solution to liberalism's problem of reconciling diverse forms of the good with moral uniformity, because the principle of universalizability does not solve value conflicts or prove that there is a human good that is truly the same for each of us.

The production of one person's good is a reason for that person to act, just as the production of another's good is a reason for that other to act. Each person cannot claim that his good provides him with a legitimate reason to act without also acknowledging that the other's good provides her with a legitimate reason to act. An agent-relative notion of values thus can be universalized in this sense, but this form of universalization is obviously not sufficient to establish *common* values or a reason for other-regarding conduct among persons. Universalization in this sense does not show one person's good to be another's good, nor does it show that the production of one person's good provides a reason for another's action. It only shows that goods are reasons for action and that we must acknowledge that in others as well as ourselves. Thus, if one person's good should conflict with another's, universalizability could not resolve the conflict.

Secondly, there is a fundamental difficulty that stands in the way of anyone who uses impersonal moral theory. The difficulty is simply that

---

[7]Douglas B. Rasmussen, "Community versus Liberty," in Tibor R. Machan and Douglas B. Rasmussen, eds., *Liberty for the 21ˢᵗ Century* (Lanham, MD: Rowman and Littlefield, 1995), p. 271.

nothing can be said in reply to those who ask why they ought to be moral in an impersonal sense. There is, in other words, no self-contradiction in asking why one "ought" to adopt an impersonal moral theory (that is why it would be good, worthy, or appropriate to do so). And since there is, *by definition*, no way that an impersonal moral theory can give a reason that is not an agent-neutral reason, it cannot provide an agent-relative reason to the person who asks why he should be moral in an impersonal sense. Any rights theory based on such an impersonal view of morality can provide neither reason nor motivation for human conduct. This is a major, possibly insuperable, difficulty faced by anyone who bases the right to liberty on impersonal moral theory.

The development of a conception of rights that is not reducible to other moral concepts, while being at the same time grounded in a recognition of a real diversity of personal goods, is what is needed as a corrective to the foregoing problem. We describe this conception of rights as "metanormative" principles. The theory is put forward within an Aristotelian framework, and in the argument a central role is given to self-directedness, understood generally as the use of practical reason.[8] It is important to realize that by "self-directedness" in this context we do not mean full blown Millean autonomy or the directedness of the perfected self where one is fully rational. Instead, we mean simply the use of reason and judgment upon the world in an effort to understand one's surroundings and make plans to act within or upon it. Self-directedness as just described is still true of the actions of the most self-perfected of individuals, but nothing in this description requires or implies such individuals or even successful conduct.[9] The protection of self-direction in this sense does not favor one form of human flourishing over any other, because it is the act of exercising practical reason that is being protected, not the achievement of its object. Further, self-direction is not something disconnected from an individual's own good, but the central necessary component of its achievement.

[8] The term "Aristotelian" is an ambiguous one. We do not necessarily mean Aristotelian as derived directly from Aristotle's own writings, but rather the tradition of doctrines perhaps somewhat loosely collected together due to similar convictions about basic philosophical principles, e.g., teleology, human nature, reason, and the like.

[9] It might be asked, "why pitch the starting point here rather than at a higher level of self-directedness?" Apart from the fact that the more perfected or successful forms arise out of practice with the more "ordinary" form, the perfected forms are too individualized to serve us in this context. See *The Virtue of Prudence*, Bern: Peter Lang. 1991, Ch. 8.

In the Aristotelian case, we argue that self-directedness is both central and necessary to the very nature of human flourishing. It is the only feature of human flourishing common to all acts of self-perfection and peculiar to each without at the same time implying those particular forms of flourishing. It expresses the fundamental core of human flourishing. Self-directedness is the only feature of human flourishing upon which to base a solution to liberalism's problem, because (1) it is the only feature in which it can be universally said that each and every person in the concrete situation has a necessary stake, and (2) it is the only feature of human flourishing whose protection is consistent with diverse forms of human flourishing.

Rights from this perspective are concerned with protecting the condition under which moral conduct — for the Aristotelian, self-perfection — can occur. That is to say, rights are principles designed to protect self-directedness. Obviously, securing the basic condition for the possibility of self-perfection is logically prior to and distinct from the actual pursuit of self-perfection. But securing that condition must be understood as essentially "negative." This is because self-directedness does not imply or guarantee self-perfection and because one person's self-perfection is not exchangeable with another's. In other words, we are *not* trying with our theory of rights *directly* and *positively* to secure self-perfection, but rather to protect, and thus prevent encroachments upon, the conditions under which self-perfection can be pursued. Our aim is thus to protect the *possibility* of self-perfection, but only through seeking to protect the possibility of self-directedness.

Since the purpose here is to structure a political principle that protects the condition for self-perfection rather than to further or encourage acts of self-perfection themselves, the consequences of actions are of little importance (except insofar as they threaten the condition that rights were designed to protect in the first place). Rights are not structured with an eye to how acts will turn out, but rather with setting the appropriate foundation for the taking of any action in the first place.

Thus, though "rights" are ethical principles, they are of a special kind. Their function is *not* to provide persons guidance in achieving good or conducting themselves properly. They are *not* normative principles in any usual sense, but are instead what we call *metanormative* principles: that is to say, they concern the preconditions for moral conduct and arise because of the need to establish, interpret, and evaluate political/legal contexts so that individuals can achieve their moral well-being in consort with others. Since the single most basic and threatening encroachment upon self-directedness is the initiation of physical force by one person (or group) against another, rights allow each person a sphere of freedom whereby self-directed activities can be exercised without being invaded by others. This translates socially into a principle of maximum compossible and equal freedom for all.

The freedom must be equal, in the sense that it must allow for the possibility of diverse modes of flourishing and, therefore, must not be structurally biased in favor of some forms of flourishing over others. The freedom must be compossible, meaning that the exercise of self-directed activity by one person must not encroach upon and does not diminish that of another. Thus, a theory of rights that protects persons' self-directedness can be used to create a political/legal order that will not necessarily require that the flourishing of any person or group be sacrificed to any other.

Rights are not normative principles in the sense of guiding us towards the achievement of moral excellence or self-perfection. And contrary to appearances, they are not ordinary interpersonal normative principles either. Rights express a type of moral principle that we must obtain if we are to reconcile our natural sociality with diverse forms of flourishing. We need, in other words, social life, but we also need to succeed as individuals approaching a particular form of flourishing. Norms which specify how to live among others and the obligations one is likely to incur in such a life are one thing; norms which define the setting for such interactions and obligations are quite another. The "obligations" one has to another in the latter case are due to a shared need to act in an orderly social/political context. The obligations one has in the former case are a function of what is needed to live well and cannot be generated apart from the particular actions, context, culture, traditions, intentions, and practices in which one finds oneself acting. Those actions and contexts call forth evaluative norms by which success, propriety, and merit can be measured and judged in particular cases. Metanorms (rights) are not, however, *called upon* by the progress of a culture or individual, but rather *depended* upon.

In this respect, the standard sort of "state of nature" analysis traditionally used by liberals may actually confuse the issue, rather than help clarify it. In the state of nature approach we are tempted to abandon the social and ask what one would be obligated to do if there were no law, society, culture, or political authority to define any duties. If one person does injury to another in such a state of nature, it looks as though only one level of obligation is present, since, by definition, there is no particular society or political context to offer any other. The normative and metanormative seem to collapse into the single duty of respecting another's natural rights. Securing the setting (non-interference), in other words, appears to be the same as undertaking appropriate conduct itself. But while asocial beings might worry about why they have any obligations at all towards others and thus would need to conjure up arguments as to why it might be in someone's interest to respect another's "rights," social beings, by contrast, would never have a radical worry about why they should concern themselves with others. They come, as it were, already concerned. State of nature approaches give us the illusion that society is only marginally relevant to a determination of what will count as moral and that *all* norms worth considering are context setting norms (e.g., rights). A state of nature approach may have some value in helping us to identify metanormative principles, but it does so at the expense of what liberal critics are most insistent upon, namely the role of social life in moral theory and moral life. Thus those critics have a point when they claim that the language of rights does next to nothing towards generating the normative rules or obligations that are necessary for a life of moral excellence. Part of our point in response is that rights should never have been meant to do that work.

Liberalism's problem can now be put another way: how can liberalism retain any connection to a substantive moral philosophy and demand so little politically? Communitarian critics of liberalism, for example, have argued that liberalism is morally vacuous because it has no room for substantive moral principles. Its minimalist and rights centered perspective leaves off the role of imbeddedness in community so central to moral life. The metanormative perspective on rights mentioned here allows for a strong connection to a substantive moral framework without lapsing into a moralistic politics. It can do so because it recognizes the difference between conditions for the possibility of certain actions and the actions themselves (and their accompanying norms). Liberalism is the political theory that limits politics to the first function and is thus two tiered. It partitions off morality from politics much as it partitions off religion from politics and for similar reasons.[10] Liberalism is not, therefore, a political philosophy in the traditional sense. It does not evaluate social orders with reference to ordinary moral norms, but rather in terms of whether the conditions for moral conduct have been secured. Liberalism does not deny — indeed it *assumes* — that moral life goes beyond specified rights and political principles. The viability today of liberalism depends upon it not closing off the path to a rich moral posture, any more than it can still remain a liberalism while politically dictating a particular form of moral living.

The idea that liberalism is not a political philosophy in the sense of seeking to evaluate social institutions in terms of their exemplification of, or contribution to, preferred moral principles does not render it a merely descriptive theory. It is both evaluative and ethical though not *morally* evaluative in the sense of determining whether persons have successfully done good and avoided evil (or in general fulfilled their moral obligations). Liberalism is, therefore, different from the ideal world as envisioned by its communitarian critics — whether of the left wing or conservative variety — and would still be, in light of the theory offered here, fundamentally defective from their point of view. This is because the two tiered sort of perspective we have been advancing suggests that politics is not significant in the exercise of moral excellence, but rather serves only to secure the conditions under which such excellence might be undertaken. The communitarian, by contrast, usually gives political life a central place in moral development. In this respect, therefore, liberalism as we conceive it does not reduce morality to a set of "liberal virtues" which consist entirely in various principles of cooperation and non-intervention and which are meant to signify what is central to a "liberal" ethics. On the other hand, liberalism does not try to inflate the language of rights to include any morally worthy form of conduct as something deserving of political attention. Instead, liberalism insists that there are related, but distinct, types

---

[10] It should become evident that "morality" is not being used here as an equivalent to "ethics." Morality concerns itself with ordinary moral aspirations, for example, finding fulfillment and keeping one's obligations. "Ethics" encompasses normative principles of all types that concern themselves with human well being. Metanorms are ethical principles but not the same as ordinary moral norms for reasons advanced here. The distinction seems more pertinent when considered in the context of the theory presented here. We do not mean to impose the distinction on ordinary usage.

of normative principles with politics concerning itself with one type only, the metanormative.

Liberalism as we conceive it is thus opposed to what might be called "regime building." Regime building consists in developing a political and social philosophy which is then used to guide a politics in shaping a certain kind of social order with a certain kind of person in it. Regime builders can be very intrusive or minimalistic in what they advocate with respect to politics and the advancement of moral life. Often the fight between "liberals" and communitarians is a fight between minimalist and robust regime builders. The endeavor to produce through political techniques, or their limitation, a certain kind of liberal character — usually one that is open minded, tolerant of diverse "life styles," concerned for the plight of classes of people (e.g., minorities) and the like — is a form of regime building as much as the communitarian who wishes to infuse individuals by political techniques with preferred norms and roles of an appropriately envisioned community. Our argument about the nature of liberalism is quite different. Liberalism is opposed to regime building. If one wishes to give a society a certain look, means other than the political will have to be taken.

### III

There is lurking in the background a powerful objection to our approach. The objection goes something like this: politics is of its nature a character forming enterprise. Political orders, in other words, always produce a certain sort of character and establish certain norms of moral conduct. Consequently, there is no possibility of drawing away from direct moral influence by means of limiting politics to metanormative principles, for a political order instantiating these will of necessity also be promoting a certain sort of moral life and ethos. If nothing else, it will have the effect of reducing morality to the metanorms in the same way that communitarians have accused liberals or reducing morality to rights.

This idea that politics is always regime building was probably first expressed in Book VIII of Plato's *Republic* where the nature of the soul is tied to the nature of the political order. Numerous authors, especially in political theory, have echoed the same idea. Yet the degree to which this is an empirical versus a theoretical claim is worth considering. As an empirical claim we would have to examine whether the order of the regimes as described by Plato (or any other theorist) is always made manifest in the way he describes. We would have to consider whether certain forms of government, e.g., modern constitutional republicanism, always produce the same types of individuals. We would have to consider whether the regime follows the character of the people or vice versa. As empirical matters, these issues are beyond the scope of this paper.

As a speculative or theoretical issue, however, it is important to recognize that from the point of view taken here, the claim that politics of necessity produces a certain sort of character to match a certain type of political order would be a question begging claim. Regime building cannot be *presupposed* in the attack on metanormativity. The exact degree and nature of the contribution of politics to moral excellence or depravity would have to be argued for. Further, the critic of the metanormative understanding of liberalism would have to show that alternative forms of inducement to moral excellence besides the political are impossible or insignificant, for liberalism holds out the belief, not that we should have no concern for the character of our society, but that there are other contexts and modes of moral inducement besides the political. Finally, even if it were true that a certain sort of politics produces a certain sort of person, the question of the plurality of forms of flourishing would have to be faced. It may be that a minimalist politics allows for the decadent and immoral to manifest itself, but it is by no means clear that flourishing comes in one form only, or that a politics that achieves a conformity of a certain type behavior has come any closer to that form than one that does not. [11]

The metanormative approach really has two positions: 1) that there is no necessary connection between politics and moral excellence, and 2) that politics *should* not be used as a tool for the direct production of moral excellence. The first is partially an empirical claim, but it is mostly a claim that the centralized and monopolized use of physical force to direct behavior at best has only an accidental bearing on the production of moral excellence, because that excellence is so much the result of self-directed practical wisdom. We do not wish to deny that force has ever brought someone to a position where they recognize the worthiness of a course of action they may not have otherwise seen. But there is no necessity here —

---

[11] Indeed, the politics of regime building betrays a profound ignorance of the pluralistic character of the human good and suffers from hubris. It assumes that knowledge of abstract ethical principles alone will suffice for the creation of moral excellence. Its ethical rationalism reflects modernity's failure to see the importance of practical wisdom and the unique character of each person's fulfillment.

indeed we would expect a certain unlikeness. That politics should not be so used is partly a function of its ill-suitedness to the task, but also a function of the individualized nature of the good. Politics must, of necessity, ignore what is individual and therefore must of necessity treat some goods as being privileged when it directly commands a certain sort of "moral" conduct.

But it might be argued that we have set up a straw man here. Those wishing to argue for the role of politics in the production of moral virtue are seeking a middle ground between the imputed laissez-faire implications of metanormativity on the one hand and the direct production of virtue on the other. Adherence to a norm through coercion is not moral action, so the argument goes, but coercion can *habituate* one to such action and therein lies the middle position. Habituation is the groundwork for moral action and without it no groundwork is laid at all, especially if character development is the central concern of ethical conduct. Saying this does not require one to pretend that actions that are a part of the habituating process are in and of themselves moral actions or manifestations of moral excellence. Hence the process of habituation is both necessary and a middle way between moral excellence on the one hand and the mere opportunity for choice-making on the other.

Yet the admission that politics does not induce moral excellence is a significant concession. If we are talking of conduct that does not truly qualify as morally excellent because of its coerced rather than voluntary nature, then *the best* that can be said for such conduct is that it is orderly. It must first be noted that there is a difference between conformity and order. Both have to do with rule governed behavior in the presence of others, but conformity is action in accordance with a norm, whereas order is adherence to a norm with some belief that the norm is appropriate or justified as a rule of action. Presumably those who see politics as a means of habituating virtue would seek an orderly form of conduct, not a conforming one. The reason is that conformity offers little hope of transformation into moral action because it lacks insight. Order by contrast, while requiring conformity on the part of those incapable or unlikely to achieve more, seems to offer the promise of movement towards moral action because of the presence of belief.

Even if we grant the foregoing rationale for the link between order and virtue, it must be noted that it is one sided. The argument forgets that just as order may be a prelude to virtue because of belief, it is just as likely to be a prelude to conformity if belief is without understanding. As Mill points out in *On Liberty*, there are many reasons for holding that politically enforced social norms generate conformity. But in essential terms, the reason to suppose a movement in this direction from politics is that the tools politics provides appeal in the end not to understanding but to sentiment alone (e.g., to fear or to social acceptance). Now it may be true that most people are moved by sentiment most of the time, but unfortunately this does not help the cause of the critic of liberalism. That critic must show that the sort of directed appeal to sentiment offered by politics is more likely to produce order than are such devices as markets and non-governmental intermediary institutions such as churches or clubs. We would suggest that in this respect politics is more likely to produce *conformity* than are these alternative ordering institutions. Furthermore, by laying only foundational norms of conduct as metanorms do, the possibility exists under liberalism that conduct within that framework can actually be recognized as moral conduct. This is virtually impossible in the regime building framework, because conformity, orderly conduct, and moral excellence would all *look* the same. That is to say, whether one acted out of a threat of punishment, a desire to conform, or from a self-directed understanding of the good would all look the same to any observer.

Politically induced habituation nevertheless seems to have going for it the removal of many examples of moral baseness that the metanormative approach could not rule out. Those in the early stages of moral training (e.g., the young) are thus less exposed to modes of living that divert them from the path of virtue. We shall ignore for the moment the issue of whether the path to virtue is a singular one. What is to be noticed about the regime building argument is that there is no way to distinguish fraudulent from real moral exemplars. Those acting in political roles may not themselves be virtuous at all, but simply orderly or possibly even conforming. There is again no way to tell the difference. Those in moral training are perhaps saved from exposure to what is base, but they are so saved at the expense of gaining much insight into the nature of virtue, since the indistinguishability of the types of actions (conformist, orderly, or virtuous) gives increasing weight to what is most readily perceived, and that is behavior. There is, as a consequence, a tendency towards conformity. The liberal order can, in contrast, point to real moral exemplars precisely because their conduct is of necessity normative without being politically directed.[12]

The regime builder's desire to connect politics with moral excellence holds out orderly conduct as the highest level of moral excellence. The liberal to the contrary leaves open a different possibility — one that recognizes a difference between orderly conduct and moral conduct. Orderly conduct is adherence to a norm because of belief in its rightness or appropriateness. Moral conduct, on the other hand, is conduct which proceeds from an understanding of the appropriateness or rightness of an action including the appropriateness or rightness of any relevant rules or norms. Moral conduct is *essentially* self-directed conduct as, we would argue, is reason itself. The distinction between moral and orderly conduct is, obviously, somewhat analogous to Plato's distinction between knowledge and true belief. It differs at least by leaving open the possibility that value might be agent-relative though knowledge is not. Yet it is similar in a way that is particularly significant, namely that just as knowledge would not be attributed to an individual without that individual possessing understanding, so too would we not attribute moral virtue to an individual lacking in practical wisdom which of necessity includes self-directed conduct. The orderly individual is open to the Euthyphro type question of whether the action is appropriate because it is believed or whether it is believed because appropriate. But with orderliness as the measure, it makes no difference which way this question is answered.[13] This is because orderliness only requires belief and nothing more, so the action would be the same in either case. The liberal, however, holds open the prospect that the answer to the Euthyphro type question not only makes a difference in the abstract but does so potentially to each and every individual in the concrete. This is because liberalism protects and does not structurally impede the second option to the question — that we believe it because it is appropriate. The first option, that it is appropriate because believed, is the orderly option.

---

[12] It is, of course, possible to suggest with Spinoza that real moral exemplars would shine through any political order, but this seems to lend more weight to our argument that the connection between politics and virtue is at best contingent than it does to the argument for their connection.

[13] This point, by the way, follows the *Meno* where Socrates notes that understanding and belief amount to the same thing in practice.

It seems paradoxical, but for this reason it is the liberal who is more directly linked to moral excellence than the communitarian critic of liberalism. By limiting politics to a context setting role, liberalism leaves the path to virtue free of confusing or misdirecting alternatives. Its main problem is that it offers no guarantees that virtue will be forthcoming. However, the guarantees of the regime builder, by the arguments offered above, are either contingently related to virtue or they form an obstacle to it, if they are not illusory altogether. The *rhetoric* of virtue may lie more with the regime builder, but its presence is no more likely to be found there than in the liberal order.

There is a final issue to consider. This is an alternative where the critic of liberalism agrees that politics should be concerned with metanorms as we have suggested, but that the metanorms needed are more robust than the ones we have allowed. The point here would be to use politics to secure the foundations for the community life necessary for moral conduct in a more direct and positive way than the negative liberty approach suggested here which protects only the possibility of moral conduct. This alternative framework would make no pretense at encouraging moral excellence or even providing a "middle way" to it. What would be provided instead are the sorts of conditions human beings need in which to flourish. These might include provisions for basic education, health, and welfare. Since the proposal is not inconsistent with our position when considered in the abstract, we shall not spend time here rebutting it in any detail. We have done so elsewhere.[14] In essence, this line of argument suffers from the confusion that what is true in the abstract — that human beings need education, provisions for health and the like — is univocally true when applied to individual cases. The plural and individualized nature of the good insures that political solutions to these problems must always fail to do more than average or aggregate, because politics has no concern for the individual, though virtue exists no where else. In any case, to adopt the line of argument about more robust metanorms is to give up the proverbial ghost, at least philosophically, on the necessary connection between politics and virtue. It is, in other words, to become a liberal!

## IV

[14] "'Rights' as MetaNormative Principles" (with Douglas B. Rasmussen) *Liberty for the 21ˢᵗ Century*, pp. 59–75.

It is every bit as much a part of our argument here to say that liberalism undermines itself — and has done so already to a considerable degree — by countenancing any element of moral skepticism or minimalism. As we have noticed, there is a big difference between claiming that politics should not be concerned to promote virtue and claiming that virtue is nonexistent or equivalent to simple forms of social cooperation. Our suggestion is quite the opposite, namely that liberalism is dependent upon a very robust notion of virtue and ethics. Without a commitment to moral robustness, liberalism falls prey to doctrines that present themselves as having justice and the good on their side. Avoiding the moral in the name of efficiency, utility, social harmony, and the like leaves the central issue open — namely, the issue of the *legitimacy* of the political order which calls upon us to address the connection between it and the human good. In the face of this issue, one of three paths remains available: a) attack the idea of needing to give an account at all of legitimacy (the positivist social science approach), b) join the ranks of regime builders and claim that morality and politics ought to be united in some significant way and that liberalism is a complete philosophy or system of thought, or c) link liberalism to a robust ethical framework, but argue for a limited politics from that perspective. Liberalism has traditionally split itself between the first and second sorts of defenses. We have, obviously, chosen the third way.

To appreciate why a liberal or limited politics is compatible with a robust ethics requires an appreciation of a point of moral ontology. The point has been implied above. Ethical norms can be of differing types and not just of one type with differing degrees of importance or obligatoriness. As we have noted, norms outlining ordinary moral obligations are one type of ethical norm, and norms which govern the establishment of a social context in which the possibility of the pursuit of moral action is protected form another type of ethical norm. We describe systems or theories which see norms as differing only in degrees of priority or obligatoriness as being "equinormative." Liberalism as we view it rejects the equinormative approach, requiring instead the tiered model we have been discussing. It does so because it recognizes that norms can have distinct roles to play — one for guiding action the other for setting contexts. If there can be different types of norms, then the possibility is open that there may be specialized or limited ways in which politics and ethics link together.

The obvious question here is, do not metanorms — however context setting they may be — guide action just as "ordinary" norms do? Differing purposes, in other words, do not necessarily require a division of ontological types any more than the differing purposes embodied in norms of honesty versus norms of charity require us to speak of ontologically different *types* of norms. Since ethical norms are action guiding principles, the answer to this objection at one level is, "yes, norms and metanorms both guide action." In fact, however, the more significant answer is, "no," because actions guided by metanorms alone are not expressions of moral excellence. They do not, at *any* level of abstraction, aim at moral excellence. Rather, they are expressions of ways to solve "liberalism's problem." Indeed, these norms are fully satisfied when followed out of ignorance or fear of force as they are when self-directedly adhered to. One merely has to have behavior that conforms to the metanorms that solve liberalism's problem.[15]

One of the central ontological facts about metanorms is that unlike regular moral principles, the motivations and intentions for following them are of little importance to their normative value, provided they *are* followed. The same cannot be said for the usual norms and values of moral conduct. A person may follow a metanorm out of a self-directed sense of the norm's applicability and worthiness, but the self-perfected basis of the conduct in this case adds little to the meaningfulness of the norm. The context is set whether one, for example, refrains from initiating force against another out of a fear of punishment or censure or whether one does so from a rational understanding of the role of metanorms. By contrast, if an act of honesty is undertaken out of fear of some reprisal, then some discounting of the act and the person's moral worth is applied. The self-perfected, or at least self-directed, qualities that seem so necessary for moral value with respect to ordinary norms can be absent from motivations to obey metanorms with little detriment to the functioning of those norms. As context setting principles for the possibility of moral action, moral action per se is not required. Morality *in general*, however, requires the metanorms because moral conduct takes place within social space and that space needs to be defined and structured in some way.

The history of political theory, from our perspective, is one of trying to make politics compatible with ordinary moral norms. In fact, politics must be about metanormative conduct, because it cannot effectively

---

[15] This is a different issue from determining the level of responsibility or form of punishment for someone who violates a metanorm.

discriminate among motives. The inability to discriminate finely about motives is one of the reasons for the unsuitability of politics. The other is its universalizing character. These points are the main reasons why politics can never serve as a means to moral excellence or self-perfecting conduct. Nevertheless, the endeavor to fit politics to that for which it is unsuited is common enough.

The traditional classical liberal has endeavored to infuse adherence to metanorms with value appropriate to ordinary moral conduct. Since metanorms do not need the same motivation as moral conduct to be functional, the endeavor to infuse metanorms with such value breeds skepticism or minimalism. That one refrains from initiating force against another or lives up to one's contracts hardly represent significant expressions of moral excellence. The classical liberal whose list of virtues are simple ones of social cooperation not only impoverishes the moral landscape, but shares with his critics the notion that whatever makes a list of worthy moral norms or principles is an appropriate area of political concern and action. The effect is to hand over to those with more robust conceptions of moral life the more compelling and exalted dimensions of the moral universe; for not only can these others account for those simple virtues of the liberal, but they have additional virtues as well. And they would be correct, by the way. The moral landscape is much richer than minimalist theories suppose.

Just as equinormativity may bring down the peaks of moral excellence or elevate the low virtues when in the hands of the classical liberal, so does it pervert the character of ordinary moral prescriptions when in the hands of the communitarian. Because politics is by its nature suited to metanorms, to politicize morality is to give ordinary moral prescriptions the intransigent, universalist, and detached quality possessed by metanorms, for this is how political rules function of their own accord anyway. Doing so, however, moralizes politics intolerably. What is known as "political correctness" today is an example of politics moralized, and it is a natural hazard of equinormative thinking. In addition, if everything is a matter of the same type of moral obligation, then we must index levels of obligatoriness. Yet politics (as opposed to political theory) does not do this very well, for it is not rooted in reason and argument, but force and sentiment. Force and sentiment may index, but presumably that mode of indexing is not in accord with what ought to be exhibited in moral conduct. Therefore, the argument that a significant element in the development of one's moral life is political activity is quite off the mark. At this juncture, however, we are one with the liberal tradition in distinguishing "political" from "social."

There is another "ontological" element to the theory we are advancing. However social we may be by nature, morality is not essentially or finally about social conduct but about self perfection. Some indication of this was given in the opening section when discussing Spinoza. The preceding arguments would hold in any case even if morality is essentially about social conduct, for there would still be the need to distinguish metanorms from moral norms. But part of our argument here is that the moral robustness presumed by liberalism is the ability to recognize a dimension of moral life that goes beyond the social to the self-perfective. In Aristotelian terms this is sometimes referred to as self-sufficiency.[16] The idea is that in the end one is left with the problem of perfecting one's own nature, and while that may take place in the company of others it is essentially a process one faces for oneself.

What Spinoza called blessedness or Aristotle the theoretical life are examples here. But our concern at the moment is not to discuss the nature of this sort of life, but to appreciate the scope of moral existence and the relationship of liberalism to it. If there is a dimension of moral life in some significant way beyond the social, then the posture of liberalism towards morality seems even more compelling. The posture of liberalism is compelling here because politics seems even less suited to promoting the self-perfective virtues than it does the social ones. One can, as Stanley Fish and others have done,[17] claim that liberalism really has no contact with such levels of existence, because it seeks to avoid any commitments to substantive issues, or one can see liberalism as making more modest claims precisely in view of the fact that it understands the substantive to be inadequately captured by the general patterns of political or social existence.

It is ironic that contemporary critics of liberalism accept the idea that morality — and even truth itself — are matters of social roles, interests,

---

[16] See Henry B. Veatch's discussion of Aristotle's criteria of human perfection or well-being, *Human Rights: Fact or Fancy?* (Baton Rouge and London: Louisiana University Press, 1985), pp. 77–85, especially p. 84.
[17] *First Things*, op. Cit., "Why We Can't All Just Get Along," and especially his reply to Neuhaus p. 38.

accepted customs, or community standards.[18] This sort of perspective is from ancient times on the kind of philosophy one would expect from "liberals."[19] Aristotle, so far as one can speak here without anachronism, put the social contractarians who took all to be agreement and convention in this camp.[20] Standards such as nature, reason, or God, which stand outside convention and are used to judge it, get reduced by the anti-foundationalist epistemology of the post-modern communitarians to social roles and practices or interests. But this is just liberalism as they themselves understand it, because just as the neutrality of liberalism is said to be unable to decide ultimately between competing claims, except in terms of cooperation alone, so is there nothing here but incommensurable commitments, all of which have no better claim than the other to truth. The result is not to enrich morality by wresting it from the abstract world of liberal rights and embedding it in a particular social context where morality can be meaningful and flourish. Instead, commitment disappears, because truth itself has done so. Societies do not flourish morally which do not see their conventions as rooted in, and answerable to, standards beyond themselves. And it is hard for one to remain committed to what one believes is grounded only in acts of commitment themselves, existentialism notwithstanding. And indirect anti-foundationalism — where one believes *as if* there are independent truths, but gives a wink when the meta-question arises of there being anything outside our belief systems — only forestalls the cynicism.

When we claimed, therefore, at the opening of this section that liberalism *depends* upon a robust moral outlook, we were suggesting that its own health requires such a perspective. Paradoxically perhaps, the more robust one's moral universe, the more readily one can appreciate the rather limited role that can be played by politics with respect to moral perfection. It is perhaps no accident that faith in politics might flourish in an era of moral skepticism and historicism. In any case, if our conception of liberalism is correct, skepticism and minimalism undermine liberalism because they make it difficult to separate the normative from the metanormative. As we have seen, this conflation tends to give too much value to the low virtues while ignoring the high ones. The moral landscape

[18] Fish in ibid., p. 38 reduces truth to convention and interest.
[19] One is reminded of Protagorous and Lycophron — classical versions of "liberals."
[20] E.g., cf. Aristotle, *Politics*, 1280b5–12.

is flattened, undermining robustness and giving liberalism the appearance of being a full moral framework in competition with other such frameworks. That in turn directs us away from what liberalism, in our view, is all about — namely, the need to limit the political because of the very scope, depth, and complexity of the moral order. Liberalism does not offer us an ethical philosophy or framework so much as it does a position on the relationship between politics and ethics, given certain truths about the nature of the good and moral life. And while we cannot argue for it here, we have the suspicion that the notion that liberalism is a complete moral and social philosophy is more at the insistence of its enemies than its friends (either contemporary or historical).

It has been argued that liberalism cannot generate its own moral values, so it must be parasitical upon moral frameworks that come from outside of it.[21] Yet, in addition, the nature of liberalism is to systematically erode the frameworks upon which it is parasitical. Therefore, liberalism is incompatible with morality, robust or otherwise. But without trying to give a full response to this here,[22] in the absence of the normative/metanormative distinction, liberalism *would* be undermining of robust moral perspectives, because it would have a tendency to postulate ordinary moral norms as metanorms and vice versa. So our point is again that failure to make the normative metanormative distinction has the perverse consequence of giving liberalism the appearance of being a complete philosophy or at least a complete moral philosophy. And again, robustness is something of a solution here: "How small, of all that human hearts endure, That part which laws or kings can cause or cure."[23]

## V

Adam Smith tells us that,

> The disposition to admire and almost to worship, the rich and the powerful ... is, at the same time, the great and most universal cause of the corruption of our moral sentiments. That wealth and greatness are often regarded with

[21] MacIntyre, A. *Whose Justice? Which Rationality?* (Notre Dame, Indiana: Univ. of Notre Dame Press), 1988, pp. 343–344.

[22] We respond to this in *Liberalism Defended*, Chs 1 and 2. See also Rasmussen. "Community versus Liberty?" op cit.

[23] Richard Neuhaus quoting Johnson: "Why We Can Get Along," *First Things op. Cit.*, p. 33.

the respect and admiration which are due only to wisdom and virtue; and that the contempt, of which vice and folly are the only proper objects, is often most unjustly bestowed upon poverty and weakness, has been the complaint of moralists in all ages. (*Theory of Moral Sentiments,* I.iii.3.1)

Much later, however, he also tells us that,

Nature has wisely judged that the distinction of ranks, the peace and order of society, would rest more securely upon the plain and palpable difference of birth and fortune, than upon the invisible and often uncertain difference of wisdom and virtue. (*Theory of Moral Sentiments,* VI.ii.1.20)

If Smith is right in these observations, numerous problems and issues are raised that would be of concern to anyone addressing our topic. If nothing else, these passages give a rather pessimistic outlook on the prospects for the public promotion of virtue. They do so because one might hold that the symbolic character of politics is central to it, and thus while there may not be a causal relationship between politics and the development of virtue, it s nonetheless important to have a public presence or display of it to serve as a polestar for its development. The symbolic nature of politics is indeed a possible objection to our entire approach here. It allows one to claim a significant role for politics without having to defend a direct causal connection between political activity and the promotion of virtue. But if people cannot recognize virtue on the one hand, and it is not displayed on the other, then the symbolic role of virtue in politics collapses. Smith's point, of course, is that social order does not depend upon government by the virtuous. Nevertheless, Smith is undoubtedly worried about the prospect for virtue.

The Smithean problem is one we have partly alluded to above when we discussed the issue of virtue versus order. Here it takes on a slightly different dimension. "Wealth and greatness" are suitable to the production of order, because social order requires leaders and managers who have public visibility which the wealthy and wellborn do have. Order is in no way dependent upon virtue. Indeed, to hope for order as a result of virtue is a mistake, because virtue is too subtle a quality to be recognized by all ranks of society,[24] but all ranks need to be simultaneously ordered. Yet it

[24] It might be said that this is the essence of modern politics, namely, that it does not depend or rest upon virtue.

would seem that without virtue playing a prominent public role, there would be little hope for its promulgation in society. Yet virtue cannot play a prominent role, because not only is it too difficult to recognize a true manifestation of it in order to place it in the public light, but even when it is in that light, it is too hard to recognize. Virtue, then, is not only completely inefficacious, it is too dim to serve as a polestar for public life. However, if virtue is not put in the public light, how can we expect it to gain a foothold in society?

We could simply decide to challenge Smith's observation head on and claim that virtue *can* be recognized and contribute something significant to social order and the general advancement of virtue itself. If Smith's point is accepted, however, it would seem that the alternatives are either to reject the idea of drawing any necessary connection between virtue and order and thus possibly end with a kind of tragic pessimism, or one could conceive of virtue in such a way as to be compatible with that which *is* recognizable in political life. The latter alternative is not unfamiliar to liberal politics. Wealth creation itself has been made into a virtue by certain strands of Protestantism or within certain versions of libertarianism such as that of Ayn Rand. Virtues useful to, or connected with, wealth creation have also been touted as virtues, such as honesty, promise keeping, or tolerance. The problem would be that if liberal orders tend to put these virtues more readily before the public, what might it be doing to less visible virtues such as friendliness or magnanimity? Does the liberal order ipso facto select the virtues to be given weight (and thus the issue raised earlier), or is it limited to a certain pattern or list of virtues? Do these "pre-selected" virtues then serve as symbols for "liberal virtues?"

It is, of course, our contention that there is no necessary connection between social order and virtue. Contrary to some assertions to the contrary, liberal orders do not necessarily shape a certain kind of soul, though the predominance of a certain kind of soul may give a particular look to a liberal order.[25]   Saying this is, however, no solution to the Smithean problem. Smith may be suggesting that virtue *ought* to have a public role, because if it does not people will end up admiring the wrong things to the detriment of virtue itself. So even if order can be produced in

---

[25] *Liberal Virtues; Citizenship, Virtue, and Community in Liberal Constitutionalism* (London: Oxford University Press, 1991); and Ralph Lerner, "Commerce and Character: the Anglo-American as New Model Man," *William and Mary Quarterly*, 36, pp. 3–26.

the absence of virtue, we would still have a problem of virtue. Virtue seems unable to be produced on any general scale when people fail to recognize it, because they admire something else. So not only is the non-liberal confronted with a problem, but so is any classical liberal who cares about the promotion of virtue.

But looking at the matter this way is to start taking off in the wrong direction again. In a political sense, we should not care about the promotion of virtue.[26] It is important first of all to distinguish here between understanding virtue as the disposition to act according to socially accepted norms, and virtue as those qualities of character that contribute to self perfection (or constitute a feature of one's eudaimonia) and that exhibit a disposition one has to the diverse situations one confronts in the course of living. Though the two understandings are not mutually exclusive, they are seldom distinguished. The former of these conceptions, however, would by itself necessarily have more of a concern about the promotion of virtue in society than the latter. If virtue is conformity to social norms, then custom, authority, institutions, traditions, and the like become central to the promotion of virtue. It is important to recognize that although the Aristotelian sees human beings in communities, the telos of an individual is not conformity to community standards per se, however salutary those standards may be — MacIntyre's "social teleology" of *After Virtue* notwithstanding. And if human flourishing were to be more individualistic than Aristotle himself might allow, the first of these alternatives is even less likely to be accurate as a description of virtue.

With a pluralistic conception of eudaimonia and a recognition that we are rooted in communities when we act, the classical liberal emphasis on intermediary institutions, such as Tocqueville describes in *Democracy in America,* take on increased significance. This is because pluralism and "rootedness" are only jointly compatible within a framework of diverse communities. The significance of this is more radical than liberals have traditionally admitted: liberalism is not at all interested in the promotion of virtue in any substantive way across society as a whole. In one respect this is almost definitionally true. If liberalism is concerned with metanorms and virtue is tied to norms or principles meant to directly guide one's conduct,

---

[26] Part of liberalism's political appeal is its realism (that is, aiming at peace and order) and its rejection of political idealism (that is, aiming at moral excellence or virtue). See ch. 5 of *Liberty and Nature.*

then clearly liberalism is not concerned with the promotion of virtue. Our point here is not, however, to beg the question by circular definitions. The point rather is to emphasize that liberalism leaves the promotion and exercise of virtue within smaller decentralized social units. Regime builders, by contrast, can be identified by their desire to encourage patterns of "virtue" on a society-wide basis.

We are compelled to ask why we should be so concerned that virtue be promoted at the level of society as a whole? If Smith is right, the answer cannot be because some contribution is being made to social order. Another answer might be that since virtue is the same for all, there is no reason to *limit* it to any unit less than society as a whole. We have argued elsewhere that what can be attributed to people in general is virtue in the most generic sense, but not virtue itself.[27] We cannot re-argue that point here. Suffice it to say that for our purposes, we deny that virtue is the same for all. Instead virtue is realized only in and through individuals and the particularized circumstances in which they act.[28]

There is the idea, advanced by Robert George and others, that social "moral ecology" may require the enforced establishment of habits of conduct that either directly promote virtue by getting people used to acting according to certain forms of conduct, or which prevent forms of conduct that may undermine the moral conduct of others. The Smithean recognition problem, however, still remains. For either the sort of "ecology" needed is recognizable by many or only by a small elite. If the latter, we can hope for little more than an imposed order by the elite, the danger of which is conformity on the part of the people it is supposedly trying to bring to virtue. If the former, we face the problem that what is recognized is not really virtue or promotive of virtue, but is instead that which results from the appeal of the great and wealthy. The first option, as George himself

---

[27] Den Uyl, *The Virtue of Prudence* Ch. 7. See also Douglas B. Rasmussen, "Human Flourishing and the Appeal to Human Nature," *Social Philosophy & Policy* 16 (Winter 1999): 1–43.

[28] Acting in general terms for abstract ends is a common phenomenon of modern society. The "cause" oriented person claims virtue by association with, and promotion of, the right causes which are generally abstract impersonal social goals of some sort. From the perspective being advanced here, the disposition to make oneself a part of a cause would be more in the nature of an issue of virtue than the actions undertaken in the name of the cause itself. This is because virtue concerns itself with one's own particular character and not with generic behaviors or attitudes.

admits, may have trouble keeping certain values that George, at least, wishes to maintain — values such as equality and independence.

The problem of virtue in society, then, is troublesome to any social order that is not organized along essentially hierarchical strands. Hierarchy establishes clear lines of authority and responsibility such that messages of appropriate or legitimate conduct can be conveyed to the desired recipients and enforced thereafter. Hierarchical social forms, however, seem anathema to any order that values liberty. George, for example, criticizes Aristotle and Aquinas for being too hierarchical in the social structures they advocate.[29] Yet there may be a reason why an interest in the promotion of virtue by political or legal means and hierarchical organization go hand in hand. Without a clearly structured hierarchy, it would seem that the Smithean recognition problem would take the form of confusing wealth and greatness with virtue, for there would be no mechanism left but persuasion to transmit the messages of appropriate conduct. Persuasion, however, is subject to manipulation by the wealthy and great irrespective of the content of their virtue.

An issue arises in this connection of whether the people in general are really much like children. The Smithean recognition problem assumes that they are children every bit as much as any doctrine of hierarchical paternalism. For Smith the childlike attraction to what "glitters" about a person results in an inevitable pessimism about the social promotion of virtue. A hierarchical paternalism is not fundamentally pessimistic about the promotion of virtue, just about the ability of people to get there unaided. It may seem that liberalism requires the opposite assumption — that people are really more like adults; but Smith's own position indicates that liberalism does not require that perspective, unless one wishes to deny the status of "liberal" to Smith. Liberalism neither requires nor forbids any general theory about the gullibility of people with respect to what is good for them or promotive of their good. The contingent connection between order and virtue means that gullibility is not an impediment to virtue in the sense of placing disorder in the way of virtue.

Liberalism does require an element to be present, however, that links the metanormative with the normative in such a way that the two are not in principled conflict. That element, and the topic of our brief concluding section is, individual responsibility.

[29] Robert P. George, *Making Men Moral* (op. cit.,) p. 36ff.

## VI

Shaftesbury tells us that in a free society one of the ways in which improvement of ourselves takes place is that "we polish one another, and rub off our corners and rough sides by a sort of amicable collision."[30] There is an ambiguity here as to whether the "polished" finished product is seen to be such from the perspective of the society in which it is refined or from standards of virtue that transcend any particular social order. Both perspectives, however, leave open and spontaneous the types and number of amicable collisions that will take place, for in a free society a great deal is left to individual choice and discretion. As they pursue their own ends, individuals "bump" into each other in unstructured and unpredictable ways. In the process of having to cooperate, they refine at least their manners and civility through a process of mutual criticism and compromise. There is little direction from authorities and the exact nature of the "collisions" cannot be determined in advance. In this respect the process is highly individualistic, spontaneous, and decentralized.

We shall not comment upon Shaftesbury's optimism that we really do become polished in such a process. For some, recent times seem to suggest the very opposite. What needs attention is not so much the image of collisions as the one that underlies it, namely, the image of independent "atoms" in collidic motion. Rather than soft-bodied malleable entities shaped by culture, social roles, and political discussion, we have instead apparently "hard bodied" self-contained units. A common criticism of liberalism has been its so called "atomism." The image of atom-like units having their rough edges worn off through interactive criticism and compromise seems to play into the hand of these critics of liberalism.

The main virtue of this imagery from our point of view, however, is the individualism of it. Individualism is a necessary feature of liberalism, and the erosion of individualism is not simply an erosion of the metanormative/normative distinction, but of virtue itself. Individualism, or what we would prefer to call "individual responsibility," is the component necessary for linking metanorms with ordinary moral norms. Without it, moral norms are not indicative of virtue and metanorms do not secure the

---

[30] Shaftesbury, *Characteristics of Men, Manners, Opinion, Times etc.* Thoemes Press reprint of the Robertson 1900 edition. "An Essay on the Freedom of Wit and Humor," p. 46.

possibility of virtuous conduct, but become surrogates for virtuous conduct itself.

We have argued here and elsewhere that virtue requires the centrality of individual choice and cannot be located externally in such factors as culture, custom, tradition, or social standards or sentiments.[31] If one is, at root, a function of one's society or culture or traditions, it is hard to speak of *one's own* virtues as opposed to "virtues" one happens to possess. To be a possessor of virtue is not the same as being virtuous, and the sense of virtue consistent with liberalism is one where virtue is a result of one's own choices. The reason, as we have tried to suggest all along here, is that not only is liberalism defined by its restraint in the legislation of morality, but by its posture towards the very nature of morality. As noted, the posture of liberalism is one most at home with moral objectivism of some sort. If, however, it is to have this posture toward the good, it must have it as a phenomenon of the individual rather than society, because politically liberalism offers the individual the widest possible latitude for conduct and thus the smallest number of pre-determined social roles.

By recognizing that virtue is itself fundamentally rooted in individual choice and responsibility, liberalism and virtue are in principle compatible. They are compatible because liberalism is dedicated to protecting that which is necessary for conduct to qualify as fully moral, since the metanorms regulate the institutional arrangements that protect the very foundations of virtuous conduct, namely individual self-direction. In this respect we can say that liberalism is the political form appropriate to the recognition that virtue is, in the end, essentially rooted in individual choice.

If virtue were in its essence a function of society rather than the individual, then liberalism and virtue could have no necessary connection to one another. For if virtue is essentially a function of the social, then we would need to insure a certain social character from which to pattern the character of individuals. Consequently, under the social theory of virtue, if virtue and social order were actually seen to be connected in a liberal polity, the connection would have to be regarded as accidental or contingent, because no endeavor was made to promote a particular pattern

---

[31] *Liberty and Nature*, p. 71. See also Douglas B. Rasmussen,"Economic Rights Versus Human Dignity: The Flawed Moral Vision of the United States Catholic Bishops," in Rasmussen and James Sterba, "*The Catholic Bishops and the Economy: A Debate* (Bowling Green, OH: Social Philosophy and Policy Center and New Brunswick, NJ: Transaction Books, 1987), p. 64.

of social roles or institutional contexts. That is quite different from saying what we believe liberalism to be saying, namely, that while liberal orders do not promote virtue, the virtue that is present is necessarily connected with liberalism's protection of an essential feature of virtuous conduct.

Part of our point, then, is to claim that self-directedness lies at the heart of virtue, moral objectivity, moral robustness, and liberalism. They are jointly part of a package of concepts that can cohere together every bit as effectively as the social virtue theories of the communitarians. If social roles and processes are at the heart of virtue, then the liberal will always appear to be less than sincere when speaking of a concern for virtue. But if individual responsibility is at the center, liberalism at least accords with the essential character of virtue.

In this connection, it is important to realize that without the primacy of self-directedness, norms and metanorms would be distinguished — if distinguished at all — in terms of some conception of social priorities. That is, when virtue is fundamentally based in social roles, or in the conformity to social patterns, or in actions stemming from the possession of certain social goods, the distinction between what is framework setting and what is not becomes a matter of which social factor is to have priority. We see this phenomenon in the discussion of whether liberty, for example, should be given greater weight over other social goods like security. But it should be evident by now that such is not the structure of our argument. We do not claim that liberty should be given more weight than other goods, but rather that liberty is a good of central importance for the foundations of *political* life. Indeed, in some respects it would be mistaken for us to give "liberty" priority as a good, if priorities are based on ends one should seek. Some goods like friendship would seem to be superior to liberty on that basis.[32]

If individual responsibility is central to virtue, and social policy should be formed with an eye to its impact upon virtue, then policies which erode individual responsibility would be ones contrary to a concern for virtue. It is widely agreed that virtues are dispositions of character that (should) pervade all aspects of one's life. If significant portions of one's life are removed from the realm of responsibility, then they are removed from the realm of virtue. Vast portions of our lives these days are removed from the

---

[32] See our reply to M.P. Golding in Reason Papers [Reply to Critics" (with Douglas B. Rasmussen) *Reason Papers* 18 (Fall 1993): 115–132.

realm of responsibility. Everything from beneficence towards others to care of one's own estate. If liberalism requires the widest possible latitude for individual responsibility, then the issue we are left with is not whether liberalism is connected to virtue or destructive of it, but rather whether the demands of liberalism for virtue are too great for creatures prone to ignorance, prejudice, and weakness of will.

# 6. *The Perennial Experiment in Liberty*

## DAVID WALSH

The core of a liberal political order is the transcendent finality of the individual which it intuits without explicitly articulating. That is both the source of the endemic confusion and of the surprising resilience of liberal democratic politics. Without a clear identification of the direction that ultimately guides and justifies its orientation, liberal political thought is prone to endless vacillations. Is liberty indeed directed toward some ultimately serious end? Can it be just as well exercised through irresponsibility and dissipation? Is there or is there not one highest good toward which all are directed? The answer to all of these questions consists in the recognition that the end of liberty is transcendent, lying beyond all boundaries and definitions. There is no clear or single goal because no immanent or mundane good is capable of answering the purpose of liberty. The transcendent character of its goal defies all specification. That may render the conception and exercise of liberty a matter of enduring uncertainty but it preserves it from the deformation of all false absolutes. Silence concerning the end of liberty is the only appropriate way of representing its transcendent finality.

## Rights Talk

The vagueness and vacuousness of the liberal political tradition is paradoxically both its weakness and its strength. We cannot gain much insight into the reality that sustains it by focusing only on the abbreviated statements of principle it supplies. Declarations of universal rights cursorily supported by the language of contractual agreement, constitutional limitations and adumbrations of bonds of trust and solidarity, are not enough. They are capable of interpretation in widely divergent directions. We are familiar with the incommensurable and interminable disputes that seem to increasingly fracture liberal societies. Culture wars and moral stridency seem ever more in evidence and we are familiar with the inability of human rights documents to resolve international disputes. It is no wonder that many thoughtful observers have despaired entirely of the liberal language being rendered into any coherent form. Following the cue of Humpty Dumpty, its words seem to mean whatever we want them to mean. The compressed character of the liberal formulae provide little guidance in resolving disagreement over priorities among rights. Even the background of mutual responsibilities which is indispensable to sustaining an order of rights virtually disappears from public consciousness.

Clearly the success of a liberal political order, as testified by its durability over time, cannot be attributed to the clarity and coherence of its formulations. If we are to understand what sustains liberal politics we must look much more at the substantive presuppositions of its practice. It is not what they say that explains liberal societies, but what they do. We must be willing to discern the animating convictions which guide the practice and even preserve liberal politics from the anarchy that seems to prevail in its theory. What is the source of its resonance, the sense of self-evident rightness which is satisfied with the most cursory explications of principle? At its core liberal politics is animated by the conviction of the inexhaustible depth of each individual human being. Everything we know about a particular individual can be enumerated and quantified. The sum of his or her contributions and costs can be calculated. Yet we know that we will never reach the totality of the person. No matter how well we know someone or how much he or she seems contained by the categories of our analysis there remains an indecipherable abyss of mystery. It is as inexhaustible to the person himself as to everyone else. That is the core recognition which resonates through the liberal political tradition. We respond to it because we recognize the truth of its valuation of the individual as an abyss of mystery beyond all finite measurement.

We sense that this is how it is appropriate to treat human beings. Any other frame of reference that sought to quantify them in terms of some finite scale would end by destroying everything of value in human life. All that is precious, that constitutes the core of meaning for us, would be lost if we placed a limit on the dignity of human beings. Neither friendship nor love could survive the imposition of conditions on what we owe one another. Once we began to think in terms of one another as reaching a point where our usefulness had been exhausted, the point where we became dispensable in the name of some social whole, then we would cease to relate to one another in human terms. It is of the essence of human relationships that we recognize the unlimited and inviolable worth of each one. They cannot be weighed against one another. They never lose the status of ends in themselves, becoming reducible to the level of a mere means to some other good. There is no good higher than the good of a single individual human being. He or she outweighs the whole universe.

It is because the politics of liberty conveys that sense of the transcendent dignity of each one that it has such astonishing strength. Contrary to the squabbling surface exhibited by liberal societies, their deeper inspiration is profound. The power of their appeal arises from the degree of resonance with the most compelling perspective on human life. No more exalted conception of human beings can be provided. It may be that the liberal tradition is not particularly good at articulating the relationship to transcendent reality which brings human dignity into focus. That may require an expansion of the meditation into the revelatory experiences and symbols we have contemplated. But the liberal tradition is surprisingly effective at evoking that transcendent resonance indirectly in the valuation it implies about human beings. One is drawn from the liberal exaltation of transcendent individual dignity and worth toward the reality of transcendent Being itself. By contemplating the awesome dignity of the individual we are drawn toward the source of that reverence in divine being.

## Depth Below Surface

A liberal political order is thus not a half-way house on the road toward nihilism. This has been a recurrent misconception in the twentieth century that has deflected attention away from the real challenge. It has discouraged the effort to deepen and solidify the liberal political order which is the only viable political form in the contemporary world. Thinking that liberal politics is merely the superficiality of rights talk many critics have despaired of finding a means of remediating it. But there is more to the liberal political tradition than the face of anarchic self-indulgence it often presents to the world. Even the historic failure of liberal regimes, both in the Russian Revolution and in Weimar Germany, cannot be taken as representative cases. The fact that these two weak liberal democracies spawned the worst totalitarian regimes of the century cannot be regarded as the inevitable fate of liberal constitutional politics. Both regimes were in fact defeated by the combined resistance of the liberal democratic West and have now been replaced by such regimes themselves. For all their apparent inconstancy there is a formidable strength within the liberal political tradition that cannot simply be dismissed, or at least not until we have a more substantial possibility of discovering a replacement.

It is not enough simply to select certain patterns within liberal politics and extrapolate them toward their logical conclusion. This is an approach favored by conservative critics who see the epidemic of social disorder, everything from sky-rocketing crimes rates to the soaring number of illegitimate births, and extend the process to the final and total collapse of order. They regard such phenomena as symptomatic of an inner flaw within the social and political tradition itself. Liberal democratic politics, they contend, gives exaggerated prominence to the notion of rights without sufficient counterbalancing attention to responsibilities. It encourages the unlimited assertion of rights without any constraining discipline of duties. Such a society cannot teach the virtues indispensable to its self-preservation. Eventually the process will have run so far that we will cease to recognize any common order or interest between us. Politics will have reverted to the naked contest of self-assertive wills. Without either the incentive to moderate our individual interests or the means of rationally resolving conflicts between them, nothing is left but the raw exercise of power. That apocalyptic vision of liberal democratic politics as "civil war carried on by other means," is what has galvanized the conservative appeal in reforming and restraining a process widely viewed as dangerously derailed.

The mistake, however, consists in attributing the blame to the inevitably corrosive tendency of liberal convictions. What such critics fail to recognize is that they too share such convictions and that their very reform efforts are intended to preserve the tradition of liberty not eliminate it. The confusion is evident in the language itself. Progressive advocates of expanded individual rights are labeled liberals, while their conservative opponents understand themselves as the preservers of liberty in the face of anarchy. The extent to which all sides revolve around the issue of free self-responsibility should alert us to the reality that they represent poles of the tension within the liberal tradition. Neither side is outside of the tradition and what they do works to preserve it. Just as the New Deal/ Great Society era was inaugurated to protect the sphere of individual liberty from social and economic forces that threatened it, the conservative reform of the welfare state arises from the same desire to invigorate the moral purpose of liberty. The reason why liberal democratic politics does not unravel into oppression or anarchy is that it continues to make such vital adjustments to changing circumstances. Conservative warnings would have been correct if there had been no conservative movement, just as progressives would have been correct in their warning if they had not succeeded in their reforms.

In each case the mistake has been to confuse the surface of liberal politics with its reality. Critics from the right or left have often tended to assume that they themselves were outside of the regime they were critiquing. They failed to realize that they were themselves one of the most central components of its self-remediation. The extent to which liberal political order embraces a considerable range of perspectives is indicative of its real strength. With the exception of the revolutionary extremes, all sides wish to see an order of liberty preserved. No substantive proposals for radical constitutional changes are advanced. Many suggestions are made for modifications but they all lie within the continuum of the fundamental rightness of a rule of law respecting inalienable rights. The moral authority of liberal democracy now reigns unquestioned throughout the world. Even regimes that are neither liberal nor democratic feel compelled to dress themselves in the trappings. To a very considerable extent the disputes we encounter within both domestic and international politics are all disputes within a liberal framework. That supremacy of the liberal self-understanding is powerful testament to the response it evokes within human beings. It is clearly not the house of cards liberalism is often assumed to be.

Even the debate about the shortcomings and defects of liberal politics must ultimately be conducted within liberal terms. This is the definitive

93

proof of the primacy it occupies. We cannot conceive of any more penetrating analysis of the crucial issues than the liberal language of fundamental rights. When it comes to specific controversies, whether euthanasia, abortion, pornography, affirmative action or anything else, it is only the arguments concerning the propriety of rights that decide the issue. We are not strongly taken by considerations of divine law or of moral imperatives. It is the appeal to the appropriate notions of fundamental rights that is ultimately decisive. Our whole notion of what is fair or just is bound up with the sense of the equal right of all human beings to equal respect and dignity. The inviolability of individual life and liberty is the turning point and the arguments that succeed in persuading us that they advance that fundamental orientation win the day. Theological and moral perspectives are tested by how far they advance or retard respect for human rights. There is no more compelling touchstone of what is right. The monopoly of moral authority exercised by liberal principles is revealed in the extent to which even religious leaders make their case in terms of promoting the fullest reverence for the person.

## Consensus on Essentials

Once we begin to see the liberal political tradition as a powerfully compressed expression of a transcendent conviction then we begin to understand the source of its strength. It has a capacity to resonate across a wide spectrum of controversies. By trusting to the transcendent truth embedded within liberal principles we can follow its intimations into the resolution of the most divisive conflicts that beset us. That may seem a rather optimistic claim given the range and intensity of debates we encounter today. But the presence of debate is itself testament to the shared sense that a resolution is possible by reference back to the common convictions we share. Each side still holds onto the possibility of convincing its opponents. The real danger is when people walk away in despair from the conversation. That is when the shooting is likely to begin, not when they are remonstrating with one another. It is those who counsel silence, the smothering of controversy, who constitute the real danger.

So long as debate continues both sides share the conviction that the question cannot be settled until it is settled rightly. That is, they have a sense of a rightness to which they must appeal. Its core lies within the liberal principles whose consequences each side struggles to unfold as the means of making its case persuasive. The preeminent example of this kind of struggle must surely be the historical one of Lincoln and the slavery crisis. What is striking about Lincoln's approach to the debate is the confidence he had that a resolution could ultimately be attained through an expansion of the consequences for a free political order. The dispute did indeed oppose two liberal principles, democratic freedom of choice in the states and the equal rights of all human beings. On its surface it was irresolvable but Lincoln was confident of the inner coherence of the liberal political order. Its principles could not be in conflict. He set out to persuade his countrymen that the democratic self-government they professed would itself be undermined by the refusal to acknowledge the equal rights of all human beings. It would lead directly to the implication that some have a right to rule over and enjoy the work of others. Slave owning was simply incompatible with a regime of liberty. It was the shared fundamental conviction to which he appealed that enabled him, even in the midst of civil war, to regard the division as destined to be reconciled.

It is when it is tested by the necessity of struggle against oppression that the inner strength of the liberal tradition emerges from its compressed depths. Tyrants from Hitler to Saddam Hussein have perennially miscalculated its apparent weakness. Of greater significance, however, is the tendency for liberal societies themselves to be deceived by the slackness of their order and the suspicion that deep down there is nothing deep down. Liberty is like the experience of transcendent being that underpins it. Neither are cashable deposits that can be withdrawn from the bank at will. Rather it is a case of the account growing in strength and substance the more it is drawn into actuality. The result is that we apprehend the full measure and significance of liberty only as we are called upon to exercise it in defence of what is of transcendent value. By exerting ourselves in pursuit of what is highest we discover both the indispensable value of liberty and our participation in a reality beyond life itself. We are free because we are open to the word of truth that outweighs the whole world. The discovery surprises even ourselves.

From the perspective of that enlargement of our souls we can reflect more clearly on the nature of a liberal political order. We can recognize more clearly the kind of abridgement it involves. Liberal formulations of rights, consent, and rule of law are a way of condensing the long meditative

95

articulation by which its existential sources are unfolded. It is a way of narrowing the public consensus to the points of essential agreement within a pluralistic social setting. This is the origin of the liberal formulations as they reached a recognizable identity in the seventeenth century. John Locke is the preeminent exemplar as he provided the formulation of liberal democracy which justified the events of the Glorious Revolution of 1688. He provided the authoritative account of the source of government in the consent of individuals who compose civil society. They are each given by God the authority to rule themselves in accordance with their individual conceptions of the moral law but, as a result of the inevitable disagreements, consent to be ruled by the laws of civil society which they themselves have made. Government is thus instituted to protect the rights of life, liberty and property which are the means by which each individual exercises responsible self-direction. The limitations imposed by government on each of us are only the minimum required to facilitate a life of freedom. There is little role for government in the broader formation or direction of the spiritual life of the citizens.

The summary essence of a liberal political order, which has remained fairly stable up to the present, sounds astonishingly spare. Generations of liberal thinkers have themselves wondered if their construction contained enough in the way of a substantive core to hold it all together. Was it, for example, merely an arrangement of convenience destined to come asunder as soon as individuals no longer found their interests served by it? How was it possible for government to promote even the minimum virtues required to sustain its order, if they could no longer play a formative role in moral and spiritual affairs? How could we be sure that individuals would not misuse the power, especially the power of the majority, to extort and burden members of minority factions? If they entered into a contract to create society, what was to prevent them from contracting to commit injustice? What indeed was to preserve fidelity to their word so that they would not simply cut and run at the first sound of trouble? Clearly a great deal more needed to be said about the foundations of liberal democracy. It was particularly necessary to find a way of connecting the essential public principles with broader moral and spiritual sources that alone could justify and animate their application.

The liberal concentration on the core elements of self-government was a brilliant solution to the problem of pluralism. The religious fragmentation of the early modern period had precipitated a political crisis as profound as any we have historically known. Indeed we often fail to appreciate the depth of the cleavages opened by the collapse of the authority of the Church. Our own pluralist conflicts are by no means more radical and we enjoy the inestimable advantage of a model of successfully resolving the divergences. Liberal democracy worked as a means of containing conflict because it relegated most of it to a private realm. Agreement was limited to the principles indispensable for lawful self-government. That provided a way for men and women of different theological convictions to remain faithful Christians without having to kill one another. Tolerance was possible within the framework of agreement on the essential political principles. But both tolerance and pluralism, while broad and destined to become broader, must always acknowledge their own limits. In the final analysis tolerance cannot be extended to the intolerant, those who wished to work for the destruction of the agreement that kept the peace.

The need to sustain the convictions behind the liberal construction itself has become the major challenge. It is never merely enough to formulate the principles, for no contract can stand on its own. It must always be backed by the inner conviction of its rightness or fairness if it is to be sustained. The history of liberal political thought is largely the history of the efforts to make the justification for its order transparent. By persuasively articulating the rightness of the liberal construction we will have found a means of educating ourselves in the virtues that sustain the order we enjoy. Of course the task of finding a compelling justification was rendered enormously difficult by the condition that the explanation must share the same neutrality as the liberal principles themselves. If it was to be a publicly available justification then it could not reach into the vexed sphere of theological and philosophical questions that the liberal consensus had sought to avoid. Needless to say the experiment has not been an overwhelming success.

Even thinkers of the genius of David Hume, Jean Jacques Rousseau, Immanuel Kant, Georg Hegel, or John Stuart Mill have been unable to satisfy the critics of their interpretations. What is indeed striking about the whole project is the sheer diversity of justifications provided and the inability of any of them to win enduring consent. The problem is one that continues all the way up to the present. In our own time, John Rawls has attempted such a comprehensive "theory of justice" to underpin a liberal constitutional order. Now twenty years later even he has largely abandoned the effort as a failure. The prevailing wisdom is that the task was impossible and that a liberal political order is merely the accidental fruit of a fortuitous historical convergence. It can have no theoretical defense because either such defenses are impossible or they are impossible under the limitations imposed by the requirements of a liberal society. The problem of liberal meaning parallels the broader crisis of meaning in the postmodern ethos, but it leads to more immediate practical consequences. If we cannot explain to ourselves why a liberal order of rights is worth preserving, it will not be possible for us to persuade ourselves and our children to retain it much longer. The theoretical crisis is reflected in a social crisis.

It is no wonder that the nature of the liberal democratic consensus is the number one subject of philosophical discussion. Discussions and books proliferate, continuing a rich historical pattern of reflection, because none has succeeded in defining its core. Why is it that a political arrangement of such worldwide popularity, and with such a demonstrable record of success, should be so uncertain of its justification? Why is liberal democracy unable even to explain itself to itself? Once we get beyond the level of political generalities about freedom, self-responsibility and human dignity we find ourselves tongue-tied. The reason is of course not hard to find, as many contemporary observers have concluded. Departure from the most general formulae requires us to acknowledge that a liberal order is not neutral between competing moralities. Sure, the point of the liberal construction is to maximize individual freedom. But even that core cannot be articulated without presupposing some view of the human good toward which freedom must be exercised. What is the point of freedom if it does not enable us to realize what is good? That unfortunately is the question on which the whole liberal consensus comes apart.

The point of the liberal abbreviations of rights and liberty, we recall, was to remain silent about the different worldviews we regarded as important. Controversy was to be removed from the public arena and corralled safely within the private domain of individual choice. What was significant and what was compelling was up to us individually to decide. Public space was to be constituted by the purely formal arrangements that made this maximal exercise of private freedom possible. Constitutional and legal arrangements were to be value neutral with respect to varying assessments of the human good. These were the sources of pluralism, of the social fragmentation that went all the way back to the theological cleavages that fractured the early modern period. Our disagreements have not lessened. How then can the liberal center hold if the divergences have invaded even its appearance of neutrality?

## Transcendent Dignity of Person

The challenge is considerable but not insuperable. Most immediately we can admit that the game of neutrality is up. Liberal democracy is not neutral with respect to all conceptions of the good, only in relation to a certain range of moral and religious disagreements. It presupposes a more embracing moral order which the respective traditions within it are capable of recognizing. Among these are the convictions that human life is precious, that personal freedom is to be respected as the means by which individual responsibility is developed, and that ultimately it is the struggle to live in accordance with the moral intimations within us that constitutes the highest life for human beings. But how to articulate this sustaining background to a liberal order without jeopardizing the peace between divergent philosophies? That is the nub of the difficulty. Clearly the answer does not lie in the direction of uncovering some ultimately neutral formulation without any presuppositions.

That is the rock on which all of our contemporary philosophical hopes have foundered. We never get beyond presuppositions. This is the limitation of our condition, we are already embedded in positions before our philosophizing begins. From another perspective this is also our liberation, we are relieved of the burden of the quest for the presuppositionless beginning. Instead we can begin where we are, immersed in a reality already structured by the pull of a mysterious meaning of which we are in search. Respect for inalienable individual liberty embodies that transcendent openness as its political expression. Even more, it resonates with the experience of human beings who may have very varied capacities or inclinations to make their transcendent finality explicit. In other words, it evokes a practical response long before it wins theoretical approval. That is why liberal democratic politics has been such a runaway success. It does not depend on convincing people in principle of its rightness. They sense its appropriateness through its continuity with the never ending unfolding of their own experience. Within the context of that practical resonance all discussion of presuppositions and arguments pale into insignificance. The appeal of a liberal order is primarily existential.

It has long been recognized that the practice of self-government is the principal means of inculcating the virtues that make self-government possible. This was Tocqueville's major insight into the importance of the associational life of society as well as of the American federal arrangement. Through the dangerous exercise of liberty, he remarked, Americans had found a way of obviating those dangers. Nor is this insight lost in the contemporary scene. Within the awareness of the limited moral resources available to government there is a clear perception that one of the few effective means available is to encourage the exercise of self-responsibility. Governmental initiatives may waste not only financial reserves, more importantly they may drain the moral initiative of society. The Tocquevillian insight into the indispensability of individual exercise of self-responsibility now occupies the center of our attention. We cannot afford to jeopardize the dignity and self-worth attained only through liberty itself.

What is less well recognized are the existential dynamics involved in taking up that challenge. When we freely bend our efforts to promote our common good it is not simply that we more efficiently accomplish our goals. We become different. The effort is one that has its greatest effect on the persons involved rather than on the policies enacted. Tocqueville alludes to without dwelling on the enlargement of soul that takes place in the strenuous exercise of liberty. It is a topic that deserves much more attention than political commentators are willing or able to give it. The change effected is not merely incidental or peripheral. It is central to the whole project of a self-governing society, for it brings into view the clear intuition of the enduring realities toward which the whole arrangement is constructed. Even without naming the transcendent goal, the straining of our efforts toward what is good and right renders the whole justification of liberty transparent. We see clearly what was only dimly intimated at the beginning. That is, that human beings are made to stretch their efforts toward what is independently good, that this is the higher life toward which we are called and the route toward our participation in a reality that transcends all others. Liberty and choice are no longer empty words once we have acquired a concrete sense of the direction in which they must be unfolded.

Such a growth of the soul occurs without philosophical articulation. It later comes to recognize philosophical formulations as more or less adequate accounts of its immediate convictions, but it does not in any way depend on the validity of such justifications. That is the secret of the liberal constructions. Its philosophical abridgements have been just sufficient to call forth the resonances required to undertake the adventure of liberty. Once the process is initiated it reveals a dynamic of its own that carries us forward toward heights of self-realization we could only dimly intuit in the abstractions with which we began. For this reason the inadequacies of the theoretical elaborations appear as incidental to the living movement of growth toward which they point. They can be accepted as approximations rather than as blueprints because the existential movement does not depend on their guidance. It is enough that they are available to give the enlargement of feeling and intelligence some fixity of definition. Theoretical articulations are necessary if the experience is not to dissipate into forgetfulness. There will be a recurrent need to resuscitate it. But that is a far cry from insisting that the theoretical difficulties must be resolved in advance or as the condition of engaging in moral growth.

Within this light the evident historical failure of the liberal political tradition to provide a coherent self-articulation must be regarded differently. It is no longer a failure. Now it must be viewed as part of the broader process by which a liberal political order recurrently awakens consciousness of the reality that draws it. The search for foundations is the theoretical counterpart of the existential practice of liberty. Despite the failure to reach any fully satisfactory account of foundations the effort to do so keeps the consciousness of foundation alive. It is not a futile exercise. On the contrary the rich history of liberal philosophical reflection from the seventeenth century up to the present is testament to the enduring character of the search in which it is involved. If it were fruitless then there would be nothing to sustain it. In contrast, each generation begins with the same faith in the goal for which it seeks and struggles to explain its inspiration to itself. The fact that none of the accounts becomes definitive does not signify failure. In each of them living contact is made with the source of the movement that underpins them. By straining toward the transcendence out of reach we gain a greater sense of its reality.

It is at this point that the appropriateness of liberal incompleteness and tentativeness becomes clear. How else can the transcendent goal of human existence be represented except through the consciousness of our failure to represent it? Liberal silence about ultimate reality may now be viewed, no longer as a regrettable failure of consensus and articulation, but as its great theoretical contribution. Far from being an absence of meaning, it can now be seen as arising from a fullness of meaning that transcends all symbolization. The insistence of many liberal thinkers that there is no highest good in terms of which all other goods must be ranked and that the liberal toleration of diversity reflects this irreducible plurality, must be viewed in this sense. It arises from the conviction that any highest good, once it is named, becomes suspect as an illegitimate contraction of the full reach of the human spirit. The latter can only be answered by a good that transcends all names. But whence comes that conviction if not from the living sense of its presence? Liberal silence about the transcendent is the one that pays its respect most profoundly.

To avoid the other danger of lapsing from silence into forgetfulness, however, it is necessary to keep the struggle toward articulation alive. Both the practical and theoretical reaching of a liberal political tradition are the indispensable means by which we actualize the resonances it contains. The incompleteness and provisionality of all attainments is not the last word. Liberal political practice and reflection is simply a way in which we work out our participation in the meaning of the mystery that guards all of human life. The appropriateness of liberal evocations must be assessed within this context. Only then does it become apparent that two correlative processes are at work within the liberal construction. There is first the concentration on the consensus necessary for moral and political order. Much of the resonance necessary for sustaining this consensus is preserved in the silence respectfully observed before the transcendent mystery of the goal of human life. That resonance, we have seen, cannot be adequately articulated but it can be evoked through the practice and reflection in which it is pursued.

## Dignity as Moral Advance

The second process at work in this liberal concentration on essentials is a heightening of awareness of the transcendent moral worth of each individual. This is perhaps the most overlooked dimension in the contemporary preoccupation with our shortcomings. But it is the key both to the inexorable moral pressure within liberal societies and to the inescapable tendency to debate moral issues within liberal terms. Human rights are not just a shorthand for the moral code of our relationships to one another. They also direct a spotlight on the central dimension of respect for the inner person that ultimately is at the core of our moral convictions. Any proposed moral order that fails to enhance the inviolable dignity of each person cannot stand before the liberal scrutiny directed on it. Liberal order heightens our sensitivity to that inescapable dimension. The point of all moral and political conventions, we have learned, is to enable the inner growth of the person toward the goal that is beyond all finite characterizations. Any preimposed limitations on the full dynamic of the human soul can no longer defend its legitimacy.

We see this dynamic working itself out in the moral controversies that widely beset us today. Invariably the most powerful arguments on either side of the abortion, euthanasia, genetic and behavioral engineering, affirmative action, capital punishment debates are all derived from the core of the liberal conception of rights. Despite the confusion that also prevails in the use and misuse of the liberal vocabulary, we cannot afford to forget that these issues are being fought out largely in liberal terms. And that is not simply because such terms are the only publicly available medium of discourse. It is much more because they are the most morally authoritative formulations available. A liberal tradition heightens our awareness of the moral dimensions of human relationships that cannot be jeopardized. It focuses our attention on what is of transcendent importance, that which cannot be lost without losing everything. We recognize that what is at stake in each of these issues is not just the rightness or wrongness of a particular action, but the whole way we understand who we are and treat one another. If we fail to respect the fundamental reality of the person in one of these instances then it calls into question the seriousness of our commitment in all others. Nothing is more important than the irrefragable dignity of the person.

Euthanasia, for example, is presented to us as an issue in which the freedom of self-determination is at issue. Does it not enhance the dignity of human life to be free to choose the time and manner of our departure from it? What could be more inhumane than to refuse the relief of suffering to those in the terminal stages of an illness? One of the reasons why voluntary euthanasia has made such headway is that it seems to appeal directly to the same liberal sentiments. All that seems to matter is that we take care to ensure that the necessary safeguards against abuse are followed. So long as a truly informed consent has been given we need have no scruples about accommodating the wishes of the terminally ill. It is only when we reflect on the consequences in practice that the darkness contained in the suggestion becomes evident. Voluntary euthanasia means that some human beings will be deciding who will live and who will die. Surely we will exercise some discrimination among those who request the services of euthanasia professionals. How will they in turn make that decision?

They can make it in the only way that any of us would. We will have to decide which lives still have some sustaining merit and which are no longer worth preserving. Even if the patient has already decided that his or her quality of life has slipped below an acceptable level, we cannot avoid entering into the same judgment if we are to facilitate their wishes. What criteria will we use? We can think of none that do not involve a process of measuring and weighing the value of human life. We will inevitably be involved in the process of defining what a person is worth. What pain or inconvenience costs too much? We can no longer use the standard of every person as an end-in-him or her-self, since they must now be assessed in terms of their aggregate contribution to themselves or others. The euthanasia situation compels such a finite reduction of the value of human life.

Once we have entered into that process we cannot appeal to safeguards to prevent abuse. Now we will recognize that the limits we impose on the practice are entirely our own. There are no longer any absolute barriers on the way in which we can treat one another. The only barriers that exist are ones we have chosen to adopt. We might shift to different criteria and inevitably different people will interpret the different criteria differently. Some will err on the side of life, some on the side of death. Either way we will have no way of distinguishing the abusive from the non-abusive because there are no fixed limits. We cannot say when evil has occurred. It is only then that we realize the abyss opened up by the euthanasia suggestion. The extension of the liberal practice of rights to the very parameters of human existence itself does not constitute a true expansion of liberty. It opens up the loss of all rights if our fate is to be decided by other human beings determining who will live and who will die, based on nothing more than their own subjective goodwill. We have lost all rights if there are no fixed limits. Once everything becomes a matter of choice we have become totally subject to the whim of others. They are the ones who decide the limits since none are already pregiven.

What is interesting about this argument is that it reaches its conclusion without appealing to any larger theological or philosophical presuppositions. It has emerged from within the liberal framework itself. Strongly resonant of course is the opening toward a transcendent order beyond human life and it no doubt appeals most to those who are in touch with more robust and explicit spiritual traditions. Behind the liberal debates there are larger conflicts of spiritual orientation being worked out. Clearly the deepest resonance of those who support euthanasia is the rebellious spirit of human self-assertion. It is the secular mentality that wants to dominate reality independently. Opposing it is the countervailing submission to an order whose source lies mysteriously beyond us. That is the attitude of trust in the goodness of the cosmos in which we find ourselves. But the debate itself can be fought out in largely, if not strictly, liberal terms. This is because the liberal language of rights is both a compressed expression of what can be more elaborately unfolded as the transcendent openness of human nature and because it represents a moral heightening of the core moral issues within that orientation. That is why we can have faith in the eventual resolution of the debates.

Just as Lincoln observed of the slavery crisis, conflicts over rights cannot be settled until they are resolved rightly. Permanent incorporation of any settlement less than the morally appropriate would cause too much of a disruption to the whole liberal construction. Such controversies will continue inexorably under their own internal moral pressure toward a resolution. In their refusal to go away we see perhaps one of the most significant dimensions of the heightening of moral consciousness involved in the liberal concentrations. There is simply no way to avoid the recognition that the elimination of the rights of one group or one area of life, infects with uncertainty the whole structure of rights everywhere. If it is a matter of governmental or popular determination in one case why not in all others? An order of rights is too deeply embedded in the transcendent order of reality for it to be swept aside by the prevailing pressures of convenience and confusion. Such deformations do and will occur but they cannot get a permanent foothold within the authoritative expression of what is right. The formidable strength of the language of rights is that it has, for all its peremptory compression of order, made the abuse of fundamental rights more difficult to sustain. One has only to look at the impressive use to which liberal moral language was put by the dissidents of the Communist era.

At the same time we can never afford to forget that the authoritative account of order constitutes only a part of the publicly available world of meaning. By far the largest part is occupied by broader cultural issues. It is a grave mistake for politics to forget this larger cultural context within which its own struggle for order takes place. The literary, artistic, philosophical debates between competing worldviews are worked out within the arena of civilizational meaning. Ultimately the liberal moral and political order depends on those wider resonances beyond itself. It is not enough to rely on the compressed illumination of the debates about rights to resolve the issues. A liberal order cannot stand alone. It depends on a wider context of spiritual traditions, intellectual vitality and civilizational meaning that it cannot create. Even to say that liberal democracy is largely a secular expression of Christianity is not to say that it can be sustained without the presence of the more robust spirituality of the world religions. The heightened intensity of liberal public language is likely to become shrill, unbalanced and confused if it is not sustained by the kind of broader faith in a transcendent order of grace and forgiveness represented by the revelatory traditions. That is why the question of cultural meaning, the effectiveness of the appeals of cultural movements, cannot be a matter of indifference from a political perspective. It is within the cultural arena that the life and death of a civilization is largely determined.

# 7. *Liberal Freedom and Responsibility*

## MARK BLITZ

The issue on which I would like to focus is simple. How can liberal democracies such as ours that are based on individualism summon the attention to the common good that they need in order to flourish and survive? My goal is to discuss the concept and practice of responsibility as a partial answer to this question. It will take some time, however, before this goal is reached. I will begin by discussing the defining elements of liberalism, concentrating on individuals rather than institutions, turn to the topic of commonalities and the common good, proceed to an analysis of responsibility, and conclude by addressing my point directly.

## Liberalism's Central Elements

The first defining element of liberalism is equality in rights. A right is an authority to choose or act. In the theory of liberalism in Hobbes and Locke, the true origin of rights is nature: hence, natural rights.[1] Nature here means two things, and neither element is restricted to liberal political thought. First, something natural is what it is spontaneously, independent of any creation or interference. We can see this if we look at our ordinary, everyday, commonsense, conversation. In it, we sometimes tell people to be natural. We mean by this that they should be uncalculating, unforced, unphony, and not artificial. In a word, they should be spontaneous. If we

---

[1] See John Locke, *Second Treatise of Government*, chapter 7, paragraph 87, and Thomas Hobbes, *Leviathan*, chapters 6, 10, 13 and 14.

push this notion all the way so that it does not refer just to this or that person or situation, we will reach full spontaneity, full self generation, full self causality, dependence on nothing else. The fully natural is the fully spontaneous.

Second, nature means what is generally or universally true of something. Commonsensically, we often say when someone acts in a certain way — she is lazy, or irresponsible, or very precise, or messy — that it is her nature, i.e., that it is a dominant or pervasive characteristic. If we push the notion of what is pervasive to its limit, we reach what is fully universal, say a natural law of physics. The fully natural is the fully universal.[2]

Taking rights and nature together, then, we see that natural rights are the authorities for choice that cover every authority to choose and that exist spontaneously, whatever we do, however we change things and make them over. In the liberal understanding, these rights belong to individuals, and they belong to each of us equally. Individuals are those who in a spontaneous way possess the authority for justified choice, and this root authority covers all people and all choices equally.

This view of natural authority could, of course, be challenged. Perhaps only communities are naturally authoritative, not individuals.[3] Perhaps some natural characteristics cover all their members, but cover them unequally, as reason covers all humans who, nonetheless, are unequally rational. The common understanding of what nature means, that is to say, does not require liberal individualism. Indeed, substantive differences here are at the core of variations among political philosophers. For, thinkers obviously have different views of what we truly mean by spontaneity and causality, of the various possibilities for universality and generality, and of what the natural things are concretely. Working out these differences belongs to the overall conceptual and historical task of political thought.

The second central element of liberalism concerns this question: who exactly is this naturally authoritative individual? Hobbes and Locke talk of the centrality of self preservation — and ultimately of comfortable self

---

[2] For related but not identical reflections cf. Jacob Klein, "On the Nature of Nature," in his *Lectures and Essays*, edited by Robert B. Williamson and Elliott Zuckerman, St. John's College Press, 1985.
[3] Consider Aristotle's discussion in Book 1 of the *Politics*.

preservation. Hobbes also talks of the fear of violent death. Every other desire is seen in this light.[4] What does it mean to flee from death and satisfy the desire for self preservation? For liberal thinkers, the satisfaction of desire is the quelling of uneasiness.[5] Fleeing death is fleeing the void, nothing, emptiness. So, what Hobbes and Locke ultimately mean is that what motivates us is the restless movement away from nothing in particular to nothing in particular, with various arbitrary resting points along the way. The self is nothing but this movement and resting, and the calculation appropriate to it. Happiness is not fulfillment oriented to set ends but, rather, is the accumulation of variable satisfactions which are stopping points from which one gathers energy for continued movement. What is good for me is whatever I judge will keep my restless motion going, perpetually.

To gain some perspective, we should briefly contrast this liberal notion of the individual self to other views. The chief is to see each of us as having his own soul. Every soul is composed of identical parts, and the soul's perfection, its happiness, would be the same for us all, if we did not fall short of this perfection in different ways. Our natural motion is not restlessness, but a combination of longing to join with something higher, purer, more beautiful and complete, ranging from sex to philosophical contemplation; and spirited self defense, where we stiffen and gather ourselves in our own independence and pride, ranging from simple courage to great statesmanship. What is desirable is not the objects that my restless motion happens to rest on and gather strength from, but these goals to which my soul is attracted, and the means to them. Moral and intellectual virtue — statesmanship and philosophy — are the two peaks, and the small hills the rest of us occasionally climb are dignified only by their likeness to these mountains.[6]

A third key element of liberalism concerns the status of property or power. Property, one's private substance, becomes decisive because it is the neutral good that could be used to satisfy any desire. The liberal self's wish to continue its restless activity is in practice largely satisfied by the movement of accumulating and acquiring power generally and property in

---

[4] See Hobbes, *Leviathan*, Chapters 13, 14, 12, 6 and 21.
[5] John Locke, *An Essay Concerning Human Understanding*, Book II, Chapter 20.
[6] Consider, for example, Aristotle's discussion of moral and intellectual virtue in the *Ethics*.

particular — not so much spending it and using it as obtaining it and holding it. Acquisition is not primarily about enjoyment but about the ever increasingly controlled and energetic movement away from death and unease.

A fourth central element of liberalism is the importance of freedom. By examining freedom at length I will develop further some of the points that I have just made. My intention is to analyze freedom generally and then to show what is specific about liberal freedom.

## Freedom

We say that a prisoner who has served his time has been freed, or that a dog chained or tethered to a pole can be set free or set loose. These primary and ordinary uses suggest that to be freed is to have a restraint eliminated: to be free is not to be, or no longer to be, restrained; to be completely free is to be completely unrestrained.[7]

We employ related meanings when we call people free spirits, i.e., unconventional ones who are not limited by ordinary ways, or speak of ourselves as free from burdens and concerns, i.e., as relieved from them, or say that we are not free to do some chore because we are busy, or involved. Indeed, the close connections and occasional substitutability of these terms, where involvements can be burdens and burdens normally restrain, allow us still to think of unrestraint as freedom's leading current meaning.

Most of the more evidently political uses of "free" also group around unrestraint. When the teenager says that she is living in a free country she means that she should not be stopped from doing what she wants; when the journalist praises free speech he means that no one should restrain him from saying what he wishes; and, when the economist praises the free market he means one in which anyone can participate, with few restrictions.

We also oppose free government more broadly to tyranny, and here we see freedom's second chief meaning. To be a free man in a free government is, taking its widest opposite, not to be a slave. To be a slave is to be restrained. Still more, however, it is to be controlled — it is not

---

[7] See Hobbes, *Leviathan*, Chapter 21.

merely to be a prisoner who is stopped from doing as he chooses, but to have to do what someone else chooses, to be dominated, forced, directed, or ruled by another for his purposes. Free government means both that citizens are not (unduly) restrained by government from doing what they choose, and that they are not subjects controlled and directed by the monarch, tyrant, or party for their own (i.e., for the "government's") ends.

To develop our understanding further, we must mention two additional facts. The first is that almost any of our actions, and some actions of other animals and of inanimate things, can be said to be free or not free. We say of someone that he freely attends school or does his homework; that he enters battle freely or is free to play the stock market; that he freely obeys the law; that he is free to leave the table or change his job. Being free is not restricted to one area of activity; anything can be free, or the object of freedom.

The second is that although we sometimes act as if our freedom is a burden, we generally believe it to be good. We almost always choose it for ourselves, and when we see it as harmful for others it is usually because they or we are being unjust.

## The Current Sense of How Freedom Is Good

To be free means not to be constrained or controlled. This is always the case, so it is therefore also true for us today. There is, however, a specific difference with liberal freedom. This difference is that liberal freedom normally is coordinated with goods understood as the objects of our wants or desires, when we can understand anything and everything to be equally desirable.

This point may not seem to advance our discussion because it looks inevitable or empty, a mere restatement of what has gone before. In fact, it is not. For, freedom as being unconstrained in satisfying desires for objects ("interests") that are in principle equal is not identical to freedom simply. Rather, it has a specific kind of neutrality that differs from freedom universally: extreme modern freedom is only one type of unconstrained awaiting or unburdened lightness. In our contemporary liberal sense, freedom is a flat, flaccid or loose uninvolvement, a being left alone, in relation to which any particular flatly desired interest or good can then be pursued and the means toward it found. Freedom as we experience

111

it is a not being restrained from pursuing, following, moving toward, or leading oneself toward objects, each of which is potentially equally desirable. This general, uninspiring, and undifferentiated untiedness colors all the restrictions and liberties involved in the attempt to satisfy concrete desires: liberal choice and the ability to choose has about it a kind of undetermined voluntariness. Such freedom is analogous to property as we have just described it — a generally useful good not tied to desires seen to be especially uplifting.[8]

This contemporary freedom is more a universal means than an end in itself, or, more exactly, it is an end, a good, precisely as a flat, placid, uninvolvement, the freedom of Nietzsche's last man. If, however, we consider further the kind of motion involved in the pursuit of interests, we can see things more subtly, and differentiate today's excess from its origin. As we have suggested, self-preservation and the satisfaction of desire understood as it is in Locke as dispelling uneasiness or in Hobbes as perpetuating oneself by fleeing from nothing (death) to nothing in particular (anything as something that one might desire) is energized or empowered precisely by the interests upon which one rests and gathers strength. Our liberal freedom strictly, therefore, is not only the flat, placid uninvolvement of our contemporary Nietzschean or Tocquevillean decay. It is also the neutral unrestriction (in which one is then ready temporarily to restrict oneself) and the not being pushed or lead around (in which one is poised to push and lead oneself around) in which a certain kind of energy and "power" accumulates and impels. But because of its flatness — in the sense that it is not a lack or restriction connected to, for, inspired, or uplifted by anything in particular — this bourgeois freedom can degenerate into flaccidity. It can decline from responsibility, calculation for the future, and freedom for these into bovine self absorption.

## Freedom and Virtue

We can clarify matters by contrasting what we have just said with the freedom implicit in virtue. For, one who seeks, say, courage and the proper disposition toward honor will not feel or be free in the same way as one

---

[8] Consider the close of Strauss' discussion of Locke in *Natural Right and History* (Chicago, 1952).

who seeks the security of simple privacy, wealth, or even responsibility. Indeed, one problem with today's discussions of freedom is that they sometimes unthinkingly consider it to be correlated only to the equal objects of desire. Therefore, the connection between, say, freedom and virtue either is mysteriously unclear or virtue is treated as a set of characteristics one simply happens to want: it is assimilated to desire rather than the other way around.

What is the freedom that is correlated to the attempt to develop a character composed of virtuous dispositions? For our purposes here, let us combine elements of Aristotle's and Plato's understandings. Each virtue is a mean with regard to a specific good: moderation to pleasure; courage to fear; liberality to wealth; pride to honor; and so on. Each of these goods has its own natural or spontaneous attraction, however short-lived or unstable that attraction might be, and enjoying it is a kind of completion; it is not, or not only, the quelling of restlessness. Even fear is as much a feeling of risk as of trembling and unease, and its overcoming is a feeling of exhilaration as much as relief.[9]

The virtuous disposition toward these goods (or dangers) is not the restless, forward moving, energetic, quelling of unease, and still less flat placidity. It is not even the serious, responsible, leading of oneself in, through, and at the forefront of greater and greater (i.e., larger and larger and in this sense more significant) enterprises. Rather, it is a completion of one's own soul through dealing properly with goods that are attractive or complete on their own. Virtue is noble, beautiful, and not only serious or even sober. Its beauty is the beauty of a symphony, in which the fitting end or completion is harmony, rather than, as it were, a straighter and deeper monotony.

Freedom here is also a type of unrestrainedness and not being pushed around. But it is not identical to the flat and sometimes unfocused relief that is oriented to accumulating goods that are the objects of numberless equal desires. Rather, it is oriented to goods that are uplifting, or (as with a political community) needing defense and protection, and to forming and

---

[9] Consider Plato's *Laches, Charmides, Sophist* and *Statesman* in addition to Aristotle's *Ethics*. One might also reflect here on Churchill's accounts of his various battles in his *My Early Life* (published originally in 1930).

continuing a character composed of dispositions to enjoy goods or deal with dangers in the right amounts, times, and places.

As opposed to the freedom of the liberal self or soul, therefore, freedom as being unconstrained and uncontrolled in the pursuit of such goods has the following characteristics. It is not experienced primarily as undirected unrestraint in relation to what is undifferentiated but, rather, as an eager, attentive, comprehension while choosing and acting to produce or enjoy specific goods, pleasures, goals, forms, or character. The quality of liberal goods as possible objects of desire, and of freedom as the general unrestraint for this possibility, is countered by freedom experienced as liberation, mastery, or joy, that is, as a gathering of strength and attentive awareness for combat, pursuit, or the immersion and shaping we practice in moderation, liberality, and magnificence; and all is tied to (and subtly ranked by) the worth and range of the activity. The freedom that is a correlate to virtue is a burgeoning and plenitude, a sense of having burst chains, or being ready for expansion or full growth, and a gathering, shrugging off, and standing firm, not merely a relief from fear. The "possibility" in these goods one chooses, that is, their not simply being ineluctably and necessarily compelling, includes the unequal way in which we have them or are attracted to and guided by them; and freedom as not being restrained or forced is experienced in our expansiveness and readiness for goods that attract, are pursued, and are attained differentially and imitatively.[10]

## Common Goods

The question to which I would now like to turn is how individual support for common institutions becomes possible in liberalism. For, little about the freedom, natural authority, motion, and satisfaction of the liberal self as I have just described them would suggest that it would support such institutions.

I will begin by elaborating the various ways in which things can be common entities, or parts of a whole. I will discuss only a few salient points because my goal is to locate a distinctively liberal common good.

---

[10] Compare Nietzsche's *Twilight of the Idols* and *Beyond Good and Evil* with Plato's *Alcibiades*. Consider also the discussions in Hannah Arendt's *Between Past and Future*.

First, some commons entities have identical members or parts. Some do not: all or several of their parts are not interchangeable. In the group or class of every thing with the number two in it, for example, all the twos are identical. In a team, however, most parts are different — quarterback, linebacker, etc. Second, some common entities have parts that can exist (well) apart from the whole; others do not. The parts of a face, for example, cannot really exist or function apart from the whole face to which they belong. Third, some common entities have parts that are equally important. In others, some parts are more significant than others. In an automobile, for instance, the engine is more significant than the door. But for a group of marbles the parts are equally significant and equally defining.

Distinct from the question of the kind of parts that constitute a common, goods can be considered common because they are commonly enjoyed, produced, or maintained. When a good is available for common enjoyment, for example, in some cases all can enjoy it equally while in others the good is used up and exhausted. Consider wisdom, a good that we enjoy differently because of different capacities, but which is inexhaustible, or a sunset, more or less equal and inexhaustible. As opposed to this, however, not everyone can be first in line for the movies, or have a house on the beach.

We can also separate the questions of parts and of enjoyment and production from yet a third way to consider common goods, namely, the nature of the tie in what is common. We may, for example, distinguish covering, binding, intertwining, linking, ordering, placing, attracting, attaching, fitting, likening and other ties that have been integral to analogies for law and statesmanship from Plato's day until our own.[11]

## Common Goods and Liberalism

My purpose now is to say a word or two about the type of commonality and common good that is coordinated with the other bases of liberalism. The first central point is that when we have common goods in the theory of liberalism — or, as we should strictly call them, common interests — we enjoy them in the same way that we enjoy other goods or interests. This is

---

[11] One should consider here the complex discussion in Plato's *Statesman*.

to say that in liberalism there is no separate natural attraction to common things. Moreover, any attachment to a good of which we are a part must be chosen and justified in terms of my individual natural authority. Just as our individual interests are attachments in which nothing is naturally compelling, but everything is a possibly variable and essentially restless attachment, so, too, with our common interests. There is nothing about us that is naturally oriented to, or essentially satisfied only by, something that is necessarily common.

Concretely, common interests in liberalism are, therefore, things in which we merely happen to be commonly interested, in two senses. First, they refer to the fact that we have individual attachments to the same types of objects, for example, good music. Second, common interests are things that are linked to the other interests of many of us, opportunities and situations in which we are mutually interested. "It is in the interest of everyone in this city that the government not close down the military base." The point of liberalism, however, is that there is no precise unchanging list of common goods, any more than there is of individual goods. There are, however, goods such as representative institutions and markets that reward individual industry that are almost always useful.

Our next task is to specify the commonality of participation in common goods, in the liberal sense. In terms of the distinctions I just made, their commonality consists in the possibility that they could be fully and equally participated in by anyone, and that those who participate in them are all equal. The paradigmatic immediate example is the structure and operation of a completely neutral economic market. Indeed, all our political institutions, voluntary associations, and professional organizations are common in this sense, as opposed to guilds, churches in theocracies, participatory aristocracies, or the democracies of which Rousseau wrote. The passionate ties and related exclusionary nature of these structures are transformed by the dominance of equal access. The rich or poor man's ancestral home is subject to the equally held bourgeois right to buy and sell property.

So: common interests in liberalism can in principle be fully and equally participated in by anyone, and they are all artificial, and not naturally compelling. Our problem is that precisely because common goods in liberalism are in this sense artificial or equal, it is a mystery why anyone would devote himself to the mechanisms that serve them if his own interests were in any way harmed. If someone else is supplying a common good, you are pleased at getting away with no effort, or a minimum effort. If your local school works well without your volunteering, why bother? But since everyone can make this calculation, how are common things ever produced and maintained?

I want to argue now that one explanation of this mystery turns on our looking away from any *particular* selfish interest that someone has and looking toward the liberal self that has and defines interests. The best description of this phenomenon, whereby the free individual driven by self interest nonetheless attaches himself consistently to long-term and common concerns such as defense of markets and free government rather than merely using these institutions, is what we call responsibility. I mentioned responsibility earlier and will turn to it in detail now.[12]

## Responsibility

What is responsibility? First, when we say that someone is responsible we mean that he can be held to account. "Who is responsible for this military disaster?" That is, whose fault is it, who can be blamed. But why are we deservedly accountable? Because we are the cause. The second meaning of being responsible is to be the cause of something, the reason that it happened. Now, accountability and guilt may make us think of sin and intention, of what I tried to do or planned to accomplish, whatever the outcome. Responsibility's third main meaning, however, points in a different direction. When we call someone responsible we also mean that he is concerned with results, and takes care that the results are correct. A responsible craftsman or accountant sees his work through to its completion, and sees that it is done well. He is dependable and reliable:

---

[12] In terms of the broader conceptual options that I have been discussing, the point is that in any form of constitutive understanding, in addition to a coherent view of what is actually natural, what the truly common things are, and so on, there will also be a characteristic kind of completed self or character that serves and secures the chief common goods, the main institutions. This virtue, and educating for it, is a central goal and motive force in the structure. For our liberalism, I will be arguing that it is responsibility that is the excellence that is best coordinated with the other elements. It takes the place of classical virtue, or religious piety, or being assigned to traditional duties, but is analogous to them.

good intentions are not enough. The roof must actually stop leaking, today, not next week.

So, to be responsible is to be accountable for results, for outcomes, not only for intentions. Accountable to whom, and for what? Primarily, when we think of responsible men as the ones who get results, we think of them as doing their job. They are accountable to those who hire them or, more profoundly and steadily, they are accountable to themselves for doing their work and obtaining results. Responsibility, however, goes beyond simply doing one's *own* job. We also think of responsible men as the ones who take charge in situations in which it is unclear whose job it is, situations in which no one is accountable. Responsible men and women in this broader sense are the ones to whom everyone turns to handle emergencies, or to organize the neighbors so that a necessary traffic light is installed. Responsible people are the ones who attempt to secure results that are good for many, for others as well as for themselves, when it is no one's job in particular to do this. Responsible men and women are often the ones urged by their friends to run for office.

This responsibility is the most interesting kind because the responsible man in this sense takes on tasks that provide a common as well as an individual benefit. The responsible man takes on common tasks, takes charge of them, and sees them through. His actions go beyond doing his job, because he makes things his job.

Such responsibility, I will argue, is the heart of active engagement by free liberal individuals in securing common interests: responsibility is the analogue in liberalism to traditional duty, religious obligation, customary self-denial, and noble virtue. To a degree, indeed, it replaces them.[13]

## Responsibility and Liberal Self Interest

My goal now is actually to develop the connection between liberal self interest and responsible attention to common concerns. I want to show that responsibility is of a piece with liberal self interest — rather than being opposed to it. It is not alien as altruism is, or pre-liberal as are ancient

[13] The vast, interesting, literature on responsibility is concerned primarily with the question of responsibility and free will. Responsibility in the sense that I have pointed out receives surprisingly little attention. A good example of the current state of discussion is Hilary Bok, *Freedom and Responsibility* (Princeton University Press, 1998).

virtue or religious duty, although it is related to them. This is why the actual term responsibility begins to appear only in the late 18th century and is first used to any extent in the *Federalist Papers*.[14]

One good way to see the connection is to examine what we are attempting to be when we try to be responsible for ourselves. When I continually and habitually drive too fast, eat too much, waste my money, fritter away my time, or fail to work hard in school, I am accused of being, and am, irresponsible. This means that what I am doing today will make it difficult to be successful tomorrow. This suggests that being responsible about myself is a disposition in which I treat myself as a possibility for continued motion and accumulation. I show foresight about my own need for foresight: as we say, I invest in myself, or treat myself as my most important job. I therefore begin to develop habits of steadiness, prudence, and circumspection, and a self defined by these qualities. Indeed, these habits are the conditions we need to exercise economic and other rights effectively: responsibility helps to produce and establish the qualities it takes to be free to succeed, to be an individual whose choices and actions are unmastered and unconstrained.

We can make this more clear by reconsidering modern freedom. The peculiar flatness of bourgeois freedom is correlated, as we have said, to the way items present themselves to us when all could be objects of desire. They are not compelling, outstanding, or remarkable things that "must" be possessed or imitated, unlike, say, honor, although they can become objects of obsession or extremism. Rather, they are in a less forceful way satisfying and energizing in the sense that they help us continue forward on our way — jobs, homes, food, and so on. If our point or purpose is self-perpetuation or self-satisfaction, however, then certain abilities and ways of thinking become necessary. One must consider the long-term, and amass the skills and substance suitable to it. One must often control or be competent in a wide range, to ward off enemies, to expand one's power, and to enjoy the proper field for the perpetuation of the expansive self that the growth of skill and a long-term point of view develops. All this takes one away from narrow, short-term calculation of satisfaction and interest to a disposition to responsibility toward oneself, and, ultimately, to engage in those situations in which the fuller sense of oneself and the interests of this

---

[14] See papers 23, 63, 70, 77, and 79.

119

self are involved. The effective preservation of self, the effective flight from death, and the effective conquest of unease require, when one is not completely alone, a wariness, carefulness, and security that come only with responsibility to self and with earning and amassing the abilities that give one self-protection. When this disposition of responsibility arises, it then becomes as significant for the liberal self as merely satisfying interest after interest: the successful and emblematic modern liberal is not merely the seeker and accumulator of material goods and pleasures, but the responsible man who is attentive to tomorrow's tasks and requirements.

In fact, healthy concern with myself and my freedom, healthy self-interest, is ultimately nothing but this collected concentration on myself as a possibility for long range accumulation and satisfaction. Self interested behavior, as understood in liberal theory and exemplified in paradigmatic lives, is not truly for the sake of any narrow attachment but for the sake of *self* perpetuation — in the way of a great capitalist accumulation.

Now, from this point of view, it is not surprising that behavior often occurs that does not serve the immediate accumulation of this or that piece of property, i.e., that does not serve individual selfishness as we usually understand it. Liberal self interested men are less attached to their discrete interests than to the naturally authoritative liberal self whose movement and resting is the basis of everything else that we find to be good. This attachment to self perpetuation, in fact, can very naturally lead them to take a long-term and common point of view, for there is no reason to believe that perpetuating the cool, measured, calculated, ongoing, expansive, attachment and accumulation that define the liberal quest for self satisfaction will be more successful on the small field of petty interest than on the broad field of service to and shaping of others. The responsible man takes charge of his own future, including the public tasks that are suitable to his own sense of his substance.

## Responsibility and the Common Good

This is the central point at which I have been driving. Taking on the task of perpetuating ourselves requires a long and wide view, not the view from any particular interest. The disposition to the long view then colors any particular interest as well: to become responsible for my self interest as it attaches to any separate interest means that I see this interest too in as wide and common an extent as my concentration and understanding allow. There is a continuum, based on responsibility for oneself, that runs through responsibility experienced as doing one's job well to responsibility experienced as making one's own the jobs that need to be done but belong to nobody. At the end of this continuum are activities that for most practical purposes serve the common good as well as would a nobler devotion.

I do not want to leave it just at saying this, because I might give the impression that I am only discussing calculation — what is called enlightened self interest. My point goes beyond this because what happens on one's journey on this continuum is that we understand and experience the self and the disposition to be responsible to it in wider and wider ways. Responsibility becomes more a matter of character than of calculation. To put this in another way, the responsible self that seeks to perpetuate itself gathers itself and stretches itself throughout its interests, and carries this disposition to new situations. As this happens, the responsible man need not normally see a contradiction between his self interest and taking the lead in the tasks that face him, even though they are common to us all and no one's in particular. For, these tasks belong to him too, in his wider self-understanding. I also do not mean to say that everyone will be equally responsible, but, rather, that the firmer one's responsibility, the steadier one's self interest, and the more prudent the exercise of one's rights, the wider will be the extent of, and the more secure will be one's grasp of, the genuine requirements of common tasks. Ultimately, I act responsibly and do the common jobs that are not mine alone because I attempt to perpetuate successfully the presence and power that are mine alone.

I also should emphasize here that responsibility hardly explains all attention to what is common in actual liberal democracies. Some comes from a combination of individually self interested calculation and law enforcement. But the outstanding examples of common service — war, politics, leading and beginning organizations — cannot be explained fully in these ways. Some of this outstanding activity also occurs because elements of the natural pre-liberal attractions remain in liberal democracies. This should not be underestimated: old-fashioned duty and obligation have not altogether disappeared. Yet, all goods, including faith, tradition, and friendship, are experienced in liberalism within a context in which each practice is voluntary and all ties are freely self-chosen. Free

121

individuals' attention (and even devotion) to what is common would not survive, or would be extraordinarily attenuated, if this attention simply contradicted the reigning spirit. Fortunately, the coordination of responsibility and self interest enables us to explain why there is often such a firm commitment to common associations in individualistic liberal democracies, where one might least expect it. Genuine responsibility is not counter to, but, rather, flows from a deep grasp of one's self interest.

## Conclusion

Whereas duty, obligation, and altruism presuppose either a set assignment given feudally or through faith, or an external divine code, responsibility does not. It is a disposition of character consistent with the essentially voluntary nature of our associations. So, it is very interesting practically, because in addition to all the remnants of bygone and natural sources of acting communally, it shows that there is a phenomenon that springs from self interest and is consistent with self interest but becomes a disposition that still on the grounds of self interest leads us to go beyond ordinary, narrow, self interest. And, it is very interesting theoretically because it helps to indicate that the various conceptual alternatives about what is natural, about the self or soul and its movements and what it experiences as free and as good, about how things are common, and about the character or disposition to serve what is common fit together coherently.

There are many practical points that flow from this argument about the nature of responsibility and its link to liberalism.[15] I will conclude by mentioning some of them. In encouraging corporate and individual responsibility, we should think of them less as what we owe others and more as expressions of the proper scope of self-independence. They are not so much matters of guilt as of pride. This means, in turn, that we should not seek the same degree of responsibility from everyone, because responsibility in the full sense of doing the tasks that belong to no one in particular is rare. We should not water it down by equalizing it. Indeed,

[15] I discuss some of these points more fully in Mark Blitz, "Philanthropy and Public Needs" in John W. Barry and Bruno V. Manno, eds., *Giving Better, Giving Smarter*, National Commission on Philanthropy and Civic Renewal, 1997; and in Mark Blitz, "Responsibility and Public Service" in Peter Augustine Lawler, Robert Schaefer, and David Lewis Schaefer, eds. *Active Duty* (Rowman and Littlefield, 1998).

we should consider responsibility primarily in the light of occupations, professions, and dispositions, rather than universal rules. The heart even of bureaucratic responsibility, in fact, is effectiveness, not accountability. For, government works better when we execute our responsibilities aggressively and check each other in doing so than when we look over our own and each other's shoulders.

# 8. *The Judeo-Christian Tradition and the Liberal Tradition in the American Republic*[1]

## WILFRED McCLAY

When asked to contribute to this volume, and to the conference that preceded it, I was given the above title as my assignment. At first blush, it was a daunting idea to approach such a huge subject, and I was sorely tempted to request reassignment, or suggest a nice, neat, and manageable topic of my own choice. For one thing, the proposed paper had nothing but problematic words in its title. "Judeo-Christian" "liberal," "tradition," and "republic" — each could make the top-ten list of our most ambiguous and contested words. Even the adjective "American" could make the list, if one wanted to be a fanatic about it, which would mean that every noun and adjective in the title would qualify.

One problem with such a title, I feared, is that I would end up spending all my time quibbling about the meaning of these words. What, for example, is the meaning of the Judeo-Christian tradition? *Is* there really such a thing? What is the nature of the union being described? Just what does that hyphen mean? Does it denote a marriage made in heaven? A marriage of the heart? Or a marriage of convenience? Or a mere cohabitation, a grudging *modus vivendi*? What kind of cultural splicing are we talking about? Can we usefully compare it to other such cultural splicings? Greco-Roman? Anglo-American? Serbo-Croatian?

And what, for that matter, does one mean by the term "tradition," which can cover a multitude of continuities between past and present,

[1] © Wilfred M. McClay

124

including purely fanciful ones, gotten up expressly for the occasion? Haven't we all seen academic books with titles like: "The Anarchist Tradition in American Poetry?" And, moreover, is the Judeo-Christian tradition the same *kind* of tradition as the liberal tradition? And what about the word "liberal" itself, whose tortured ambiguity is surely the result of a conspiracy by academic political theorists to keep themselves gainfully employed in perpetuity? Or "republicanism," of which John Adams observed in 1807 that "there is not a more unintelligible term in the English language" — and this was more than a century and a half before the historians and theorists got their hands on the concept, and started applying it to everyone in sight: antebellum feminists, populist agitators, shopkeepers, artisans, and trade unionists?

So I thought I had good reasons for shifting the topic onto less problematic ground. But the conference organizers knew what they were doing. They were well aware that academics, like politicians, specialize in translating questions they can't answer into ones that they can. Translation can be betrayal, as the old adage has it, and the most important questions do not always pose themselves in just the manner we would like. One of my graduate-school teachers used to speak of something he called "Greene's Law," which asserts that, the more susceptible an inquiry is to precise formulation, the more likely it is to produce trivial results. This surely takes the matter too far, and in any event is probably a self-refuting proposition. But he had a point. Not all ambiguities can or should be cleared up in advance, particularly when one is using a public vocabulary. Ambiguous words may play the same role in our speech that ambiguous coalitions play in our politics — and coalitions are often a good thing, and certainly are inevitable. We have to be willing to swim through unsought turbulences if we are going to venture out in the ocean of public discourse, rather than merely doing our laps in the serenity of the university pool.

So in the end I chose to forgo the joys of semantic quibbling, and try to address this unwieldy topic exactly as it was posed to me — even if I did wind up insisting on some semantic quibbles in the end. But the real underlying questions here, I think, are clear enough, especially when one considers them in the larger context of our conference and volume. I take it as a given that the moral condition of the United States in our day is sufficiently worrisome, to a sufficient number of us, to warrant some sustained reflection on where we are, how we got there, and where we need to go next. And I take it to be my particular task to reflect, in a very exploratory way, on the evolving relationship between our nation's dominant religious traditions and its dominant political traditions, and ask what that evolving relationship might have to do with our present and future condition.

That story is complex, and has been formed as much by the requirements of prudence and custom, or sheer historical serendipity, as by the invocation of explicit principle. Take the question of religious establishment. Although we take great pride in our history of religious liberty and pluralism, the record suggests that this history owes a great deal to economics and geography — to British North America's large initial endowment of dissenting Protestant faiths, to its pragmatic willingness to recruit a religiously and ethnically diverse immigrant labor force, and to a spacious continent's ability to accommodate a diversity of distinct communities. American religious tolerance was a concrete fact before it became an abstract virtue. Although our First Amendment explicitly forbade the Congress to establish a national religion, it did not prevent the continuation of existing state religious establishments. Indeed, one can reasonably argue that our constitutional order has supported various *informal* establishments all along. Americans have moved through various stages of such informal establishments. In the beginning, there was a non-denominational Protestant establishment. That was replaced, beginning roughly sixty years ago, by a non-faith-specific "Judeo-Christian" establishment. This latter establishment, never firmly rooted to begin with, now increasingly finds itself on the defensive, challenged and superseded by a non-Judeo-Christian, non-believing establishment, one that owes far more to the desiderata of secular liberal ideology than to the moral legacy of biblical revealed religion.

One might say that these latter two forms of establishment are the two competing ways that a heavily Protestant and Christian American culture has tried to take respectful account of non-Protestants, and particularly Jews. The first way tries to emphasize and affirm, through the umbrella concept of "the Judeo-Christian tradition," the things that Jewish and Christian believers have had in common, and that have been so profoundly constitutive of our civilization. The second way attempts to transcend the points of division by breaking down the traditional faiths, separating the

126

grain of their universal moral teaching from the chaff of their particular religious doctrine, and then banning explicit religious identity as a legitimate element in public life. The second of these ways has been in the ascendant in recent years, and may well remain the stronger of the two. It may take the form of John Dewey's post-Protestant "common faith," or it may take the form of a more openly militant or dismissive secularism. But what stays the same is its relatively low regard for the substance of the Judeo-Christian tradition, except in the most vague and inconsequential sense of the term.

Even so, what has been especially interesting and surprising in recent years has been the way that the concept of the Judeo-Christian tradition, which began life as a diffuse, even evasive, term, has gained in concreteness and persuasiveness at precisely the same time that the pure secularist alternative has come to seem more and more culturally dominant. This is not merely because the Owl of Minerva is taking flight at dusk. It is because the sense of common cause in opposition to a militant secularism has been gathering strength. So strong has it become that it is now even conceivable, as Peter Kreeft has argued in his interesting book *Ecumenical Jihad*, that we may in the coming century see the Judeo-Christian tradition come to be expanded into an even more inclusive "Abrahamic" tradition, which would include elements of conservative Islam in its portfolio.

I suspect that this may be a pipedream, for reasons we need not get into today. Then again, I am making no bets against it. For if it did happen, it would hardly be more surprising than what already *has* happened, by way of making the Judeo-Christian tradition a much more meaningful concept today than it ever was in the past. In the term's heyday, in the 1940s, 50s, and 60s, there were good reasons for critics, particularly Jewish critics such as the writer Arthur A. Cohen, to flail away at what they called the "myth" of the Judeo-Christian tradition, and to decry efforts to blunt and efface the vast and historical differences between Christians and Jews. Such critics disliked the term's tendency to accommodate and subsume all such differences beneath the big tent of a smiling American consensus — a consensus that, on closer examination, looked a whole lot like a thin and highly secularized liberal Protestantism. Protestants have always been very good at the game of advancing their worldview while presenting it as a neutral matter of "acculturation," "assimilation," or "Americanization." In any event, the attacks of writers like Cohen had their effect, and the term fell into dishonor and disuse — almost as much dishonor and disuse as the concept of sin. And yet, even if the term is used less today, there is every reason to believe that, ironically, it now really *means* more.

It is important, too, to point out that the Judeo-Christian tradition and the liberal tradition, properly understood, are neither opposites nor enemies. They are different. They exist in tension in some respects. But they also are compatible, and may even be mutually supporting. The Judeo-Christian tradition, grounded as it is in the biblical revelation, provides crucial resources for the formation of souls. Without something like it, a liberal political order would find it exceedingly hard to produce the kind of resilient, self-reliant, and morally responsible individuals it needs. And the traditions of a liberal political order, by separating political institutions from religious institutions to a greater or lesser degree, underwrite the freedom of choice and the liberty of conscience that are the very heart of a vibrant religious faith and practice — at least, as they exist in the West. Both traditions, rightly understood, support the dignity and moral agency of the individual person. Both traditions also acknowledge the inherent limitations of human judgment. Both assert the fatal partiality of the individual understanding, and the need for countervailing constraints upon the human will. Both can be so understood as to exist in a relatively harmonious balance. And both are susceptible to variations or misinterpretations that may put them sharply at odds with one another.

One way of getting at this problem is to distinguish between two ways of understanding the concept of the "secular," only one of which is an enemy of religion. There is, on the one hand, a way of understanding the secular idea as an opponent of established belief and a protector of the rights of free exercise and free association. On the other hand, one can understand the secular ideal as a proponent of established unbelief and a protector of strictly *individual* expressive rights. The former is a fairly minimal, even "negative" understanding of secularism, a freedom "from" establishmentarian imposition. The latter is a more robust, more "positive" understanding of the secular order, one that affirms secularism as an alternative faith, at least so far as the public realm is concerned.

The first of these possibilities, which sounds almost identical to the language of the First Amendment, suggests that it is at least theoretically possible for there to be such a thing as a non-established secular order, one that is equally respectful of religionists and nonreligionists alike. Such an order preserves the core insistence upon the freedom of the uncoerced individual conscience. But it does respect the religious needs of humankind, and does not presume that the religious impulse should be understood as a merely individual and private matter — as if it were a private language, in whose tongues each of us babbles solipsistically about "the mystery of life." It would, on the contrary, understand that religion is also a social institution, for whose flourishing the rights of free association are just as important as the rights of individual expression.

Such subtle distinctions have generally been lost on the more militant secularists, the establishmentarian secularists. In many cases they honestly cannot imagine that they are imposing anything on anyone, which is why they consistently style themselves heroic defenders of civil liberties — or, more modestly, just People for The American Way. Indeed, that organizational name, whose breathtakingly self-aggrandizing qualities surely equal any parallel offense committed by the erstwhile Moral Majority, perfectly expresses the unstated presumptions of our informal secular establishment. (Is there, by the way, a more forlorn epithet today than "Moral Majority?") Their efforts have been aimed at creating and enforcing the naked public square. Such a regime seeks, under the principle of strict and complete separation of church and state, to exclude religious thought and discourse from any serious participation in public life, and to confine religious belief and practice, as much as possible, to the realm of private predilection and individual taste.

To this analysis, two things must be added. First, the ideal of secular establishment has never carried the day entirely, even with all its impressive victories in the courts and halls of government and academe. Prayers are still uttered at the opening of Congressional sessions. God's name appears on our currency and in the oaths we take in court. Chaplains are still employed by the armed services. The tax-exempt status of religious institutions remains intact. Belief in God remains pervasive, and church and synagogue attendance rates remain high, at least relative to other Western countries. The president of the United States freely invokes "his" God and faith, and totes his Bible around conspicuously on a regular basis, and no complaints are heard from the ACLU. The point is, this is still not an entirely secular country, one that has been sanitized of any form of public sanction for religion. The quality of our belief is another matter, of course, to which I'll come in due course.

Second, the secular establishment, with its strict-separationist dogma, seems to be losing much of its unquestioned binding force. This is largely because the social and cultural problems of the nation have come to seem beyond its power to address. This is now even reflected on the level of law and government and ideas. The recent welfare-reform legislation included an option for "charitable choice," which opens up the provision of social-welfare services to faith-based organizations, operating on a contract basis but supported by the taxpayers. The rise of school-choice initiatives promises to produce a similar leveling of the playing field as regards religious and non-religious schools. So did the Supreme Court's recent *Agostini* decision, which would appear to ease us away from the strict taboo against public support for parochial and other sectarian schools. The Court's 1995 *Rosenberger* decision put college-campus religious organizations on the same footing as non-religious organizations, with the same access to student activity fees. Even the Court's widely lamented decision in the 1997 term to strike down the Religious Freedom Restoration Act (RFRA) as unconstitutional may not have been such a bad thing, since the bill as written appeared to underwrite an entirely individualistic idea of religion.

Quite simply, the governing elites of this country, even when not themselves religious believers, have begun to understand that we cannot afford to dismiss what people of faith have to offer, if we want to have any hope of solving problems such as substance abuse, teen pregnancy, family breakdown, and the like. Even many liberals who flatly deny conservative assertions that the Great Society "failed" are fully open to the fresh possibilities of faith-based organizations, perhaps because they perceive that such social problems as we face are so clearly problems of the heart and will, and therefore will require inner transformation. This openness is particularly evident among those addressing these social problems in the context of the African American community, where a rich tradition of evangelical Protestant theology and practice, full of the dramatic language of renewal and redemption and salvation, is a crucial resource that can be tapped for this very purpose.

This is an arena in which the tenets of secular liberalism have rebounded upon themselves. Secular liberals, along with many of the rest of us, have a reflexive hostility to any public criticism of minority groups, a taboo that uses a pose of "compassion" to mask an attitude of breathtaking condescension. But this taboo now works powerfully against their own secularist ideology, since so many African Americans are people of very robust and often highly supernaturalist Christian faith, and people who are determined to express that faith in the public realm. Talk about the cunning of history!

The mask of compassion slipped a little when that most quintessential of liberal Protestants, the Episcopal Bishop of Newark, the Right Reverend John Shelby Spong, recently chided the highly conservative and pentecostal African bishops in the Anglican Communion for their childlike "primitive" views on matters of sexuality. Perhaps they and others like them will make the American Episcopal Church their next mission field. But make no mistake: these are not the kind of people that John Dewey had in mind in his search for a "common faith," the kind of people who would free the religious sensibility from its ties to supernaturalism. Although if these are people who do not fit The American Way, then one wonders who does.

Of course, the core of the problem with liberal theology, whether Protestant, Catholic, or Jewish, white or black, is that it is so easily retailored to conform to secularist political agendas. That is, indeed, the very core of what the Social Gospel was all about, the translation of religious questions into political causes. One sees this clearly in all the mainline Protestant churches, whose ecumenism consists in agreement about the essentially trivial character of religious differences, and the primacy of political and social ones. But such ecumenism has in turn given rise to what might be called an "ecumenism of the orthodox," exemplified by such initiatives as Evangelicals and Catholics Together and such journals of opinion as *First Things*, *Touchstone*, and the like.

These unprecedented developments reflect a growing solidarity, across interdenominational and even interfaith lines, of those who want to do two seemingly contradictory things: first, to reaffirm the central distinctives of their respective faiths; and second, to bracket, rather than efface, some of those very distinctives, not only for tactical reasons, but in order to affirm the core elements of the biblical revelation. These elements include: radical monotheism, the createdness of the natural order, the belief that the cosmic order is also a moral order, of which humans are aware, and to which they are accountable — and yet against which they find themselves in perpetual rebellion, and therefore perpetually in need of saving reconciliation and restoration. For "orthodox ecumenicals," such elements of Judeo-Christianity are understood to be fundamental, and to undergird all purely secular considerations.

That last example suggests that there may be something more complicated going on than a mere swinging of the pendulum back in the direction of traditional faith. Are we then entering new territory? If so, is it because we are so fully in the grasp of a nakedly secular orthodoxy, whose views about such matters as the origins and dignity of human life, the status of the family, the meaning of human sexuality, marriage, reproduction, and so on, place no binding moral limits on human action? Has the secular ascendancy created an entirely new correlation of forces? Is it possible that erstwhile antagonists will now become closer allies than ever before, in unprecedented ways, unimaginable in the past? This, it seems to me, is already happening, and this very development is giving a deeper and more precise meaning than ever before to the concept of the Judeo-Christian tradition, one that does not require the collapsing of difference in the search for a watery lowest common denominator.

In this regard it is illuminating to consider the discussion (if one can call it that) that we have had in this country regarding the possibility of human cloning, a form of asexual reproduction that is *clearly* at odds, in ways that even *in vitro* fertilization or surrogate motherhood were not, with the biblical understanding of human procreation. This discussion erupted in public in 1997 with the successful cloning of a sheep in Scotland, an event that produced immediate expressions of horror over the now very real possibility that such procedures could be adopted for the reproduction of human beings. Opposition to such research seemed pervasive, including that of President Clinton, who promptly banned the use of federal monies for such inquiry. But soon the tide began to turn, and the biogenetic research lobby found its voice.

It also found surprising allies. There was, for example, a December 1997 op-ed piece in the New York *Times* by the eminent Harvard law professor Laurence Tribe, which expressed his support for experimentation with the possibility of human cloning. What makes this case especially interesting is that in 1973, he had emphatically declared himself *opposed* to cloning, as a technique incompatible with the dignity of the individual person. But now that the technological means are almost within reach, and after a quarter-century of defining deviancy down, the matter appears differently to him. More powerful than his fear of damaging the dignity of the individual person was his fear that the prohibition of cloning might serve to open a Pandora's box of reactionary sentiment, ultimately serving to cast a pall of doubt over all those who are experimenting with "unconventional ways of linking erotic attachment, romantic commitment, genetic replication, gestational mothering, and the joys and responsibilities of child rearing."

One can only hope that there is still a critical mass of Americans left who find this last statement both ludicrous and horrifying. Is there a better example of the deterioration of the untethered, unconstrained version of the liberal idea than this celebration of what is, in fact, nothing less than human disintegration? Tribe's firm, if abstract, commitment to the dignity of the human person has given way, in the course of the past quarter-century, to a *carte blanche* commitment to the sovereign right of the individual person to do exactly as he or she pleases with his or her body — even if doing so violates and dishonors the divine spark it carries. Few cases put the matter more forcefully and inescapably. Few better illustrate the inability of strictly liberal understandings of the human person to resolve these issues satisfactorily. Few better predict the very bad places that its unconstrained logic will lead us.

Bioethical issues are especially revealing in these matters, because they take us straight to the heart of what is distinctive in the Judeo-Christian understanding of the human person, as a *created* being whose characteristics are an *endowment* (cf. the language of the Declaration of Independence) that comes from the Creator God. It is a divine gift, not a human-engineered product. The biblical faiths are incarnational and sacramental, by which I mean that they affirm the flesh, the body, the givenness of our physical being, because our bodies are uniquely carriers of the *imago Dei*, the image of God. Tribe's statement usefully concentrates the mind, and makes the case, by negative example, for the reality of a Judeo-Christian tradition, which stands in opposition to, and in judgment of, the prospect of a hypertrophied liberalism. That latter prospect offers us no answers and no hope — only a long, dark corridor, at the end of which crouches a specter called The Abolition of Man. In the presence of that spectral apparition, the difference between Christians and Jews, Protestants and Catholics, seems small indeed.

Such a statement suggests that the way that we must go about reappropriating and reasserting the Judeo-Christian tradition will be complicated. And it will. As I've already suggested, it will require moving in two opposite directions at once. I'm reminded of the bumper-sticker slogan, "Think globally, act locally." Something on the same order will be required, though the right slogan eludes me. Think ecumenically, act confessionally? At any rate, the point is to balance a recommitment to the real particularities of real existing and historically rooted faith communities, with a simultaneous, and genuinely unprecedented, recognition of the overriding importance of the ground they share. This formulation corresponds nicely, I think with Gilbert Meilaender's distinction, made elsewhere in this book, between locatedness and freedom, or situatedness and universality.

Such a tension is hard to manage. Indeed, its management would likely be impossible without the resources that the liberal tradition has provided us. For it is *that* tradition that has given us the best way of thinking about how to live in a world containing a diversity of goods, no one of which can be allowed to trump all others. Yet another example of the cunning of history — that a tradition whose original reason for being was anti-theocratic should prove so essential to the preservation of healthy religious commitments. Just as healthy religious commitments are needed to preserve the health of liberalism.

This analysis also suggests that my initial distinction between two types of secularism might need to be modified. For even the secularism of non-establishment, which treats belief and unbelief with equivalent public respect, must contain the right kind of formative presuppositions if it is to be sustainable. And those presuppositions would seem to be broadly Judeo-Christian. Is this so? And is it true in a way that means we all have to be Jews or Christians of some sort? The very fact that such a question springs instantly to mind shows how much of our thinking about such matters is controlled by the imperatives of radical individualism. But even so, it is a vital and legitimate question. And one possible approach to an answer is to point to the revived interest in the concept of natural law (and what Reformed Protestants sometimes call "common grace") as a medium within which believers and nonbelievers can deliberate about, and reach normative conclusions about, matters of common concern. Whether one regards the language of natural law as some kind of moral firmament or as merely a useful lingua franca, this renewed interest represents a very promising development. Even a non-theistic form of natural law represents a reassertion of the absolute and universal, precisely the sort of reassertion of immutable limitations on human prerogatives that is profoundly threatening to the way we now do business.

And yet I wonder whether natural law will be enough. It seems no coincidence to me that the language of the Declaration of Independence is grounded not only in the God of natural religion but in the biblical God, the God of revelation who *creates* and *endows* and *judges*, and in whose eyes alone the visible injustices and inequities of nature are resolved into ultimate equality. Even Thomas Jefferson, who was known neither for his piety nor his orthodoxy, averred that he trembled at the thought that God is just — a statement suggesting that, at least at that particular moment, he did not have an Aristotelean Prime Mover in mind.

It was President Eisenhower who once allegedly said that "Our government makes no sense unless it is founded in a deeply felt religious faith — and I don't care what it is." The statement has been roundly ridiculed ever since, beginning with Will Herberg's book *Protestant Catholic Jew*, as a laughable example of Ike's garbled syntax and fuzzy thinking. But the fact of the matter is, he *did* care what it was, and would likely have said so, had such alternatives as goddess worship, Scientology, wicca, and transcendental meditation — not to mention the multiple apostasies from his own tradition — been widely available in his day. When the Judeo-Christian tradition was in effect the only tradition on offer, there were certain things that did not need to be said.

Now perhaps they do, and they need to be said for liberalism's sake, as much as for anything else. In years past, liberalism needed to establish a certain distance from our religious traditions. Now that distance appears to have become too great. At the same time, however, the Judeo-Christian tradition itself needs to be rescued from those who would incorporate it into liberalism, and thereby reduce it either to the continuation of politics by other means, or to smarmy platitudes, cost-free forgiveness, and acres of cheap grace. Like partners in a happy marriage, the Judeo-Christian tradition and the liberal tradition will have nothing to offer one another

135

unless they maintain their differences, as well as recognizing their similarities. To reduce one to the other is to betray them both.

# 9. *Rationality v. Morality?*

## CATHERINE HELDT ZUCKERT

There is a long-standing tradition or suspicion in the West, originating in ancient Greece, that rationality — both scientific and philosophical — has an invidious effect on morality. In this paper I propose to address that suspicion. I will begin by reminding you of the character and content of one of the first, if not THE first attack on rationalism in the name of traditional morality — the satirical critique the comic poet Aristophanes makes of the philosopher Socrates in *The Clouds*.[1] Then I will try to show you just how easily such a critique can be applied to contemporary intellectual discourse. And, finally, I will draw out what I see to be the consequences or implications of the contemporary application of the Aristophanic critique. If, as Leo Strauss argues, in the *Clouds* Aristophanes warned the philosopher Socrates about the probable popular reaction to his philosophical teachings, and Plato shows that subsequently Socrates not only absorbed the lesson but also changed his mode of teaching accordingly, it seems that contemporary philosophers have somehow forgotten that old lesson.[2] Rather than minimize the opposition or tension between philosophical inquiry and law or religion, contemporary philosophers shout their critiques from the rooftops — or via the internet by means of amazon.com. I shall argue, however, that Plato did not entirely solve the problem. In Plato's dialogues the morality of the family or city

---

[1] Aristophanes *Clouds*, in *Four Texts on Socrates*, trans. Thomas G. West and Grace Starry West (Ithaca: Cornell University Press, 1984).

[2] Leo Strauss, *Socrates and Aristophanes* (New York: Basic Books, 1966), pp. 3–53, 311–314; *The Rebirth of Classical Political Rationalism* (Chicago: University of Chicago Press, 1989), pp. 103–83.

remains in conflict with the morality of reason or philosophy. Later philosophers of the Enlightenment were more optimistic about the possibilities of grounding morality on reason alone, but their efforts have been subjected to enormous criticism from even later philosophers who, emphasizing the limits of reason, fail to provide their readers with much positive practical guidance. In the late twentieth century we seem, therefore, to be facing essentially the same problem that divided Aristophanes and Socrates inasmuch as reason seems to be primarily critical or debunking whereas religious morality appears to be based on irrational belief and particularistic attachments.

Let me turn then, first, to the *Clouds*. The play opens with a scene in which we see a middle-aged Athenian man named Strepsiades unable to sleep; he is worrying, because he does not know how he will pay his debts. He looks at the cause of his worries, his son, peacefully sleeping next to him. Having made money on his farm, the rustic Strepsiades had moved to the city and married a woman of breeding and "airs" which she had passed on to their son. Like Alcibiades, their son Pheidippides had taken up horseracing. When he stirs, audibly murmuring in dreaming about the horseracing that is the source of his father's financial difficulties, Strepsiades awakens him and asks: "Will you do your old man a favor?" Obviously as fond of his father as the indulgent father is of his son, Pheidippides says, "Sure." But, when Strepsiades suggests that his son should attend classes at the school where they teach people to make the weaker argument the stronger and so to escape their creditors in court, Pheidippides rebels. He will not become one of those pasty-faced intellectuals! He is as proud of his tan as he is of his physical prowess. Although he is fond of his father, there are limits to his affection. He will not shame himself before his peers on his papa's behalf. (We should note before we proceed to scene two that Aristophanes shows that both father and son are morally corrupt before either encounters Socrates. Neither voices any compunctions about defrauding their creditors. Nor does either seem to take the gods by whom they swear very seriously. Both father and son appear to be concerned primarily, if not entirely with their own safety, comfort, and status.) Unable to persuade his son to study the unjust speech, Strepsiades decides to go to Socrates' "think-tank" and enroll himself as a student. When he knocks at the door, the old man is accosted by a student who describes the bizarre investigations of the things in the heavens and under the earth in which he and his fellows engage under the direction of Socrates without asking any questions about the new arrival, his interests, abilities or concerns. And when Strepsiades goes inside he sees that the inmates look as unhealthy — pale and thin — as Pheidippides feared he would become. They care so little for the necessities, much less comforts of their physical existence, it seems, that Socrates worries about providing food only when someone feels the pangs of hunger. Not having used forethought to provide, he has to employ the tools of his geometrical science to pilfer a cloak to trade for victuals. These students of philosophy do not appear to be constrained by the precepts of ordinary morality — or law — any more than the vulgar old father.

Strepsiades thus feels enough at home not to flee when he is introduced to his would-be teacher, sitting in a basket suspended above the earth from which Socrates arrogantly looks down on other "ephemerals." If one wants to understand the higher things, the philosopher suggests, one must literally associate with them. He thus seeks to live in their element — in the air, rather than on earth. As presented in Aristophanes' *Clouds*, Socrates is something of a natural scientist. He does not therefore believe in or worship the traditional Greek gods. Possessing the rhetorical art of defeating any interlocutor in argument by revealing the contradictions in his position, the philosopher does not fear prosecution for the capital crime of impiety. Without inquiring much into Strepsiades' motives or investigating his ability to undertake the desired studies in physics and rhetoric, Socrates thus proceeds to introduce the old man to the worship of new gods — the Clouds, who mimic the powers of imaginative speech inasmuch as they are able to take a variety of shapes, reflecting not only the appearance but also the characters of people they see. He announces, moreover, that the old god of justice, Zeus, does not exist. Thunder and lightning are explicable as purely natural or physical phenomena.

Strepsiades readily adopts Socrates' atheistic teaching as one of the apparently necessary steps or means of achieving his own unjust end — the defrauding of his creditors. A tough old farmer, Strepsiades proves himself able to endure the physical deprivations Socrates imposes on his would-be students. Strepsiades does not, however, have the mental agility or memory to master the basic elements of speech, pre-requisite to learning the rhetorical arts he so wishes to possess. Having tried to instruct the old man,

Socrates gives up in disgust and dismisses him. The Clouds suggest that Strepsiades send his son. He does.

Insisting that his father will regret it, Pheidippides reluctantly returns with Strepsiades to Socrates' school. Rather than deliver his teachings himself, this time Socrates sponsors an exhibition — a debate between the just speech, which argues on behalf of traditional Greek morality — modesty, physical training, courage and moderation — and the unjust speech, which shows that such traditional teachings are contradictory. All human behavior (and that of the traditional gods as well) can be shown, ultimately, to be forms of pleasure-seeking.

Strepsiades happily enrolls his son and goes home to confront his creditors — now certain that he will be able to defeat them in court with the art his son is acquiring from Socrates indoors. We do not hear what Socrates tells Pheidippides, but we learn the effects from Strepsiades' account of his confrontation with his son at the dinner party he holds to celebrate Pheidippides' graduation, as it were. When Strepsiades asks his son to display some of his learning by reciting a bit of poetry, from Aeschylus, for example, Pheidippides refuses. Why should he work to entertain them while they eat? Why should he sacrifice or subordinate his pleasure for theirs? After they have eaten, Pheidippides agrees to recite some poetry by Euripides rather than by Aeschylus; he chooses a selection describing incest that outrages his father, who threatens to beat him. Taking the stick from his father, Pheidippides further exhibits what he has learned from Socrates by proposing to show that he has a right to beat his parent. What gave you a right to discipline me as a child, he asks Strepsiades. Wasn't it your superior wisdom? If you and I both agree that I am now wiser than you, don't I have the same right to discipline you? If you do, Strepsiades objects, you can look forward to suffering the same discipline from your son. But, Pheidippides objects, I don't have to have a son. Strepsiades is persuaded. Unlike other animals, human beings are not regulated by natural instinct; we can choose to have sex and/or to have it in a form that leads to procreation. Because we are not regulated by natural instinct, we have to construct our own rules. Family organization among human beings is, in other words, neither necessary nor simply natural. It depends in crucial respects upon convention or law.

Strepsiades is willing to serve his beloved son; in one way or another he has been doing so for a long time. But, when Pheidippides proposes to demonstrate both his justice and his affection for his father by proving that he has an equal right to beat his mother, the pretentious upper-class woman who gave her son such fancy tastes, Strepsiades rebels. He will not countenance the revolution in status of the older and younger generations when a different sex is involved. It was Pheidippides' decision to sing about incest rather than the military valor of old heroes that initially aroused Strepsiades' ire. Now he sees the possibility that Pheidippides will prove that incest is natural; it regularly occurs among animals. But if incest is allowed, the ties of affection between father and son are endangered. Not only do father and son become potential rivals; no father can be sure that his supposed heir is actually his son. At this point, the father rebels against the new teaching about nature. He first turns his ire against his new gods, the Clouds. They defend themselves by reminding him that they have simply allowed him to proceed in such a way as to discover his own mistake. They support his tendency to return to the old ways, however, to learn the importance of belief in the gods. Unable to punish Socrates legally, because the philosopher is still supposed to be able to win any argument, inside and well as out of the courtroom, the father turns to force. Calling upon Hermes for assistance, he proceeds to burn Socrates' school down with its scholarly inhabitants inside.

When I taught the *Clouds* this fall, a student observed: Strepsiades sounds as if he is a member of the "religious right." He appears, above all, to be concerned about what have become popularly called "family values." And in the face of challenges he cannot rationally answer concerning the foundations or necessities of these "values," he discovers a need he had not previously felt to appeal to religion. Like some of the protestors at abortion clinics, he also shows himself ready to use force when his arguments or position, which can be shown to be self-contradictory, fail. (With regard to those who would kill physicians who perform abortions, one might ask whether one acts in a logically consistent fashion when one takes life in the name of the sanctity of life.)

At any rate, I promised to update Aristophanes' comedy to show how the critique he levels at Socrates can be applied today. I have tried to use some local color in my re-telling of the plot of the *Media moguls*. Since I have never lived in Pennsylvania, I fear that I may have erred in some of the details.

141

Our story begins with the worries of a father named Sam. He had once been an Indiana farmer, but had sold his land for a good profit when the Russians were still buying American grain and prices were high. He then moved to the East Coast where he fell in love with the daughter of an impoverished old family from main-line Philadelphia. At the urging of his wife, they moved to the suburbs, around Swarthmore. They named their one son William — it was a compromise between the Fitzwilliam she hoped for and the plain "Bill" her husband preferred. ("Bill" was good enough for the President, wasn't it?) Although his mother was an Episcopalian and his father a lapsed Presbyterian, Will attended Friends' schools and then enrolled at Haverford. (Swarthmore was too academic and political; aspiring to be a gentleman rather than a scholar, Will chose to attend the more relaxed, more socially acceptable nearby college.) His real love was horses — breeding and racing — so he wanted to remain close to the farms in Maryland. The credit card companies accommodated his passion to an extraordinary degree. They kept sending him different applications for student accounts. Once he reached the limit in one, he could simply apply for another. It was the accumulated debts on these multiple accounts that was keeping his father awake at night. Sam's capital had been eaten away by the expenses of living in the eastern corridor; he didn't know how he could continue to pay tuition for his son's college education and keep up with his recreational debts.

Sam thought about hiring a "shyster" lawyer, but he couldn't find one foolish enough to take what appeared to be an open & shut, losing case on a contingency basis, and Sam didn't have funds to pay fees. Declaring bankruptcy was an option, but his wife objected to the possible social opprobrium. Since William was about to graduate with good grades and high test scores, because he was bright, Sam thought — we can send him to law school. He can borrow more to pay the tuition; he'll learn how to get us out of debt. William was not interested in law school, however, not even in enrolling at Penn. He'd had enough of the academic life; he wanted the healthy life of the outdoors. Sam saw no alternative, therefore, but to try to enroll in night school himself. He hadn't taken the LSAT's and didn't think he would do very well if he tried. The Kaplan prep courses were expensive. Sam decided, therefore, to begin his studies with an adult education course at a local college. He took the train down to the city and enrolled at Temple for a course on the "philosophy of law." At the first session, the instructor announced that they would not be reading dry, antiquated studies of the "natural law" or jurisprudence. They would jump immediately into modern theories of interpretation. They would thus begin by reading Nietzsche, who announced very clearly, "God is dead. We have killed him." It is up to us now, the old man heard from the young instructor, to create our own standards and goals.

Pursuing his study of legal rhetoric, Sam purchased and perused the works of Stanley Fish and Jacques Derrida. From Fish he learned that the law is simply and purely conventional. It is what people — especially judges — are persuaded that it should be. Those who can persuade, the rhetoricians, have ultimate power, even though that power depends mediately upon the "certification" of specified kinds of people having a distinctive kind of education that entitles them to become members of the community of experts — the experts who are authorized by society more generally to make rules in the relevant area.[3] Sam thought he got the "gist" of Fish, but Derrida lost him. Sam simply didn't know what to make of all that talk about the "hymen," "margins," "differance" (spelled incorrectly or so he thought) and the "force" of law revealed in the process of decision.[4] Having failed the final exam, Sam thus went back to William and pleaded with him to save what was left of the family fortune. If William didn't go to law school and take on the case, he would not be able to fund his passion for the races.

Reluctantly, William agreed. Having been given a liberal education at a prestigious institution and graced with a good deal of natural intelligence, William had a good academic record and scored well on the LSATs. He was admitted to Georgetown Law School where he was initiated into something called "critical legal studies" by Mark Tushnet.[5] The central contention of this somewhat loosely defined school of

---

[3] Stanley Eugene Fish, *Doing What Comes Naturally: Change, Rhetoric and the Practice of Theory in Literary and Legal Studies* (Durham, N.C.: Duke University Press, 1989), *There's No Such Thing as Free Speech and It's a Good Thing, Too* (New York: Oxford, 1994).

[4] Jacques Derrida, *Margins of Philosophy*, trans. Alan Bass (Chicago: University of Chicago Press, 1982), pp. 1–28; *Dissemination*, trans. Barbara Johnson (Chicago: University of Chicago Press, 1981), 175–286, "Force of Law: 'The Mystical Foundation of Authority,'" in *Deconstruction and the possibility of Justice*, ed. Drucilla Cornell, Michel Rosenfeld, David Gray Carlson (New York: Routledge, 1992), pp. 3–67.

[5] Mark Tushnet, *Red, White, and Blue: Critical Analysis of Constitutional Law* (Cambridge, Mass.: Harvard University Press, 1988).

contemporary legal scholarship was that all previous judicial decisions and laws could be shown to be riddled with contradictions. By bringing out these contradictions, a lawyer would discredit the precedents and so create room for a new, more liberal, if not more just form of law. If all previous laws and decisions could be shown to be exercises of power rather than the dictates of reason, the obligation to obey would surely be weakened, if not entirely erased.

William was a bit skeptical; he thought his father might come to regret his son's learning such fashionable gibberish. But at the continued urging of his parent, he enrolled. In law school he learned that all decisions are historically contingent; as circumstances change, so does case law. Family law is and has been particularly circumstantial. At one time, married women could not own property or even control the use of the wages they themselves earned. Children were equally dependent upon the will or whims of their father. Now, some adults co-habit rather than marry, because the income tax laws make it advantageous for wage-earners to file separately rather than jointly. Mothers, fathers, aunts, uncles, grandparents and "foster-families" fight for custody of children in courts, and the laws vary from jurisdiction to jurisdiction. There does not even seem to be a definition of "family" that can be agreed upon in court or in public discourse.

In law school William acquired the rhetorical or argumentative skills along with the substantive knowledge necessary to show effectively in court that his father should not be held liable for his son's debts. William was not so sure he wanted to take the burden or the bankruptcy on himself, however; he had learned something, after all, about the conventional or perhaps truly non-existent, certainly non-necessary character of family ties. Why should he be the fall guy? At the party his father threw to celebrate his graduation, William thus refused his father's request to play a Mozart sonata on the piano. Instead he went to the stereo and put on a Busta' Rhymes CD. Sam and his friends initially had trouble making out the words that accompanied the beat. But when Sam began to understand the lyrics about stuffing one's old man and mother f--king, he was outraged. He dragged William outside and threatened to hit him. "Not only am I younger and stronger," William cooly responded, "I am also smarter and able, therefore, to put you in your place. With what right did you discipline me when I was young? Didn't you claim to reprimand me for my own good on the basis of your superior knowledge? Now, I'm doing the same for you." Aware of his own inferior intellectual ability, Sam was about to admit his own need to be introduced into the new age. But when William tried to comfort his father by adding that he would straighten out his mother as well, Sam could not longer take it. When sons no longer merely rebel against their parents' authority but threaten to act out the rap songs about mother f--king, the family is destroyed. Every man will be Oedipus; no man will ever be sure the child that bears his name is his. Sigmund Freud was definitely right about *Civilization and Its Discontents*.

Taking his cue from his more educated and liberal suburban neighbors, Sam had dismissed the members of the Christian coalition and the Minutemen as looney extremists, maladjusted misfits who had irrational reactions to the modern world. Now, he thought, they are right. If God is dead, everything is allowed. Sam took off in his car for Virginia to buy a gun.

What, then, is the moral of the story — first in its ancient and then in its up-dated, modern form? In the *Clouds*, it seems, the comic poet Aristophanes warned Socrates: You may think that you are immune from legal prosecution — for theft or impiety or corrupting the young — because you can talk your way out of court. Legal prosecution is not the only or even the most immediate and fearful form of persecution, however. Men who are much less clever than you can resort to physical force — and they will, if and when they see you taking what they hold dearest from them. These men are not moral or law-abiding or religious; they are not moderate or controlled. Precisely for that reason, they will attack you — irrationally and violently — when they perceive the danger you and your teachings represent to that which they love or desire most. But they will do so in the name of morality, law and order, and pious belief in the gods.

As a result of Aristophanes' warning, perhaps, Plato shows that Socrates gave up the scientific investigations of things in the heavens and under the earth that he had pursued as a youth and turned to a study of the human things. He did not deny the existence of divinities or flaunt lesser laws. On the contrary, he insisted on the existence and need to learn about the eternal truth. When he criticized the traditional teachings of the poets, Plato showed that Socrates criticized them, as in the *Republic* (377c–382e), for depicting gods acting against the norms or requirements of family — engaging in incestuous affairs or fighting — son against father or brother against brother — for rule. Nevertheless, in his *Apology of Socrates* (19a–e, 23c–24a) Plato has the philosopher say that, even though he never did any of the silly things Aristophanes showed in his comedy, the anger of the fathers would nevertheless convict him. It is not the questions raised about the existence of the gods by his teachings about nature but the example he sets for the young by asking questions that has gotten him into trouble. The young men who listen to him interrogating others go home and ask their elders to justify their commands and practices. Unable to respond to the questions of their sons and daughters, parents become irate and repeat the age-old accusations of philosophy.

Let us turn now to our own time. Is it still the case that philosophy undermines morality and so provokes the anger of the elders by raising unanswerable questions? There are, of course, still youths who take great delight, at age eight or nine, at responding to every reason their parents give them for a rule by asking, why? And in response to the reason given, they cleverly reiterate, why? again and again, ad nauseam. Such behavior is truly exasperating, but it does not represent the problem I or Aristophanes or Plato have been addressing. The problem in the case of the bratty kid is that he or she refuses to listen or consider seriously any answer that is given. The more serious problem arises when the people asked to respond to the question realize that they don't have an answer; they begin to fear that there is no reason or justification for their most heartfelt commitments or desires.

Here, however, the situation appears to have changed markedly from that which Aristophanes and Plato described. Rather than bragging about the omnipotence and consequent invulnerability of scientific knowledge like Aristophanes' Socrates, twentieth century philosophers of virtually all schools have emphasized the limitations of our knowledge — both philosophical AND scientific. Rather than denying the grounds or legitimacy of faith in God, such an emphasis on the restricted powers of human reason would appear to open the door again to revelation. Most philosophers refuse to walk through that door, however. They are, it seems, too impressed with the power of modern natural science. Modern natural science cannot tell us why the things they test in laboratories happen, these philosophers admit, but modern technology enables us to achieve extraordinary, remarkable effects. Average life expectancy has increased dramatically. Our knowledge may be limited, but our power has increased.

Even though both contemporary philosophers and scientists admit that they cannot give an account, much less an adequate one of the origins or first principles or "foundation," few turn to revelation. There are exceptions, of course, like Emmanuel Levinas.

If a parent, distressed about the immoral effects of the atheistic instruction his child was receiving at the university, were to turn to religious authorities, moreover, he would find that the character of religion has also changed fundamentally since the time of Aristophanes in at least one relevant respect. Strepsiades could appeal to his pagan gods for sympathy in anger at the alienation of the affections of his own son, because these gods were tied to particular peoples or nations. They themselves were worshiped and received worship largely if not exclusively on the basis of an appeal to love of one's own. Scriptural religions — Jewish, Christian, or Muslim — do not acknowledge the legitimacy of such a claim. Although all three religions emphasize the importance, indeed sanctity of family, they do not honor the strength of the bonds some people feel to others merely because of a blood relation; in all three religions family ties are sanctified as expressions of love of God and his goodness. It is not love of one's own that is respected per se; love of one's own must be justified in terms of something higher and more general.

As the need for "justification" suggests, most representatives of the major world religions would not admit that their beliefs and practices rest on faith alone. On the contrary, they argue, if people would but look into their own hearts, or at the world in which they live and the lives of people in it, they would be driven, by reason, not only to posit the existence of a first cause or "Maker" but also to believe in his beneficence. That is, like the Pope in his recent encyclical on *Fides et Ratio*, they would suggest that reason and faith are not contradictory or incompatible; quite the reverse. Faith may provide the unquestionable premises and has ultimate authority. Nevertheless, there are too many false prophets and superstitious cults to let all claims to divine inspiration go unchallenged. People have to use their reason to sort such claims out.

Why, then, do we, like Strepsiades and Sam, persist in the sense that rationalism and religion — to say nothing of morality and "family values" — are opposed? The problem seems, ironically, to be more on the side of reason or philosophy than on the side of revelation. If we look back a moment at the character of Plato's presentation of Socrates in response to

147

the Aristophanic critique, we begin, I believe, to see why. Plato's response to Aristophanes may be said to be twofold. On the one hand, in the *Apology of Socrates* Plato has his teacher deny that he did or taught any of the ridiculous things the comic poet attributed to him. Rather than engaging in scientific investigations of the heavens and things under the earth, or teaching the art of speaking, Plato's Socrates serves as the famous "gadfly." He goes around challenging his fellow Athenians' acts and opinions, asking them to show that they seek truth and prudence rather than wealth and reputation. It was, indeed, this questioning that got him into trouble with the public authorities. So far from being a "clever speaker" able to talk his way out of any legal dispute, moreover, Plato's Socrates is condemned to death after his first and only appearance before a jury.

In his *Apology* Plato's Socrates thus appears to be pre-eminently a seeker of wisdom, not someone who possesses it, that is, a scientist. Insofar as his questions undermine the authority of traditional teachings without offering anything in their place, such questions could appear to be corrosive and corrupting as the effects of earlier scientific investigations of nature. In the *Republic* Plato thus shows, Socrates also offered a positive alternative — not merely an alternative teaching about how people should live, but an explicit defense of justice. Precisely because this positive teaching seems to be so different from the life of pure inquiry that Socrates appears to represent in his description of his activity before the jury, many scholars attribute the arguments Socrates gives in the *Republic* to Plato.[6] Whether these arguments be Socratic or Platonic, they nevertheless constitute a positive reason-based philosophical teaching defending an extremely stringent set of moral regulations. They certainly do not serve to justify pleasure-seeking, on the part of individual or community; on the contrary, in the *Republic* as well as in the *Philebus*, Plato's Socrates explicitly denies the identity of pleasure with the Good.

Nevertheless, it is also clear that neither Aristophanes nor his character Strepsiades would be happy with the legal regulations of community life proposed in Plato's *Republic*. There the philosopher appears seriously to recommend the abolition of private property and the

---

[6] E. g., Julia Annas, *An Introduction to Plato's Republic* (Oxford: Clarendon Press, 1981); Terrence Irwin, *Plato's Ethics* (New York: Oxford University Press, 1995); Richard Kraut, "An Introduction to the Study of Plato" in the *Cambridge Companion to Plato* (Cambridge: Cambridge University Press, 1992), pp. 1–50.

family that the comic poet had mocked in his presentation of female rule in his *Assembly of Women*. It is not just, Plato's Socrates argues, to prefer oneself or one's own to the common good. From Strepsiades' point of view, the just Socrates might be even worse than the earlier unjust sophist insofar as he does not merely alienate the affection of the young from their parents but also justifies such alienation in terms of moral or political virtue.

Plato's contention that justice requires complete identification of self or one's own with community did not go unchallenged for long, of course. His own student, Aristotle, criticized the argument of the *Republic* insofar as it suggested that the best city is the most unified city. On the contrary, Aristotle pointed out, human beings form associations or partnerships precisely because each alone is not sufficient. They do better working together than they do separately when each performs a different function or task. Plato himself emphasized the benefits of such a division of labor at the beginning of his discussion of the "true" city in the *Republic*. His famous proposals that citizens should hold all property, including all women and children in common, makes no one particularly attached to or responsible for anyone else. Self-love is natural, Aristotle urges; it is only excessive love of self that is bad.[7]

Rooted in a teleological view of nature, Aristotle's account of the different parts, not only of the city, but more fundamentally of the household or family, did not appear to be tenable after modern natural science raised serious questions about the viability and basis of an understanding of nature in terms of ends or purposes. But Aristotle was not, by any means, the last philosopher to defend the importance of the family as an institution. In his *Second Treatise of Government* (Sections 77–83) John Locke also argued that family organization is necessary for the survival of the species. Women with dependent children need support; and the man finds the arrangement convenient. Family organization is both natural and rational, Locke concludes, inasmuch as it serves the interests of all members — husband, wife, and child. Denying that such family groups are necessary for the preservation of the species, Jean Jacques Rousseau nevertheless argued that ordinary human beings develop the "sweetest sentiments of human existence" in such associations. Marriage and family promise to provide an ordinary man like Emile a kind of

---

[7] *Politics* 1260b–1264b.

happiness he will not find living by himself or striving to advance in politics or society.[8] Georg Wilhelm Friedrich Hegel went even further and grounded human ethical life as a whole in the commitment to cleave to one another that married couples make.[9] When freely entered upon, the marriage contract not merely facilitates the development of deeply affectionate or sentimental ties; it embodies the distinctive human ability to make and keep promises.

In sum, even this brief account of the history of political philosophy shows that there has been no dearth of rationalist defenses of the institution we call family. On the contrary, philosophers have argued for its importance, if not necessity on economic, erotic, educational, self-interested, affective and moral grounds. I am forced, therefore, to return once more to the initial question: why do we still suspect rationalism of undermining what are popularly called "family values?"

The answer to that question, I would finally suggest, is to be found in our view of rationalism or philosophy itself. As I suggested earlier, there are two sides or faces to Plato's classic depiction of philosophy in the character of Socrates. On the one hand, Socrates appears to question everyone and everything. He appears, in other words, to be a critic and skeptic. That was the trait or effect of his activity to which he thought his fellow Athenians most objected. Both his students Plato and Xenophon thus showed that Socrates also presented a stringent moral teaching. As I have indicated, however, that teaching was subsequently subjected to a great deal of criticism by later philosophers. Those philosophers all argued for the importance of human beings' acquiring self-control or moderation, courage, wisdom and justice. That is, they virtually all argued in favor of some kind of morality. To be sure, some of the modern philosophers also insisted on the fundamental status and importance of human freedom. One — Karl Marx — even argued, like Plato, that the realization of human freedom required the abolition of religion and the family, along with all other institutions embodying the division of labor required by economic

[8] *Discourse on the Origin and Foundations of Inequality among Men* in *The First and Second Discourses*, ed. Roger D. Masters (New York: St. Martin's Press, 1964), pp. 146–47; *Emile*, trans. Allan Bloom (New York: Basic Books, 1979).
[9] G. W. F. Hegel, *Philosophy of Right*, trans. T. M. Know (New York: Oxford University Press, 1975), section 158–169.

necessity. All these philosophers would remind you, however, that freedom or choice is a presupposition of morality. So is a perception of order or regularity in the world, especially in human relations. If we can have no knowledge of the effects of our actions, we can hardly be held responsible. If we can have no knowledge of the effects of our actions, we can hardly be said to choose in any meaningful sense. As the philosophers who exalt human freedom would remind you, liberty is NOT license. Reason and freedom are as intrinsically related as reason and morality.

THE reason we human beings have to fabricate laws or other kinds of moral and political restrictions on our own behavior is that we are not regulated instinctively by nature to the same extent or in the same way other animals are. As Aristophanes shows, clever young men can use the non-necessity of moral rules and legal regulations as reasons not to follow them. But these are not good reasons. Individual people have always and often sought to rationalize the means of fulfilling their own desires or avoiding painful obligations. Rationalizations of selfish desires can be shown, however, to be just that. Sophistical arguments, as they are often called following Plato, can be defeated only by better, critical arguments. The "just" speech in the *Clouds* is defeated by the unjust speech because the "just" speech relies entirely upon tradition, not upon nature or investigations of what is truly good. Pleasure-seeking has been shown to be an inadequate definition of human life by many, many authors.

Rationality is not an opponent of or even antagonistic to either morality or legal order. On the contrary, both morality and legal order presuppose rationality. We have come to believe that there is a tension, if not opposition, between rationality and morality, in the first instance, because we have too many reasons, too many contradictory philosophical doctrines or systems that tell us that different, somewhat incompatible goals are good. It is difficult to sort all the arguments out, and we see what early modern philosophers like Hobbes and Hume emphasized: human beings do not act simply or even primarily on the basis of reason. We do what we do largely on the basis of inherited opinions and feelings. Like Strepsiades and Sam, we react with our "guts."

That is precisely the reason we need rational guidance and legal regulation. But philosophy as now practiced does not appear to be a promising source. Confronted with a plethora of positive philosophical moral doctrines, people faced with a need to say what philosophy itself is find the common denominator or element in the criticism of other, especially previous opinions. At the end of the long history of Western philosophy when those who call themselves philosophers do not claim to possess knowledge or wisdom, properly speaking, philosophy appears primarily in the guise of "analysis" or "critique." As such it takes things apart or, to use some fashionable jargon, it deconstructs rather than building, defending, or justifying. It appears to many people today, as Socrates appeared to many of his Athenian contemporaries, to be merely debunking or destructive. That surely is the aspect of modern philosophy that contemporary legal theorists like Tushnet, Fish, and Derrida have sought to exploit. They have not sought to expose the conventional or contradictory bases of law merely for the sake of private profit or pleasure, however; Tushnet and Derrida at least are trying rather explicitly to expose and so to eradicate sources of injustice. Because the grounds of the current order — both natural and political — are not clear, distinct, or certain, these legal theorists attempt to protect human freedom and foster a more egalitarian, if not a more inclusive society by showing that all order or orders are tenuously based. If their exposes have more deleterious than beneficial results, the proper response — the only truly effective response, I submit — is to show that this is the case. We can admit that moral rules and legal regulations have limitations and exceptions, but still insist, nevertheless, that it is better not merely to have regulations but also to have more reasonable laws than it is to have few, none or completely arbitrary, irrational dictates. As Plato's Eleatic Stranger pointed out early in the history of political philosophy and American pragmatists like William James have argued since, there is a kind of knowledge, be it imperfect and not always entirely articulated, implicit in human practices adopted on the basis of trial and error over time.[10] What we need to do is to make that practical wisdom explicit, to acknowledge its limitations and to seek incremental improvement. And to seek improvement, we have to articulate our standards of good as well as the reasons for them. The reactions of

---

[10] Plato *Statesman* 300 b–c; William James, *Pragmatism* (Cambridge, Mass.: Harvard University Press, 1975). In other words, "pragmatic" thought does not have to be subject to the postmodern interpretation or "twist" that Richard Rorty gives it in *Consequences of Pragmatism* (Minneapolis: University of Minnesota Press, 1982). The pragmatism of William James and Charles Peirce is not simply a matter of "tradition" or an individual "narrative."

Strepsiades and Sam against teachers who raise questions about the basis of traditional mores and morals are both unjust and irrational. Philosophers or intellectuals like those writing for this collection of essays should perhaps beware of arousing such passions; but taking precautions against dangerous behavior does not require us to concede its legitimacy. The only way to find answers to questions is to seek them — with reason. In the late twentieth century we may have over-emphasized the skeptical thrust of the search for wisdom. It is time, I believe, for us to begin emphasizing the positive, the constructive moral and political function of human rationality.

# 10. *Liberalism, Postmodernism, and Public Philosophy*

## PETER BERKOWITZ

Critics charge that the liberal spirit is hegemonic.[1] Supporters sense that liberalism is imperilled. To understand why it is worth defending, it is important to see that liberalism is both. Few politicians today dare to run for high office under liberalism's banner. In public discourse "liberal" has become a term of abuse that Republicans hurl and Democrats dodge. Despite their conflicting motives, the hurlers and dodgers form an unholy alliance. This unholy alliance conspires to confuse the liberal spirit with, and hold it hostage to, the governing ambitions, policy positions, and political fortunes of the left wing of the Democratic Party. One result is that fewer and fewer know, or are likely to experience the incentive to discover, that liberalism also names a proud tradition of moral and political thought. This tradition arose in the seventeenth century, it has borne many blossoms in many countries, and notwithstanding all its varieties it has consistently championed goods that are as fundamental to the political hopes of majorities on the right today as they are to those on the left: individual liberty, human equality, religious toleration, and systematic intellectual inquiry based on the free exercise of human reason.

Despite contemporary liberalism's tarnished reputation, the principles for which the liberal tradition has always stood continue to exercise a powerful influence over American hearts and minds: no candidate can hope to succeed on the national stage who denies the fundamental importance of

[1] This section is based on "Liberalism Strikes Back," in *The New Republic*, December 15, 1997, pp. 32–37.

individual freedom or questions the ideal of equality before the law. Moreover, while disputes rage about the scope of freedom and what government may or must do to secure equality for all, even the thorniest controversies between left and right in contemporary American political life take place in large measure within a liberal framework.

The primacy of liberal principles can be seen in the battle over abortion and in the struggle over affirmative action. Proponents of a woman's right to choose "to terminate her pregnancy" appeal to the familiar liberal principle of personal autonomy: the individual woman alone, it is argued, should have the final say when it comes to decisions about her own body and life. But to a considerable extent opponents of abortion also build their case on the liberal ground of respect for the individual; but they place a different individual in the forefront of their considerations. Many who oppose abortion do so not on the basis of government's obligation to legislate morals or promote the good life but rather couch their opposition in terms of respect for the right to life of the fetus or unborn child.

Similarly, in the struggle over affirmative action, the contending camps often disagree over the interpretation and application of a principle they hold in common. Proponents of affirmative action argue that in a society haunted by the legacy of slavery, racism, and sexism, taking race and sex into account in hiring and promoting is necessary to achieve equality. In reply, critics also invoke the principle of equality, contending that haunting legacy or no, legally mandated preferences based on race or sex violate government's obligation to provide each citizen the equal protection of the law. One could repeat this exercise with similar result in connection to the debates over the right to suicide, welfare reform, tax policy and other fiercely contested issues on the contemporary agenda. In each case one would find liberal principles decisively shaping both sides of the dispute. Indeed, wherever liberalism has taken root, its fundamental premise of natural freedom and equality has informed not only debates over public policy but the design of political institutions, the development of law, and the beliefs and practices that guide individuals in their private lives.

Although they are inseparably connected in liberal thought, freedom and equality must remain in tension with each other. The protection of individual freedom — even or especially on a level playing field — leads to inequality as individuals, through the exercise of their different

155

capacities and powers, achieve unequal results. And because it requires the imposition of constraints on what individuals may do with their property and themselves, the quest for equality results in a diminution of the freedom to do exactly as one pleases. These familiar tensions notwithstanding, freedom and equality are part and parcel of the same fundamental thought in the liberal tradition. All individuals equally are thought to be by nature free. And each is free because all equally lack the right to rule over any other.

None of this means that liberalism has ever devised conclusive arguments on behalf of its fundamental premise. Indeed, the perceived failure of the tradition to do so has led many contemporary liberal theorists to eschew discussion of first principles, as if one could make troubling theoretical and metaphysical questions vanish simply by refusing to speak about them. In recent years some leading liberals have become so aggressive in their evasions that they have confused the tactic of avoiding, for political purposes, complex and contentious arguments in support of their first principles with the extreme insistence that liberalism altogether lacks theoretical foundations.

It is a mistake, however, to define or defend the spirit of liberalism while ignoring its fundamental premise. Belief in the natural freedom and equality of all human beings is not by a long shot all there is to liberalism, but the premise is fundamental because it orients and organizes liberal thinking. It also links the diverse strands that make up the liberal tradition. And it provides a principle for distinguishing liberalism from other traditions of moral and political thought.

Reference to liberalism's fundamental premise, for example, helps bring out what liberalism shares with democracy, which is devotion to freedom and equality, and what it adds to democracy, which are limitations, in the name of the rights of individuals, on the freedom of majorities. Reference to liberalism's fundamental premise also explains why Hobbes, who, in *Leviathan*, establishes the natural freedom and equality of all as one of the bases of the true science of politics[2], should be seen as a member of the tradition. And why Nietzsche, who, in *Beyond Good and Evil*, honored freedom as a prerogative of the few and diagnosed the doctrine of

---

[2] *Leviathan*, Chapter 13–14.

human equality as a poisonous conceit,[3] should not. It helps set liberalism apart from classical political philosophy, which did not affirm that all human beings were by nature free and equal, and the Bible's affirmation that human beings are indeed fundamentally equal but not by nature or reason but because God made us that way.

Another mistake is to reduce liberalism to its fundamental premise, as if the liberal tradition embodied a monolithic world view and one could, from this premise, draw all pertinent conclusions about its governing style, vitality, and worth. As Judith Shklar pointed out, the liberal tradition is also defined by and should be defended in terms of its "overriding aim," which, in her words, is to "secure the political conditions that are necessary for the exercise of personal freedom."[4] Liberalism's fundamental premise does not dictate one right path to the attainment of its overriding aim. Indeed, in the effort to devise political institutions and promulgate laws that equally respect the individual freedom of all, the liberal tradition has produced a rich diversity of emphases, approaches, and arrangements.

Seen in the light of both its fundamental premise and its overriding aim, liberalism is a tradition that extends over centuries, cuts across national boundaries, and finds eloquent advocates in parties of the left and the right. It is wide enough to include not only such standard-bearers as Locke, Kant, and Mill, but also thinkers more eclectic and difficult to categorize such as Montesquieu, Madison, and Tocqueville. It is a tradition that has articulated a set of characteristic themes including individual rights, consent, toleration, liberty of thought and discussion, self-interest rightly understood, the separation of the private from the public, and personal autonomy or the primacy of individual choice; has elaborated a characteristic set of political institutions including representative democracy, separation of governmental powers, and an independent judiciary; and, less noticed these days but vital to understanding liberalism's possibilities and prospects, has provided a fertile source of reflections on such non-political supports of the virtues that sustain liberty as commerce, voluntary association, family, and religion.

Listening to liberalism's leading critics in the academy, though, one might never guess that liberalism is a complex and many-sided tradition.

---

[3] *Beyond Good and Evil*, sections 29–33, 212, 219, 259.
[4] "The Liberalism of Fear," in *Political Thought and Political Thinkers*, ed. Stanley Hoffmann (Chicago: University of Chicago Press, 1998), p. 3.

Communitarian critics reproach liberalism because, they claim, it disassociates citizens, drains the morality out of public life, and degrades politics to the play of selfish interests. Feminist critics rebuke liberalism for tolerating beliefs and practices that have denied women opportunities and perpetuated their status as second-class citizens. And postmodern critics condemn liberalism's core institutions and key concepts for working to conceal the contingency of established arrangements and thereby deprive individuals of the full range of choices that should be available to them.

There is truth in these charges. However, all this reproaching, rebuking, and condemning seems to have left its leading critics little energy for appreciating liberalism's solid achievements. These achievements, such as protecting personal rights and securing the equal protection of the laws, are ones that liberalism's leading critics take for granted and would not, at least for themselves, dream of abandoning. Nor have the critics set aside much time to consider to what extent these solid achievements would be imperilled by the pursuit, without the backdrop of liberal limits and guarantees, of communitarian, feminist, or postmodern goals.

Truth be told, academic liberalism must shoulder a fair portion of the blame for allowing the complexity and many-sidedness of the liberal tradition to fade from view. And the professors must take some responsibility for disarming liberalism in the face of aggressive assaults on its good name. Although recent years have seen the emergence of a new generation of scholars devoted to recovering neglected dimensions of the classic liberal tradition, on the whole academic liberalism has concentrated its energies on the articulation of a narrowly procedural liberalism. The liberalism that dominates in the academy is one that is primarily concerned with articulating technical principles and applying them to contemporary moral dilemmas but which takes little account of the unruliness of human passion, the practical force of higher aspirations, the non-political requirements of politics in a liberal state, and the impact of the laws on the character of those who live under them.

It would be wrong to trace the narrowness of contemporary liberal theory to the fact that liberals have sought to sustain themselves at the universities through a steady diet of Locke, Kant, and Mill and, at best, have served themselves rather stingy portions of Montesquieu, Madison, and Tocqueville. More telling is the stingy portions of Locke, Kant, and Mill with which academic liberals have contented themselves. In the universities, liberals continue to do their own tradition an injustice by uncritically conforming to the custom of studying only the Locke who teaches about the principles of legitimate government in the *Second Treatise* but not the Locke who, in *Some Thoughts Concerning Education*, examines the virtues that support liberty; of attending almost entirely to the Kant who expounds the principle of autonomy in the *Groundwork* while neglecting the Kant who articulates the virtues of moral character in the *Metaphysics of Morals*; of focusing exclusively on the Mill who, in the first three Chapters of *On Liberty*, celebrates individual choice and the need for new experiments in living, while leaving out of focus the Mill in Chapters 4 and 5 of *On Liberty* who recognizes society's interest in cultivating the "social virtues," and stresses the role of the state, the family, and voluntary associations in fostering the virtues of freedom. How can one blame liberalism's critics for attacking a desiccated vision of liberalism when contemporary liberals themselves have done so much to read out of the record the complexity and many-sidedness of their own legacy?

Greater self-knowledge is today one of the keys to repairing the liberal spirit and restoring its luster. In coming to know itself more fully, liberalism also will attain a better grasp of both the progeny it has produced and the criticisms it has provoked. And it may well come to see that its leading critics are in fact none other than its own fickle and rebellious children.

The lineage of liberalism's leading critics can be brought into focus by considering the goods which they criticize liberalism for damaging. On examination, the search for a usable communitarian political theory can, in many cases, be seen to be motivated at bottom by the conviction that respect for the dignity of the individual requires more attention than contemporary liberalism has been inclined to pay to associational life, moral virtue, and active participation in democratic self-government. To a considerable extent, feminist criticism seeks to illuminate the ways in which liberalism has not only failed to deliver equality for women but maintained barriers to its delivery. And postmodernism, in its more sober moments, has won genuine insights into the subterranean exercises of power by which the norms and terms of debate in liberal society silently restrict individuals' freedom of thought and choice. Yet what are individual dignity, equality, and freedom but central planks of the liberal platform?

159

What I want to suggest is that communitarianism, feminism, and postmodernism, even when they explicitly define themselves in opposition to liberalism, continue to derive much of their appeal from the manner in which they develop or extend liberalism's fundamental premise, the natural freedom and equality of all, and are driven by liberalism's governing moral impulse, defense of the dignity of the individual. At the same time, outstanding defects in the approaches to politics of liberalism's leading critics can be traced to their disregard of crucial lessons taught by the liberal tradition — and in many cases forgotten or poorly articulated by contemporary liberals — about the beliefs, practices, and institutions that protect — and limit — individual freedom and secure — and define the meaning of — equality before the law. In short, many of liberalism's progeny have denounced or denied their parents and scorned their patrimony, but then continued to live off — and run down — the family legacy.

This is an old story and a serious problem, though by no means unique to liberalism. According to Socrates' account in Book VIII of Plato's *Republic*, all regimes contain the seeds of their own destruction. Typically, the cause of destruction is the one-sided or defective education fathers provide their sons. Oligarchic fathers — narrow, disciplined, and devoted to the making and preserving of wealth — raise spoiled sons whose love of luxury and hatred of authority brings about change from oligarchy, the regime in which the wealthy few rule, into democracy, the regime in which all citizens rule and each is free to do just as he pleases. By teaching their sons to listen only to their own most immediate desires, democratic fathers prepare them for nothing so much as quiet submission to a ruthless tyrant. And something similar, I wish to suggest, has occurred in connection to the liberal spirit. By so successfully teaching respect for the dignity of the individual, equality before the law, and freedom from external, arbitrary authority, liberalism has raised a generation of critics who specialize in identifying the ways in which liberalism itself denies the dignity of the individual, sanctions inequalities, and deprives individuals of choice. Those inclined to dismiss out of hand the dialectic by which parents instill in their children qualities that threaten their way of life should consider that the angry and rebellious children of the 1960s were raised and educated by the middle class, solidly bourgeois parents of the 1950s.

Several reasons justify the effort to give liberalism its due. First, liberalism clarifies the contemporary intellectual scene by providing a framework which reveals that what appear to be rival and incompatible schools of thought in fact share a formal structure and governing moral intention. Second, giving liberalism its due means a substantial gain in self-knowledge, both for those who think of themselves as liberals and for those who do not recognize the liberalism of their ways. Third, the liberal tradition has untapped resources for understanding more precisely how to defend, and sustain a political life that rests upon, the premise of natural freedom and equality, a premise whose power not many would wish to deny and whose authority few can honestly resist.

## II

Postmodern theory provides much evidence in support of the thesis that liberalism provides the moral sources for the critical schools that now wish to overthrow it.

Some postmodern theorists deny that postmodernism has a stable core, asserting that the term is in large measure the invention of hostile critics who seek to dismiss a great variety of critical positions by collapsing them into a single opinion or perspective.[5] So argues University of California at Berkeley Professor of Rhetoric and Comparative Literature, Judith Butler, in the opening paragraphs of her influential article, "Contingent Foundations: Feminism and the Question of Postmodernism."[6] And yet she goes on to affirm the following as axiomatic: "power pervades the very conceptual apparatus that seeks to negotiate its terms, including the subject position of the critic";[7] "there is no ontologically intact reflexivity to the subject which is then placed within a cultural context";[8] "*agency is always and only a political prerogative*" [italics in original].[9] Of course the translation of such abstract, technical language into more ordinary terms is always a tricky business, but it certainly sounds as if Butler is affirming a

[5] This section also draws on "Liberalism Strikes Back," in *The New Republic*, December 15, 1997, pp. 32–37.
[6] "Contingent Foundations: Feminism and the Question of Postmodernism," in *Feminist Contentions* (New York: Routledge, 1995).
[7] Ibid., p. 39.
[8] Ibid., p. 46.
[9] Ibid., pp. 46–47.

core set of beliefs commonly associated (and not only by hostile critics) with the postmodern viewpoint: that there is no human nature, that truth is socially constructed, and that reason is the tool of will and an expression of power.

But there is more to postmodernism than this radical theoretical stance. There is also a governing moral intention, and Butler again is instructive. Her position, she is at pains to insist, "is *not* the advent of a nihilistic relativism incapable of furnishing norms, but, rather, the very precondition of a politically engaged critique."[10] A politically engaged critique "subversively" deploys the tools of "deconstruction" on familiar terms and categories in order "to displace them from the contexts in which they have been deployed as instruments of oppressive power."[11] And it seeks to expose "insidious cultural imperialism" and the "ethnocentric bias" of allegedly universal moral principles.[12] Postmodernism, in short, is and understands itself to be a movement of liberation. What postmodern theorists often fail to appreciate, however, is that as a movement of liberation it is not the antithesis to, but rather a descendant of, liberalism.

Postmodernism in effect demands the radicalization of the "grand, leading principle, toward which every argument" of *On Liberty* (according to the epigram that Mill placed at its head) was directed, namely, "the absolute and essential importance of human development in its richest diversity." Put aside for the moment the important question of whether postmodernism's radical critique of reason sustains or subverts its moral agenda. Although I am aware that not all would embrace such a description, I believe it fairly captures the spirit of postmodernism to say that it seeks to advance the work of human freedom by liberating the individual from hidden fetters of language and thought, especially the terms and theoretical stance in which the liberal tradition has sought to vindicate individual liberty. This unity of theoretical outlook and moral intention is no less present when one turns from the postmodern feminism of Judith Butler to the seminal writings of the French theorist Michel Foucault or to the self-styled "postmodernist bourgeois liberalism" of Richard Rorty.

The threat to freedom, for example, is the driving concern of Foucault's well-known critique of the conventional understanding of the

[10] Ibid., p. 39.
[11] Ibid., p. 51.
[12] Ibid., pp. 39–40.

relation of an author to his work. In "What is an Author?" Foucault portentously states that the view that the author is in the business of conveying a meaning or expressing an intention "allows a limitation of the cancerous and dangerous proliferation of significations within a world where one is thrifty not only with one's resources and riches, but also with one's discourses and their significations."[13]  Of course Foucault means to mock the conventional understanding that (allegedly) looks on the proliferation of meaning as "cancerous and dangerous"; and he intends that the thriftiness he attributes to the traditional view be understood as miserly and narrow-minded.  The theoretical question of the relation between author and intention matter is of practical interest to Foucault because the traditional answer, in Foucault's view, licenses severe restrictions on freedom: the traditional view of an author "is a certain functional principle by which in our culture, one limits, excludes, and chooses; in short, by which one impedes the free circulation, the free manipulation, the free composition, decomposition, and recomposition of fiction."[14]

Anxiety over the diminution of freedom is also at the heart of Foucault's influential discussion in *Discipline and Punish* of panopticism. Bentham's Panopticon was a prison or asylum designed so that all inmates are visible from a single central point. It provided for Foucault a model of the "disciplinary projects" characteristic of modern society.  Never mind that Bentham's Panopticon was never built.  For Foucault, the Panopticon symbolizes the mechanisms by which enlightenment or liberal modernity enslaves individuals to invisible forces, in particular to oppressive conceptions of normalcy, health, and happiness that are actually, according to Foucault, neither necessary nor desirable.[15]  It is seldom clear what exactly Foucault sees in individuals such that freedom from false and confining opinions — or in his terminology "regimes of truth" — is their just desert.  Nor is it clear for what or to what he wishes to set individuals free.  But precisely here, in his devotion to freedom and his studied refusal to identify a determinate goal for it, Foucault aligns himself with the

---

[13] "What is an Author?" in *The Foucault Reader*, ed.  Paul Rabinow (New York: Pantheon Books, 1984), p. 118.
[14] Ibid., p. 119.
[15] Discipline and Punish: *The Birth of the Prison* (New York: Random House, 1979), pp. 195–308.

doctrine which Isaiah Berlin famously called negative liberty and found at the center of the liberal tradition.

The best known popularizer of postmodernism in our country, Richard Rorty, is explicit about the roots of his doctrine in liberalism.[16] Until recently University Professor of Humanities at the University of Virginia, and now at Stanford, Rorty is among the most famous academics of the age. Trained in analytic philosophy at the University of Chicago in the 1950s, Rorty became a professor at Princeton University and rose to prominence within his discipline. In 1979 he attracted wide attention with the publication of *Philosophy and the Mirror of Nature*. Scandalizing much of professional philosophy while earning the admiration of scholars of literature, postmodern political theorists, and proponents of Deweyan pragmatism, Rorty argued that philosophy as understood by thinkers from Plato to Kant — as the love of wisdom, or the search for truth, or the attempt to understand the ultimate principles of the cosmos — was a vain and fruitless undertaking.

Armed with this radical critique or repudiation of metaphysical speculation, and drawing on Heidegger, Wittgenstein, and Dewey for theoretical and rhetorical support, Rorty turned to political themes in the 1980s. In influential papers such as "Postmodernist Bourgeois Liberalism" and "The Priority of Democracy to Philosophy," he contended that liberal democracy in America can get along perfectly well without "philosophical presuppositions." This was a good thing, too, because there were, Rorty casually and constantly assured his readers, no first principles or transcendent order, certainly no natural right or "Laws of Nature and Nature's God," from which liberal democracy could derive support.

In *Contingency, Irony, and Solidarity* (1989), Rorty elaborated what he thought to be the significance for liberal democracy of the abandonment of foundations in philosophy. For one thing, antifoundationalism yielded a great advance in understanding the human condition. By emancipating ourselves from the belief in a human nature, by freeing ourselves from dependence on metaphysics and theology, we can at last come to see ourselves as we truly are. To be sure, Rorty caused much confusion by repeatedly suggesting that he was abandoning the very idea of truth, or, alternatively, in keeping with the pragmatism expounded by John Dewey,

---

[16] This discussion draws on "Can Liberalism be Saved," in *Commentary*, June 1998, pp. 75–78.

by indicating that he was converting the meaning of truth from correct representation of reality to what is useful in the promotion of liberal principles and democratic values. Yet all along Rorty actually advanced a particular conception of what really constitutes human beings. He argues that we truly are creators of language and creatures of the languages we make. Since language is a social affair, socialization "goes all the way down."[17] And since there is no natural order or ultimate reality to which language might refer, who we are and what we love, our defining desires and most considered convictions, are entirely contingent, a function of time and chance.

The alleged discovery of the radical contingency of the human self, for Rorty, has few if any costs and great benefits. While he recognizes that "most nonintellectuals are still committed either to some form of religious faith or to some form of Enlightenment Rationalism," Rorty hopes (in a manner that suggests a faith in an up-to-date form of Enlightenment Rationalism) that the nonintellectuals can some day be emancipated from such falsehood and delusion so as to join forces with intellectuals like Rorty and participate in the construction of a "liberal utopia."[18]

Rorty's liberal utopia is dedicated to the production of a new kind of human being, whom Rorty calls "a liberal ironist." Because he believes that "nothing has an intrinsic nature, a real essence" and that "anything can be made to look good or bad by being redescribed," the liberal ironist is drawn to the ideal of self-creation (as developed, according to Rorty, in the writings of authors such as Nietzsche, Heidegger, and Proust). This ideal, which Rorty believes ought to govern private life, can be seen as a radicalization of the liberal idea of autonomy. But since at the same time he hates cruelty as the worst vice, the liberal ironist is also attracted to the idea of human solidarity with those who suffer (as defended, according to Rorty, by thinkers such as Marx, Mill, Dewey, Habermas, and Rawls). This ideal, which Rorty thinks ought to inform public life, can be understood as a radicalization of the liberal commitment to human equality and the dignity of the individual. Rorty acknowledges that private self-creation and the public quest to diminish cruelty can conflict, but preferring the authority of imagination to that of reason, he envisages a "'poeticized'

---

[17] *Contingency, Irony, and Solidarity* (Cambridge: Cambridge University Press, 1989), p. xiii.
[18] Ibid., pp. xv–xvi.

165

culture" that will "give [] up the attempt to unite one's private ways of dealing with one's finitude and one's sense of obligation to other human beings."[19] In what could be seen as a failure of imagination, Rorty finds no reason to believe that the conflict between the ideals of self-creation and the reduction of suffering will be tragic or destructive, and he can conceive of no compelling need for human beings to unify, or fashion a disciplined whole out of, their private and public purposes.

Rorty has devoted much of his career to interpreting works of philosophy and literature, and to writing, even when dealing with morality and politics, about abstruse theoretical matters. In a slender new book, based on the 1997 William E. Massey Sr. Lectures in the History of American Civilization that he delivered at Harvard University, he turns his attention to the history of the American Left in this century and its contemporary tribulations. In *Achieving our Country*, Rorty proudly proclaims himself a leftist intellectual. He identifies America with the hopes and projects of what he calls "the reformist Left," which, he argues, dominated during the first two thirds of the century. And he criticizes the drift over the last 30 years of what he refers to as "the cultural Left" into abstruse theory and its withdrawal from engagement with concrete politics. To counteract the drift, he urges the Left to renew its pride in the great strides the United States has taken in the twentieth century to secure social justice for all. But the road ahead, he cautions, is still long. To complete the work of building a freer, more equal, more inclusive polity, he urges a return to the pragmatic and participatory spirit of the reformist Left. And he advocates a revival of admiration for the thought of Walt Whitman and John Dewey, whom he regards as kindred spirits and the reformist Left's great intellectual precursors.

Indeed, for Rorty, Whitman and Dewey are nothing less than the "prophets" of a new, passionately secular, civic religion. Their democratic faith is not meant to coexist with Judaism and Christianity in accordance, say, with old-fashioned liberal pluralism, but rather to replace them as the one true faith. "Whitman," according to Rorty, "thought that there was no need to be curious about God because there is no standard, not even a divine one, against which the decisions of a free people can be measured."[20]

[19] Ibid., p. 68.
[20] *Achieving our Country: Leftist Thought in Twentieth Century America* (Cambridge: Harvard University Press, 1998), p. 16.

Likewise, "Dewey's philosophy," Rorty explains, "is a systematic attempt to temporalize everything, to leave nothing fixed."[21] In effect, the religion of democracy is the faith that underlies Rorty's liberal utopia.

Rorty puts forward a definition of an older Left that is broad and partisan but useful: "I propose to use the term "reformist Left" to cover all those Americans who, between 1900 and 1964, struggled within the framework of constitutional democracy to protect the weak from the strong."[22]   This Left, Rorty argues, sought to improve America by criticizing existing arrangements in light of what it regarded as best in the American tradition.  It is wide enough to include progressives, New Deal Liberals, and many who saw themselves as socialists: not only John Dewey and Herbert Croly, but also Irving Howe and John Kenneth Galbraith, W. E. B. DuBois and Eleanor Roosevelt, Martin Luther King Jr. and Arthur Schlesinger, Robert Reich and Jesse Jackson. One could wonder, however, how many of these figures would endorse the utopian — some, even on the reformist Left, might say idolatrous — vision of America that Rorty draws from Whitman, and presents as not only "ubiquitous on the American Left until the Viet Nam War" but also as an accurate reading of America's founding spirit (though he also says that correct readings of a nation's past are not possible) and as a guiding vision for the future: "We are the greatest poem because we put ourselves in the place of God: our essence is our existence, and our existence is in the future.  Other nations thought of themselves as hymns to the glory of God.  We redefine God as our future selves."[23]

In presenting the case for the reformist Left, Rorty recounts, with passion and evident patriotism, many proud moments in American political life.  He also throws into sharp relief how far the contemporary or "spectatorial Left" has fallen, especially the academic or cultural Left.  To be sure, Rorty believes that the cultural Left on campus has many achievements to its credit.  For example, he has only approval, on the grounds that it has contributed to the improvement of relations between men and women, for preferences for women in university hiring.  And he has only disgust for what he swiftly dismisses as the neoconservative critique of political correctness.

---

[21] Ibid., p. 20.
[22] Ibid., p. 43.
[23] Ibid., p. 22.

Nevertheless, Rorty himself offers a devastating portrait of the Left that dominates the academy. The contemporary academic cultural Left is all theory and no practice. It is a producer of "rationalizations of hopelessness."[24] It has become a hyper-sophisticated, mocking spectator of American life. It sits in final judgment and finds the United States guilty of unforgivable sins and utterly incapable, within the present constitutional order, of correcting its flaws or improving the condition of its citizens.

What is needed on the Left now, Rorty advises, is to break free from the idea, made famous by Foucault, that every last belief, practice, and institution in the West has been irremediably corrupted by invisible but pervasive webs of arbitrary ideas and contingent constraints that oppress and confine even when they promise to liberate and empower. This Foucaldian view, on ready display in the scholarship issuing forth from humanities and social science departments across the country, is, as Rorty observes, a recipe for quiescence that transforms politics into a silly spectator sport and turns democracy into a farce. Rorty therefore admonishes his colleagues on the Left to put down their Lacan, Foucault, and Derrida, to turn their attention to passing laws and effecting change that will improve the lives of real people, and, for inspiration and guidance, to embrace the democratic faith of Whitman and Dewey.

Although much more could easily be said, Rorty's calling of his allies on the Left to account is hard-hitting and heartfelt. Yet Rorty somehow omits to explore his own considerable influence over almost two decades on the academic Left, and the connection between the ideas he has prolifically expounded and the vices he now trenchantly exposes. One hard question that Rorty does not confront is whether the very democratic faith that he wishes to revive is not itself in part responsible for debilitating the pragmatic and reformist strands in American political life and, at the same time, aggravating the tendencies within modern democracy toward resentment and paralyzing disgust with the status quo.

That the democratic faith that Rorty preaches has baleful consequences for democratic politics is suggested by the manner in which his own practice betrays his principles. He speaks eloquently in favor of a more inclusive politics, an increased solidarity between intellectuals and workers, a greater respect for the variety of ways of being human. Yet, to take one example, he himself can scarcely refer to the right side of the

[24] Ibid., p. 38.

168

political spectrum in this country — that is, to approximately half of his fellow citizens — without indignation and anger. To the Left, some of whose mistakes and excesses he manfully acknowledges, he gives the sobriquet, "party of hope." But to the Right he refuses the dignity of a defining principle or identifying virtue. It is not that Rorty suppresses his judgment. Conservatives, in his account, form the party of indifference, greed, bigotry, and military chauvinism. Such is his antipathy that even though he takes an uncompromising stand against communism, deplores the weakness for Marxism on the Left, and does not hesitate to use the term "evil empire" to describe the former Soviet Union, Rorty cannot bring himself to utter a respectful word or give any real credit to the Republican party or conservatives in America.

Perhaps though it is not only that Rorty's practice betrays his principles. Perhaps Rorty's practice also discloses the real meaning of his principles, or, as pragmatists like to say, their "cash value." When democracy is transformed into a civic religion as Whitman and Dewey prescribe, those who refuse to conform, who insist on maintaining a distinction between democracy and religion, or between democracy and justice, or between democracy and the human good run the risk of arousing the ire of the pious and getting themselves branded, in the name of the prophets, enemies of the one true faith. Where, as Rorty urges, religion and politics are blended in such a way that democracy becomes the highest value, there democracy becomes despotic, dissent becomes schism, and such bipartisan goods as liberty of thought and discussion, religious toleration, and the dignity of the individual get placed in great peril.

Rorty has a habit or technique of deflecting criticism by maintaining that he has nothing to say to (and by implication nothing to learn from) those who happen not to share his preferences. Such a stance conveniently relieves one from grappling with a great variety of vexing issues. But it does not dissolve the need to understand the implications of, and the conditions for respecting, one's own preferences.

Rorty prefers to equate liberalism with his brand of postmodern liberalism. In doing so, he receives some support not only from contemporary usage but from the progressive and romantic tendencies in the thought of John Stuart Mill. Yet there is a powerful strand in Mill's thought which Rorty's paeans to democratic individuality may superficially resemble but which seems to make scarcely a dent on his analysis of

American politics. This strand concerns not the right of both the Right and Left to be heard in a liberal democracy but the need:

> Unless opinions favourable to democracy and to aristocracy, to property and to equality, to co-operation and to competition, to luxury and to abstinence, to sociality and individuality, to liberty and discipline, and all the other standing antagonisms of practical life, are expressed with equal freedom, and enforced and defended with equal talent and energy, there is no chance of both elements obtaining their due. . . .[25]

This is the liberal spirit at its finest speaking. It is a spirit that not having repudiated reason, reasons judiciously. It is a spirit that, not having given up on truth, seeks out the partial truth in contending perspectives. It is a spirit that, not having abandoned an appreciation of limits, resists the democratic impulse to absolutize democracy and traduce discipline and excellence. And it is a spirit that, not having turned its back on politics or the people or genuine pluralism, resists the arrogance that views one party or approach as the sole carrier of decency and justice in America.

---

[25] *On Liberty*, in *Essays on Politics and Society*, ed. J. M. Robson (Toronto: University of Toronto Press, 1977), Chap. 2, pp. 253–254.

# 11. *Issues Facing Contemporary American Public Philosophy*

## CHRISTOPHER WOLFE

The second part of the twentieth century saw the United States engaged in a struggle with totalitarianism, and its public philosophy was deeply influenced by the sense that it represented a Western civilization against a new barbarism.[1]   With the stunningly quick demise of communism toward the end of the century, this struggle was succeeded by one internal to the West, one which in fact raised questions even about the unitary character of the West.   Rather than an end of history with liberal democracy triumphant and unchallenged,[2] questions about the very nature of liberal democracy emerged more forcefully.

One interesting perspective on the post-communist world is that of *Time* magazine's 1994 Man of the Year, Pope John Paul II.  Karol Wojtyla became pope at a time when communism still seemed strong and sometimes aggressive, and he participated in changes that helped lead to its downfall.  More recently, he has focused his attention on the situation of the post-communist world, from a rather broader perspective than many others (being less confined by national and temporal horizons), and has identified key civilizational questions.   Western liberal democracy triumphed in the Cold War, and it did so under the banner of freedom.  But what is this freedom? Is it an end in itself? Or is it, by its nature, oriented

---

[1] An eloquent statement of this perspective was the foreword to Whittaker Chambers' *Witness* (Random House, 1952).
[2] Francis Fukuyama, *The End of History* (Free Press, 1992).

toward some other end: toward knowing and living what he calls the truth about the human person.[3]

This relation of freedom and truth is the question at the heart of America's current culture wars, and it is these issues that are central in the battle over American public philosophy as we enter the new millennium. In an American Enterprise Institute Bradley Lecture, "Toward a New Public Philosophy," James Ceaser discusses the current situation of American public philosophy, in which there is a struggle to establish a successor to the earlier regnant New Deal liberal public philosophy (represented by John Dewey and Herbert Croly). In discussing the efforts of conservatives to craft a public philosophy in our time, he observes that

> the final reaction of conservatism has been against the form and shape of the culture. It was connected to the practical question of the causes of recognized social problems and pathologies, such as crime and poverty. But the reaction has gone much further to the very character of that culture. And conservatives have been unsure about where exactly to place the blame. Is it just Big Government? Or is it the consequence of the process and policy of secularizing society? And are the causes to be found primarily in what liberalism promoted, or do the sources go back further still, even to our own founding?[4]

These are large questions, and the right questions.

I will not attempt to give broad answers to these questions in this essay. Instead, I would like to make a beginning to that large task, by identifying sets of issues that will be, I think, the key issues for America as it enters the 21st century. The resolution of these issues will define American public philosophy. They are the issues for which any claimant to the mantle of American public philosophy must provide guidance. Eight of these issue sets are substantive: life, death, and personhood; marriage, family, and sexuality; the role of women in society; education and culture; race; religion; citizenship and immigration, and political economy.[5] Five

---

[3] See especially his encyclicals *Veritatis Splendor* (1993), especially sections 31ff., and *Evangelium Vitae* (1995).

[4] James Ceaser, "Toward a New Public Philosophy," an American Enterprise Institute Bradley Lecture (March 8, 1999) (the quotation is from the next to last paragraph).

[5] For reasons of space, I will confine myself in this paper to a discussion of domestic issues,

are more structural or procedural: the role of the judiciary; the marketplace(s) and centers of private power; the roles of civil society and government; federalism and decentralization; and common core values.

## Life and Death and Personhood

The first set of issues concerns life and death. Abortion, euthanasia, reproductive technologies, and justifiable killing (the death penalty and war) are prominent issues here.

Abortion, despite the almost unanimous efforts of national politicians, remains a live issue, and perhaps the most profoundly divisive issue, in American politics. Ironically, the battle between liberals and conservatives on this issue seems to reverse what in the past was the ordinary structure of debate. In the past, it was not uncommon to find religiously-oriented moralists deeply suspicious of modernity and all its works (including modern science) pitted against modern progressives for whom modern science was a new kind of orienting framework for life — a worldview, or even a religion, if you will. (The Scopes trial was the classic instance of such forces squaring off.) On the issue of abortion, however, it is the moral traditionalists who have been able to invoke the wonders of neonatal technology and who often rely on the relatively straightforward scientific facts about the beginning of an individual human life from the point of conception. The progressives find themselves in the position of using scientifically awkward circumlocutions for the conceptus, such as blob of tissue or products of conception.[6]

But perhaps appearances may be misleading. The underlying worldviews may still be the same, but the difference is not so much over when human life begins as over the significance to be accorded what is concededly some form of human life, at its various stages. Thus the debate typically centers on a purported difference between human life and

---

leaving to the side the very important questions of the role of the United States in international affairs.

[6] Stanley Fish (no conservative!), who formerly viewed the abortion issue as pitting the modern scientific view against traditionalist religious moralizing, publicly recanted that position on a panel at the 1998 American Political Science Association annual meeting. Without becoming pro-life himself, he acknowledged that the pro-life advocates were the ones effectively invoking science, while the pro-choice advocates were generally avoiding scientific facts about human life, relying largely on moral assertions.

personhood. Science, of course, has nothing to say about this, strictly speaking, since it is a philosophical (or theological) matter. Nonetheless, there is a certain rationalist and utilitarian worldview that is often associated with science that tends to minimize the importance of merely potential (relatively un-actualized) human life, especially in view of other factors in the balance, above all, personal, economic, and sexual freedom for women,[7] and, sometimes, the negative value accorded human lives under conditions considered to be inconsistent with human dignity.

Euthanasia is an issue that has only begun to be discussed, though only one state (Oregon) has authorized assisted suicide. Not only the suffering of terminal illnesses, but also the decline of human powers in old age, are thought by some to rob human life of its dignity, especially in a society whose medical resources permit greater prolonging of life (not always wisely). As with abortion, un-actualized human capacities are not thought to provide an adequate ground for an inviolable human dignity. In fact, the disappearance or serious decline of such actualized capacities are grounds to argue for death with dignity, to argue, that is, that dignity may make death — freely chosen — an appropriate or even desirable choice.

The logic of euthanasia starts with individual autonomy, the right of a person to choose to end his own life (if necessary, with the assistance of others). But if the right to life is not really inalienable — if it can be given up — then it is hard to see why any absolute barrier should be erected against third parties making such decisions in at least some cases, beginning with instances of incompetent patients (as seems to be happening in the Netherlands).

Arguments for euthanasia are typically made in the name of compassion — indeed, the basis for such acts in compassion may be viewed by some as the basis of their moral justifiability. There is reason for concern, however, that judgments based on compassion may end up being based on feelings or a utilitarian calculus dominated by gut preferences — at the expense of reason — and whether such judgments are appropriate.[8] And a process of reasoning that is selective about which

---

[7] On the worldview of pro-choice activists, see Kristin Luker, *Abortion and the Politics of Motherhood* (University of California Press, 1984).

[8] On emotivism, see Alasdair MacIntyre, *After Virtue* (University of Notre Dame, 1980), especially ch.1. I do not mean to suggest that compassion is always simply a feeling. Properly understood — and perhaps in spite of its etymology — the word compassion can

human lives can be regarded as having human dignity, or that even may use human dignity as a ground for actively ending certain human lives, must be viewed, at a minimum, with caution, and at a maximum, with fear, especially when we consider the human capacity for rationalization (e.g., concluding that lives that happen to be very expensive to sustain are not really lives worth living at all). When we factor in a likely future scenario in which medical advances continue to extend life, and when the burden of supporting the aged falls very heavily on a smaller number of younger people, it would be surprising if pressures for expanded euthanasia were not to increase.

What is at issue here is what human dignity means. It is generally agreed to rest on something other than the achievement of a given person, an actualization of his or her human powers — for a basis of that sort would easily authorize denying the dignity of countless human beings. But if it rests on capacity or potential, on what grounds can it be denied to human life at any point after conception? The pro-choice (abortion and euthanasia) answer is largely framed, for rhetorical purposes, as an issue of individual autonomy, allegedly bracketing the substantive question of the status of the incipient human being. But can such a question truly be bracketed, or is the bracketing itself not an answer?

In a different area of scientific technology regarding human life, scientists have been able to develop remarkable technological means to assist infertile couples in having children, and medical research has just entered into a new era of striking capacities for genetic manipulation and cloning. A compassionate concern for the plight of such couples has seemed to many a sufficient justification for using such technologies. But these capacities raise the specter of human beings making other human beings, and it is not clear how this will affect our attitudes toward the dignity of human life. Does it matter whether a human being is engendered as the natural outcome of an act of intimate union between two human beings, or from an act (however much based on compassion) of scientists, doctors, and tests tubes?

And, finally, what are the implications of different understandings of human dignity for certain forms of justifiable killing, such as capital

be understood to include a rational moral judgment about the propriety of relieving suffering.

punishment and war?[9] When the representatives of the political community inflict death as the just punishment for a crime, it can be argued that this penalty not only defends the community and innocent lives, but also vindicates the dignity of the one who suffers the punishment, on the grounds that it affirms the reality of his free will and appeals to his intellect to recognize the evil of his action and repent.[10] But where does this leave the connection between human dignity and the inviolability of human life? Is this only a different way of arguing that human dignity does not attach to human life *per se*, but only to human life under certain circumstances? It is true, of course, that capital punishment is inflicted on human beings who have freely chosen seriously evil actions, which is not arguably the case with earlier issues such as abortion. But this leaves open a number of questions: whether the benefits of capital punishment (relative to other forms of punishment, such as life imprisonment) are so great as to require the death penalty; assuming that society can still protect itself by other methods of punishment, whether the foregoing of capital punishment might contribute to a deeper appreciation of the worth of all human lives; whether the imposition of the death penalty, even when justified, may have corollary moral effects that we should seek to avoid, such as reinforcing a spirit of vengeance or a utilitarian spirit in calculating whether to kill a person. The issue seems to me much more complex than either death penalty partisans or opponents are usually willing to acknowledge.

Those same issues are raised in the context of justified killing in war. Such questions about the limits of justified killing have always been with us, of course, but several features of the contemporary world make them even more complex. First, the extraordinary destructive power of modern weapons (especially nuclear weapons, but also conventional weapons, and biological and chemical weapons as well), capable of obliterating whole populations, tempts people today to abandon rational moral limits on the use of military power, for example, those based on the hard-won distinction

[9] Perhaps justifiable killing questions could be extended to include the issues of personal security that are central to discussions of crime and gun control, though these important public policy issues are less immediately connected, I think, with the central issue of human personhood and dignity, and its implications.

[10] John Grisham's novel, *The Chamber*, which seems generally to reflect anti-capital punishment beliefs, may actually be viewed as a depiction of repentance induced by the approaching imposition of the death penalty.

between combatants and non-combatants. And while there are difficult questions and grey areas regarding collateral damage and the relation of particular non-military personnel to a nation's military activity, it would be dangerous simply to believe that the end of a nation's self-preservation justifies *any* means. Second, modern technology (nuclear, biological, and chemical weapons) potentially offers to large numbers of small nations, and even to very small groups of terrorists, the capacity to inflict extraordinary carnage on large populations. It is not hard to imagine such acts, and the brutal responses in kind that fear and anger might produce. (If ends justify means, would our moral principles regarding torture of terrorists, for example, hold firm?)

In these life and death issues, it is the very meaning and significance of human life, the human person, that is called into question, perhaps more dramatically than at any previous time. Answers to these questions will be shaped by a key element of a public philosophy — its philosophical anthropology.

## Marriage, Family, and Sex

The second set of issues revolve around marriage, family, and sex. This must be a matter of great importance, given that the family is the cell of society, the primordial human community on which all others are based. The facts here are disturbing to almost everyone, at some level. Divorce has very much become a way of life for Americans. From being a relatively rare event, it has become both relatively normal (if still painful), and embodied fully in law, through no-fault divorce. Americans can now be said to be monogamous only in the sense that people have one spouse *at a time*.

In addition to families suffering broken marriages, there are many families that never experience marriage. Cohabitation has gone in a generation or two from being a rare and shameful lifestyle to the more or less normal pattern for younger Americans (though very many of them will go on to get married). Illegitimacy has reached extraordinary heights, cutting across racial and class lines, with powerful social consequences.[11]

[11] See Charles Murray, "The Coming White Underclass," *Wall Street Journal* (October 29, 1993).

In recent years, moreover, there has been a move to redefine marriage and family to encompass homosexual relationships, and more broadly to legitimize homosexual activity as one among many sexual lifestyles.[12]

There are some who argue that considerable variation in family forms is natural and unproblematic — there is no "family" but only different kinds of "families." There is some truth in this, undoubtedly, since families have differed in various ways from place to place and time to time. The question is what the outside limit to this variability might be, if families are to serve their purposes.[13]

Social science evidence seems more and more to confirm harmful effects of family non-formation or breakdown in America. While it is essential to recognize that many single-parents struggle heroically to provide a good upbringing to their children, and that human beings can be remarkably adaptable under non-ideal conditions, it is also necessary not to shirk the fact that a considerable range of social pathologies are significantly correlated with divorce and illegitimacy.[14]

Given these problems, the great question facing this generation of Americans is: why does our society seem to have so much difficulty sustaining stable family life? Certainly, it is easy to see that there are objective conditions that make some form of marital breakdown understandable, as cases of spousal abuse demonstrate.[15] There are many other, less dramatic, forms of ill-treatment of spouses by each other. And there is the simple fact of the emergence of irreconcilable differences or merely growing apart (especially when life expectancy increases dramatically).

And yet, presumably, human nature has not changed so drastically in recent eras — many of these factors must have been present throughout

---

[12] See Wolfe, ed., *Homosexuality and American Public Life* (Spence Publishing Company, 1999) and *Homosexuality and American Public Policy* (forthcoming, Spence Publishing Company).

[13] See Wolfe, ed., *The Family, Civil Society, and the State* (Rowman and Littlefield, 1998), especially chapter 1, Elizabeth Fox-Genovese, "Thoughts on the History of the Family."

[14] See *The Family, Civil Society, and The State*, especially Parts I and II.

[15] What form such a desirable breakdown takes would depend on the underlying conception of marriage. For those who consider marriage a species of voluntary contract, divorce would be the logical response. For those who consider marriage a natural institution, the qualities of which are independent of human will and include indissolubility, the form would be legal separation.

human history. There must be other factors, then, that account for the relative increase of divorce and illegitimacy. Some of them include the following. First, divorce feeds on itself, since it raises the question, for the children of divorce, whether permanent human commitments are really possible. Second, marriage has lost the support of its close tie to sex. When the powerful urges of sex are confined by notions of legitimacy to one marriage, they provide a strong auxiliary support. When sex is readily available outside marriage (without social sanctions), as it has become, there is both less incentive to enter into marriage and more temptations to leave it (especially for men). Third, more modern and relativist ethical notions — Alan Wolfe's formulation of Americans' new Eleventh Commandment, Thou shalt not be judgmental[16] — may be used to justify extra-marital sex and childbearing, on one hand, and exiting from unsatisfactory marriages, on the other. A particularly influential form of this ethic has been the liberationist or autonomist ethos associated with more recent forms of liberalism, particularly since the 1960s. Fourth, liberalism's tendency to ground human relationships in voluntary contracts rather than status may result in a diminished sense of certain fundamental duties that arise from nature rather than human will, among them the duties of parenthood. Fifth, materialism and affluence may incline people to resolve difficulties by moving out of unpleasant situations rather than remaining in them and working through difficulties.

But perhaps we should ask, not just "why unstable family life?," but also "how was stable family life ever possible?" There are plenty of ordinary human inclinations and objective circumstances to explain why two people would not want to live with each other for a lifetime. We have to recognize first, of course, that there was no golden age of marriage, in which family life was basically trouble-free. The relatively more stable family life of the past had its own unhappy share of pains and difficulties, infidelities and desertion. But family life was more stable partly because of the strong social supports that helped to resist or overcome the more centrifugal tendencies in marriage. Among these, religion — in America, specifically Christianity — was among the foremost. We might expect, then, a decline in marital and family stability from the facts that a) religion exercises less power over the everyday lives of many people in our society,

---

[16] Alan Wolfe, *One Nation After All* (Viking, 1998).

and b) many religious communities have come to accommodate more modern (and looser) conceptions of family life and divorce. The largely religious ideals of the past, moreover, were typically supported both by the power of social conventions and of law.

Finally, as a transition to the next topic, we can point out that family instability is partly caused by the fact that women who did not have the economic resources to live independently of a male wage earner, are now much more able to do so, either through their own earnings, or through the substitute provider, the state. Alternative sources of support have therefore made it possible for women to leave difficult or unsatisfying marriages to which they once would have been tied by economic necessity.

That the nuclear family has become less stable is generally (though not universally) accepted. Increasingly, social scientists are acknowledging a variety of detrimental consequences correlated with family instability. Most people probably would agree that greater stability of family life is desirable. On the question of whether this instability is basically a necessary evil, however, or basically an evil to be rectified, there is, unfortunately, little agreement.

## The Role of Women in Society

There is widespread agreement today that changes of this century regarding gender have been in many ways a great victory for justice: the past confinement of women to the private sphere of the home by legal and social pressures unjustly denied many women opportunities that should have been available to them.[17] The opening up to women of education, employment outside the home, and participation in public life is acknowledged as a good by virtually everyone in our society.

And yet these genuine advances are not without some more questionable consequences as well. One may view them somewhat as the protagonist of Saul Bellow's *Mr. Sammler's Planet* looks at modern developments:

[17] For the record, though, I would deny that this injustice is fairly characterized as an oppression of women by men. It reflected an erroneous (because too rigid) conception of sexual differentiation shared generally by both men and women.

. . . it has only been in the last two centuries that the majority of people in civilized countries have claimed the privilege of being individuals. Formerly they were slave, peasant, laborer, even artisan, but not person. It is clear that this revolution, a triumph for justice in many ways — slaves should be free, killing toil should end, the soul should have liberty — has also introduced new kinds of grief and misery, and so far, on the broadest scale, it has not been altogether a success.[18]

We are especially struggling for answers as to who foots the bill for the liberation of women from those unjust traditional constraints, and short-term answers are unsatisfying.

Children, in particular, it seems, pay a large part of the price, despite efforts of social scientists to discount the significance of altering traditional child-care arrangements. The reallocation of resources in the family, especially the precious resource of time, away from children to other activities (most notably, work outside the home) has come at the expense of children.[19]

Another group that has suffered from this change is those women who choose to stay at home full-time with their children — either during childbearing years, or permanently — and whose work is generally not accorded high status in our society. What conclusions, after all, should we draw from social studies that claim to prove that full-time mothering has no significant benefits, relative to the work of low-paid substitutes in day-care centers? And what is the inevitable effect on school girls of anti-stereotype-programs that encourage them to be more than "just" mothers and homemakers? Under these circumstances, college women today who desire to have children and be full-time homemakers (at least for part of their lives) must hesitate to admit to this goal, for fear of the subtle or not-so-subtle contempt it would engender in their peers and in society at large.

Likewise, mothers who arrange their employment around (subordinate it to) child-raising responsibilities not only forego career advancement and higher salaries in doing so, but also find this price exacerbated by the lower status society often accords them. For many women, the difficulties of combining outside-the-home employment and the responsibilities of child-

---

[18] Saul Bellow, *Mr. Sammler's Planet* (Viking Press, 1969), p. 228.
[19] See Peter Uhlenberg and David Eggebeen's very interesting article, "The Declining Well-Being of American Adolescents," *Public Interest* Number 82 (Winter, 1986), pp. 25–38.

raising can make the once supposedly glorious "having it all" a burdensome "having to do everything for everybody."[20]

Of course, an alternative proposal is that men foot the bill, by making a more balanced contribution to the home and the raising of children.[21] It is clear, I think, that paternal involvement in the home is essential.[22] What is less clear is what form that involvement ought to take, and whether the contributions of men and women to the home are, or should be, more or less interchangeable. Whatever the particular balance between work and family for husband and wife in a given marriage — different couples will certainly work out different ways of such balancing — should we expect or desire a significant movement away from our current situation, in which mothers, in the vast majority of cases, still undertake the primary responsibility (in terms of time, and relative to employment outside the home) for childraising?

The evidence so far suggests to me that a) most men are unwilling to undertake roles in the home that would make it impossible for them to work full-time, b) men in general are not as capable as women in the work of raising young children; c) the realities of pregnancy, childbearing, and nursing may not demand, but do support arrangements by which mothers will undertake the primary role in childraising; d) what men are capable of doing in the home is not enough to make it possible for most women to meet child-raising responsibilities without having to limit or subordinate

[20] For a recent discussion of the difficulties in balancing different aspects of a woman's life, see Danielle Crittenden, *What Our Mothers Didn't Tell Us: Why Happiness Eludes the Modern Woman* (Simon & Schuster, 1999).

[21] See Susan Moller Okin, *Justice, Gender, and the Family* (Basic Books, 1989).

[22] This is true not only for those who tend to be critical of sex role differentiation, but also for traditionalists whose beliefs are grounded in such differentiation. The profound importance of paternal involvement in the home, and especially in the raising of children, is an essential part of reflective conservative efforts to defend both marriage in general (versus illegitimacy) and heterosexual marriage in particular. I should also make this important point: to say that paternal involvement in the home is essential is not to say that single-parent homes are necessarily bad homes. There have been and are, obviously, single-parent families in which a mother (usually) has done an admirable job in raising the family. It is only to say that single-parent homes labor under the burden of lacking something very important — which is ordinarily a key factor — and that efforts to cope with the absence of a father are necessary. At the same time, however, I should candidly admit that the importance of paternal involvement does suggest that a society with many single-parent families, in the aggregate, is likely to experience a higher level of various social pathologies.

the demands of other employment, at certain times; and e) most women, despite feminist objections, recognize all of the above and are quite willing to assume the lead in raising children, accepting certain limitations in other areas (work outside the home) — but they also believe that society artificially and unnecessarily increases that price.[23]

Of course, there are various experiments afoot to deal with this difficult issue — various kinds of accommodation in the workplace, and ways of doing work in the home — and many women (and men) make extraordinary efforts to meet the various responsibilities of work and family that they have undertaken. But it remains to be seen how successful these efforts will be in reconciling the needs and desires of women and men with the best interests of children.

## Education and Culture

Perhaps because equality of opportunity is the linchpin connecting democracy's two most fundamental principles, freedom and equality, education has always been a central concern of Americans. That each person should have the opportunity to receive a basic education is one point on which there is consensus in our society. But education has also become a central battleground of various social forces in the nation. While an important part of education — especially the basic skills of reading, writing, and arithmetic — is relatively noncontroversial, there are other aspects of education that guarantee controversy in a culturally pluralistic society.

Elementary and secondary public schools originated, in great measure, with a very public task: not only providing basic skills, but also educating the citizenry in the principles of republican government. Throughout American history, the public schools have transmitted the civil religion of the nation, with its scriptures (Declaration and Constitution), its history,

---

[23] How many of the above observations (if true) are results of natural inclinations, and how many are the results of social conditioning, is hard to say, of course. (Given certain basic biological facts about child-bearing, it seems plausible to me that there are important elements of each, the latter both reflecting and reinforcing the former.) Even if they are the result of social conditioning to some significant extent, that does not mean that they could be easily changed or that the benefits to be gained would outweigh the costs.

and its saints (e.g., Washington and Lincoln). This role was thought to be especially important in a nation of immigrants from non-republican lands.[24]

Recent divisions within the United States on cultural issues have, unsurprisingly, been reflected in debates about the content of education. When America was largely a Protestant Christian nation, the existence within schools of Christian practices (reflecting the practices of local majorities) such as school prayer and Christian teachings (e.g., the Ten Commandments) was commonplace and uncontroversial. There was always the anomaly of Catholic schools — which objected precisely to the Protestant character of most public schools — but such schools were precisely that, an anomaly. The post-*Everson* secularization of public schools, especially the school prayer decisions of the early 1960s,[25] therefore came as something of a shock to many Protestants, especially evangelicals and fundamentalists, and the issue of religion and the public schools has been actively contested throughout recent decades.[26]

But the controversy has spread beyond religion, because modern secular intellectuals often apply the same corrosive analysis to traditional moral values, which are often held similarly to offend proper liberal neutrality. For example, in *Board of Education* v. *Pico*, the Supreme Court ruled that local school boards may not remove books from school libraries simply because they dislike the ideas contained in those books and seek by their removal "to prescribe what shall be orthodox in politics, nationalism, religion, or other matters of opinion."[27] Moreover, certain political theorists argue that it is precisely the purpose of at least post-elementary schooling in a liberal society to offer the individual student a wide range of theoretical possibilities, which will necessarily entail challenging the moral ideals of students' families.[28] Add to this mix the increasing salience

---

[24] In many cases, this public purpose was rather explicitly anti-Catholic, as Charles Glenn shows in *The Myth of the Common School* (University of Massachusetts Press, 1988).

[25] *Everson v. Board of Education* 330 U.S. 1 (1947), and *Abington School District* v. *Schempp* 374 U.S. 203 (1963).

[26] Among other cases, see *Wallace* v. *Jaffree* 472 U.S. 38 (1985), *Edwards* v. *Aguillard* 482 U.S. 578 (1987), and *Lee* v. *Weisman* 120 L.Ed.2d 467 (1992).

[27] 457 U.S. 853 (1982). The quotation is from *W. Va.* v. *Barnette* 319 U.S. 624 (1943), which, Michael Sandel argues, is the key decision importing the liberal neutrality of the procedural republic into constitutional law (*Democracy's Discontent*, pp. 53–54).

[28] See, for example, Bruce Ackerman, *Social Justice in the Liberal State* (Yale University Press, 1980), and Stephen Macedo, "Multiculturalism for the Religious Right? Defending

of topics such as sex education and AIDS education, and the potential for controversy obviously becomes very great.

A combination of dissatisfaction with public school policy on religious and moral grounds, and a sense that public schools have failed educationally (either generally, or in certain places, such as major urban school districts) has led to a growing movement — vociferously opposed by teachers' unions and religious separationist groups such as the ACLU — for policies that facilitate school choice, such as voucher programs and tuition tax credits. Education will therefore continue to be a major public policy issue in various ways.

But education in a broader sense goes beyond the classroom. One of the profound civilizational changes in the twentieth century, especially in affluent post-World War II nations, has been the extraordinary expansion of leisure made possible by modern economies. A forty-hour work week for many people leaves many hours of time in which to pursue other activities.[29] Moreover, childbearing is typically confined to a more limited range of life, due to decreased family size. And people are living much longer beyond the time during which the care of children consumes much of their activity.

Now, in principle, this additional leisure time could be an extraordinary opportunity for intellectual and moral development. One could hope that succeeding generations take more and more advantage of leisure to develop capacities that human beings in earlier ages had no opportunities to develop, for example, intellectual and moral development through reading literature, listening to and playing music, observing and engaging in various fine arts.

Under the circumstances of expanded "non-work" time, the importance of popular culture and of entertainment has been greatly

Liberal Civic Education," *Journal of Philosophy of Education* Vol. 29, No. 2 (1995), pp. 223–38.

[29] I can only acknowledge briefly here one important omission in my discussion here, namely *work*. In this paper I focus primarily on the issues that are associated with what is often called the culture wars, as opposed to economic issues. But work is more than just an economic issue. It is also itself a cultural issue, since it involves profoundly important questions about the way in which people will seek their life goals. Moreover, the organization of the economy and work ought to reflect the priority of persons to things: the fact that the most important product of any process of work is the worker himself.

magnified. The media, especially the visual media (movies and above all television), have come to play an enormous role in many people's lives. This is not primarily because of any conscious attempt by people in the media to persuade their viewers to think a certain way (though there is a tendency for people in the media to hold distinctive worldviews and these views do get reflected in their productions[30]). The deeper effect is more indirect, a function less of logic than of what might be called a sociology of knowledge and values.

One example: prime-time television series typically tell stories, and watching a television program is a form of entering that story imaginatively. For at least a short time, the world in which we live is the world represented in that imaginative portrayal. What is in those worlds is important — sex and violence, of course, but also friendship, fear, insecurity, humor, and a multitude of other things. At least as important, however, is what is *not* in those worlds, either because it is difficult to portray, or because its authors cannot, or do not think to, or choose not to portray it (which, in turn, may be because of their own preferences or because of what they believe to be the preferences of their viewers). Some aspects of human life, not surprisingly, are therefore significantly under-represented in the worlds fashioned by the media. These include: sex that is embedded in a context of marriage and child-bearing; intimate prayer to God, the frustration, tedium, and satisfaction of ordinary, unexciting, but necessary work; the broad range (bell curve?) from ugliness to beauty among human beings; the personal confrontation with the fact of mortality.

In general, it seems fair to characterize the content of popular culture as superficial. So much of the leisure time that might have offered unparalleled opportunities for intellectual and moral development seems wasted on passive activities that are hard to view as increasing the quality of human life.

Another, more extreme aspect of the search for ways to fill leisure time is drugs. There has never been a time in human history when human beings did not seek to deal with stress or boredom by manipulating their consciousness chemically. What is different now perhaps is that affluence

[30] See, for example, Robert Lerner and Althea K. Nagai, "Family Values and Media Reality," in Wolfe, ed., *The Family, Civil Society, and the State*.

and time, and perhaps also spiritual and moral vacuums in people's lives, have expanded the range of opportunity for such indulgence.

Should we be surprised at the low to mediocre quality of most leisure-time activities in our contemporary society? Classical political philosophers, after all, would have noted that in democracies the common man — with his very common desires — sets the tone. Is this inevitable in a democracy, and should it therefore be accepted? Or can democracy be high-toned, and, if so, how?[31]

One of the striking aspects of cultural life today is the fairly widespread faith — no less deep for being often unnoticed — in the cultural invisible hand. There is an alliance here between those on the right who have a general faith in the market, with those on the left who have traditionally shared a great faith at least in the intellectual marketplace. There are occasional dissenters on both the left and the right — e.g., cultural conservatives hostile to markets in debased sex, and liberals and feminists who would regulate the cultural marketplace on behalf of less powerful or marginalized groups. But, given most Americans' reluctance to support any form of government censorship, a rather open cultural marketplace is what seems to remain.[32]

In some cases these issues go beyond the marketplace, when they involve government sponsorship of cultural activities. For example, the National Endowment for the Arts has come under political attack in Congress, due to its funding of some controversial art and exhibitions (e.g., a picture of a crucifix in urine). While few people would argue that the government has an obligation to fund specific forms of art, there are some who contend that, once government offers sponsorship of cultural activities, it may not choose to withhold funding from a particular activity because of its ideological content.[33] This would seem to leave Congress simply with the general decision about whether or not to fund art, while the specific decisions about which art is to be funded would be left to peer

---

[31] These are important themes in Allan Bloom's *The Closing of the American Mind* (Simon and Schuster, 1987).

[32] Whether this reluctance to support at least a moderate form of censorship is reasonable can be doubted. See Harry M. Clor, *Public Morality and Liberal Society* (University of Notre Dame Press, 1996).

[33] See the various opinions in *National Endowment for the Arts* v. *Finley* 140 L.Ed.2d (1998).

review within the arts community (or at least among the elites who are dominant within it). The question here is whether the determination of government arts funding by such elites itself meets the criterion of neutrality on the basis of which explicit government decisions about content are considered legally dubious. That art elites can and do consistently make neutral judgments apart from content seems implausible.

# Race

A central issue of American life from the beginning, race has continued to be a source of cultural divisions in the post-civil rights revolution era. Conservatives, who were often reluctant to endorse government (especially federal) intervention to promote racial equality until the mid-1960s, generally consider racism to have been defeated (despite lingering and ineradicable pockets of it), and have embraced the standard of legal equality of opportunity and color-blindness. Liberals tend to discount advances in racial equality, believing that racism is still powerful and pervasive, and that much more extensive government intervention is necessary to rectify the effects of past racial discrimination and to enforce true racial equality.

The dominant contemporary issues are affirmative action and multiculturalism. Conservatives generally deplore the principle of race-based decision-making in government (or even private) affirmative action plans, which they consider unjust and likely to perpetuate racial divisions and stereotyping.[34] They are optimistic that, at least in the long term, race-neutral government policies and formal legal racial equality will ensure equality of opportunity and guarantee that people are treated on the basis of their individual qualities rather than their race.

Liberals view affirmative action as a minimum requirement of justice to level a playing field heavily tilted against traditionally disfavored racial minorities, due to the effects of past discrimination and due to subtle but still powerful racist attitudes today.[35] Moreover, according to some, only conscious and extensive efforts to foster a multicultural society that

[34] See *Adarand* v. *Pena* 515 U.S. 200 (1995), especially Justices Scalia's and Thomas' concurrences.
[35] *Regents of the University of California* v. *Bakke* 438 U.S. 265 (1978), opinion of Justice Brennan.

celebrates difference will be able to make inroads against these attitudes. This may require the use of government power to suppress public manifestations of disrespect for certain groups, for example, prohibitions of hate speech.[36]

Each side, in its own way, may represent a kind of utopian thinking. The idea of multicultural diversity as its own end, a good *in itself*, can only subsist in the absence of a candid evaluation of different cultures, since all human cultures are a mixture of good and bad, more and less attractive elements. Western culture has a monopoly neither on human cruelty, greed, and rapacity, nor on the good, the true, and the beautiful. But the need to have standards by which to evaluate the better or worse aspects of all cultures implies some universal standards that transcend particular cultures — standards difficult (but perhaps not impossible) to come by, in a pluralistic society.

On the other hand, is it possible to achieve a pure, cosmopolitan color-blindness? Individuals need to be judged on their own merits, certainly, but can race be filtered out of human consciousness so easily? Does political prudence require ignoring racial differences under all circumstances?

It may be that liberalism (including what Americans call conservatism) of its nature has difficulty with certain kinds of particularism, and race and nationality are among these, since they seem fundamentally irrational, irrelevant to rational perceptions and evaluations of people and actions. But particular identities may, from another perspective, be more rational than liberals think, since they often provide some of the most powerful and satisfying forms of human solidarity and community. (One only has to think of sports teams and the loyalties they can engender.) How to permit these particular identities (often a melange of race, nationality, and culture) to flourish, without permitting them to be the ground of unjust discrimination, is a perennial, vexing question of political life.

## Religion

---

[36] See the ordinance and its background in *R.A.V.* v. *St. Paul* 505 U.S. 377 (1992), and the controversy over various university hate speech codes.

In the ancient world, the problem of church and state was unknown, though the problem of law and religious conscience was not (as we see in Sophocles' *Antigone*). With the coming of Christianity, and the distinction between an immanent political order and a transcendent spiritual order, the relationship between Church and State became a central question of Western political theory and practice.

America, in fact, was in some measure born out of European church-state problems, since many of the early settlers came precisely to find an opportunity to practice their religious faiths. In early colonial times, however, this did not necessarily mean that they sought religious liberty in the form we think of it today. A colonial Christian commonwealth did not necessarily accord a broad freedom of worship to other Christian denominations. Yet by the time of the American founding religious liberty had broadened considerably, and the main political divisions regarded religious establishments in the states. At the same time, there was general agreement that Americans were "a religious people whose institutions presuppose a Supreme Being"[37] — manifested, most obviously, in the Declaration of Independence's reference to Creator-bestowed natural rights, and in the emphasis on the importance of religion and morality in Washington's Farewell Address (echoing the Northwest Ordinance and various state constitutions).

The original understanding of church and state in the United States grew out of a particular society — one that was sociologically and intellectually (Protestant) Christian. This considerably narrowed the range of unresolvable tensions (though without completely resolving them[38]), and made it possible, on some accounts (notably Alexis de Tocqueville's), to derive considerable political benefits from religion, while maintaining a general separation of church and state. For example, Tocqueville noted that religion (by which he meant the Christian religious groups in early nineteenth century America) had the benefits of countering the typical modern democratic tendencies toward individualism and excessive

---

[37] As Justice Douglas noted in *Zorach* v. *Clauson* 343 U.S. 306 (1952).

[38] Consider the existence of considerable strains of nativism, anti-Catholicism, and anti-Semitism, the fate of Mormon polygamy, and the unpopularity of certain religious minorities (such as the Jehovah's Witnesses) that made them central figures in many modern religious liberty cases.

emphasis on physical well-being, which were dangerous both to the political community and to human beings themselves.[39]

The twentieth century has seen (besides an increasing number of unchurched but generically Christian Americans) increasing numbers of non-Christians, partly through the increase of religious minorities such as Muslims, and greater attention to the heretofore invisible Indians,[40] but more importantly perhaps, through the growing numbers of agnostics and atheists, especially among intellectual elites. The Supreme Court has undertaken the task of fashioning a new First Amendment for this more diverse society, but hardly anyone considers it to have done this satisfactorily.

The Supreme Court began its attempted adaptation of the First Amendment to the new religious sociology of the mid-twentieth century with *Everson* v. *Board of Education* in 1947.[41] A key step in this case was mandating not only federal neutrality among different religions (the command of the original First Amendment[42]) but also federal and state government neutrality between religion and non-religion. In its attempt to achieve this illusory goal of neutrality, the Court has lurched back and forth between more separationist and more accommodationist readings of the Amendment. Its secularizing decisions (especially beginning with the school prayer decisions of the 1960s) — together with decisions in some other areas undermining traditional morality[43] — were said by some to have privatized religion and to have created a naked public square.[44] At the same time, the expansion of the public square — especially the welfare

---

[39] Wolfe, "Tocqueville and the Religious Revival," *This World,* (Winter/Spring 1982) No. 1, pp. 85–96.

[40] One example of broader, and more intractable contemporary tensions can be found in *Lyng* v. *Northwest Indian Cemetery Protection Association,* 99 L.Ed.2d 534 (1988), in which Indians sued to prevent the federal government from building a road through a National Forest, on the grounds that Indians practiced religious rituals there that depended on privacy, silence, and an undisturbed natural setting. The federal government owned the land in question, but ownership and religious ritual have meanings and legal standing in Anglo-American law quite different from Indian notions of property and religious ritual.

[41] 330 U.S. 1 (1947).

[42] See Gerard V. Bradley, *Church-State Relationships in America* (Greenwood Press, 1987).

[43] See especially the obscenity and privacy decisions, such as *Memoirs* v. *Mass* 383 U.S. 413 (1966) and *Roe* v. *Wade* 410 U.S. 113 (1973).

[44] Richard John Neuhaus, *The Naked Public Square* (W.B. Eerdmans Pub. Co., 1984).

state — in modern America, had the effect of confining religion to a smaller and smaller private sphere, since government carried the principle of church-state separation with it as it expanded dramatically throughout the century.

One of the important effects of this secularizing process was to mobilize heretofore less politically engaged evangelical and fundamentalist Protestants.[45] This mobilization of the Religious Right, in turn, further stimulated elite fears of Christian domestic *jihads* (fears that gradually seeped into other strata of American society).[46]

While the Court more recently has been less separationist in a number of areas,[47] at the more theoretical level, it is striking that the Court has tended to minimize the distinctive character of religion, viewing it more and more as one subcategory of deeply held opinions[48] or of speech.[49] Religious freedom has gone from being singled out by the Constitution for special protection to being a rather indistinct element in a more broadly defined liberty.

The current conundrum facing any public philosophy is whether (and how) it is possible to guarantee a broad religious liberty (which, especially in a pluralistic society, involves both free exercise and non-establishment of religion) without in some sense advancing the particular religious view of secularism. Do modern fears (especially among elites) of manifestations

---

[45] Nathan Glazer, "Toward a New Concordat?" *This World* (Summer, 1982), No. 2, p. 109.

[46] See Alan Wolfe, *One Nation After All* (Viking, 1998). While these fears are generally unfounded, I think, it is true that some attempts to have the United States declared a Christian nation would not return to the original understanding of the First Amendment, but would reject its principle of nonpreferentialism — a principle that allowed favoring religion in general, but not particular religions.

[47] See, for example, *Agostini* v. *Felton* 138 L.Ed.2d 391 (1997), loosening the requirements for certain sorts of public support for parochial school children.

[48] See for example Justice Sandra Day O'Connor's concurrence in *Kiryas Joel* v. *Grummet* 114 S. CT. at 2497: "That the government is acting to accommodate religion should generally not change this analysis. What makes accommodation permissible, even praiseworthy, is not that the government is making life easier for some particular religious group as such. Rather, it is that the government is accommodating a deeply held belief." See also Gerard V. Bradley, "Is the Constitution What the Winners Say It Is?" a paper delivered at the conference "Reining in Judicial Imperialism," Washington, D.C. (October, 1998).

[49] See, for example, *Rectors of the University of Virginia* v. *Rosenberger* 515 U.S. 819 (1995).

of religion in the public square preclude any non-sectarian natural theology being an essential part of the public philosophy? Or are we still a religious people whose institutions presuppose a Supreme Being and can that fact be publicly recognized — and can religion be generously accommodated — without endangering religious liberty and the political equality of citizens of all religious beliefs?

## Citizenship and Immigration

A combination of the foregoing considerations hooks up with another major contemporary policy question, namely, citizenship and immigration. Culture, race, and religion are sources of difference in society, and can be viewed as fostering a diversity that enriches our nation. Indeed, there is a significant tradition in America of looking to immigration as a source of great benefits, with its contributions to the American melting pot. This diversity was possible, without undermining the core unity required for community, because the United States was unusual in the way it was founded on a certain set of ideas, especially the principles of the Declaration of Independence and the Constitution. In embracing those ideas, immigrants could quickly become Americans in more than a formal sense.

In principle, unity based on ideas should be able to transcend many differences. For example, race, by itself, should be irrelevant with respect to those ideas. But culture and religion are categories that involve precisely ideas and ways of life that reflect underlying ideas. Earlier immigration came primarily from Europe, and immigrants thus shared the heritage of "Western civilization" with their new fellow citizens, which helped to mitigate the tensions that arose from various differences, e.g., language, and in many cases the difference between American Protestant Christianity and immigrants' Catholicism.

Questions arise today from two sides. Either of these, by itself, would be much more limited in its consequences, but taken together they magnify potential concerns. First, immigrants today come from a very wide range of cultures, many of them involving cultural differences broader than those present in earlier waves of immigration. For example, the proportion of European immigrants, or immigrants from countries shaped by Europe (e.g., Latin America), has declined, as the proportion of immigrants from non-European nations and cultures (e.g., Asia and the Middle East) has increased.

Second, and more importantly, there has been a significant loss of consensus within our nation about precisely the ideas that determine what it means to be an American. If the core unity of the nation has been maintained by educating new Americans in the principles of our regime (form of government, broadly speaking), what is the likely result of increasing division within America over the meaning of those principles? How much unity is necessary to sustain the political community, and how is that unity to be secured? Under what circumstances (if any) would immigration jeopardize that unity, and what reasonable measures (educational and otherwise) might harmonize a generous policy on immigration with the requirements of national unity?

## Political Economy

I end this discussion of substantive issues by mentioning only briefly the area that has probably been the most prolific source of public policy questions in American history.[50]

Questions in this area include the balance between work and family, kinds and conditions and amount of work and the personal development of the worker, the relations between employers and employees (or between owners, managers, and workers), worker participation in ownership and direction and profits of enterprises, the availability of employment for all workers (and the availability of enough workers for jobs), the roles of businesses, unions, government, and individuals in worker (re-)training and education programs, especially in the context of rapid reallocation of resources in a modern market economy, wages and benefits (for both full-time and part-time workers), entrepreneurial freedom and the appropriate extent of government business regulation, the impact of various forms and amounts of taxation, and the adequacy of private and public provision for unemployment, illness, and old age. (Moreover, these could be multiplied by attention to numerous and complex questions regarding the international economy.)

[50] Part II of Michael Sandel's *Democracy's Discontent* (Harvard University Press, 1996) is an extensive survey of such issues in American history.

At the present time (mid-1999), the salience of political economy issues is muted somewhat by the fact that the United States has been in a period of extraordinary economic growth, frequently confounding forecasters' predictions of slowdowns. It will not always be so, of course, and in more depressed economic circumstances these issues will likely become greater sources of dispute.

## Structural Political Issues

In the preceding sections, I have focused on substantive issues of public philosophy. It is also important to note, however, that there are other, structural political and procedural questions intertwined with the substantive ones.

## The Judiciary in the Culture Wars

Perhaps the most notable is the question of the role of the judiciary in American political and social life. Cultural liberalism is strong among elites, and judges have been among the most effective implementors of elite intellectual and cultural values. This is most obviously true of the Warren Court, in its decisions on religion, obscenity, and privacy.[51] But the subsequent Burger and Rehnquist Courts, despite their conservatism relative to the Warren Court in some areas, have also shared elite cultural values in many areas. The Burger Court — though comprised largely of Republican appointees — transformed gender equal protection law, dramatically expanded privacy rights, and maintained a high wall of separation in public schools while limiting the permissibility of public support for parochial schools. The Rehnquist Court backed off overruling, and then reaffirmed the central holding of, *Roe* v. *Wade*, held that nude dancing is entitled to some First Amendment protection, and (without overruling *Bowers* v. *Hardwick*, a Burger Court decision that upheld the power of states to prohibit homosexual sodomy) overturned a state constitutional amendment designed to prohibit nondiscrimination laws for homosexuals.[52]

---

[51] Wolfe, *The Rise of Modern Judicial Review*, revised edition (Rowman and Littlefield, 1994), ch. 12.
[52] Ibid, chapters 13 and 14. Wolfe, "Burger Court Disappointments," *This World* (Fall, 1986)

In the face of these judicial interventions, Congress and the President did relatively little. In fact, it was not clear how robust was their sense that they had any *right* to oppose such judicial actions. Judicial review was certainly important in early American history, but at that time there was still widespread recognition that constitutional issues were not the sole preserve of judges, as Lincoln's response to the *Dred Scott* decision made clear.[53] By the end of the twentieth century, however, judicial power was so identified with constitutional questions that Attorney-General Edwin Meese's repetition of Lincoln's argument caused something of a furor.[54]

The Supreme Court did, unanimously, reject a call to strike down a state ban on physician-assisted suicide — but only after lower federal courts upheld such a right.[55] Will some of those lower court judges, or others like them, be on a future Supreme Court that revisits the issue? They might, or might not — but the point is that it is utterly conceivable that the Court may reverse its decision in the future.

It is worth noting, too, the asymmetry of modern Supreme Court decisions on cultural issues. The Court has served as an engine of liberal social reform in some areas, e.g., obscenity, privacy rights — especially abortion — and (with *Romer* v. *Evans*) homosexual rights. In other areas, the Court has rejected the invitation to advance such causes, e.g., homosexual sodomy rights in *Bowers*, euthanasia. But an examination of the opinions shows that there is no debate between cultural liberals and cultural conservatives on the Supreme Court. The debate is between cultural liberals and anti-judicial activists. For example, there has never been a Supreme Court "pro-life" opinion, though a claim that laws tolerating abortion violate the equal protection clause is more plausible than a claim that laws prohibiting abortion violate the due process clause. Perhaps the justices opposed to a constitutional right to abortion are correct in basing their opposition on anti-judicial activist grounds, and in refusing

No. 15, pp. 59–65. Recently, the Rehnquist Court has become more aggressively conservative in some ways, but it is typical of it that the conservatism is largely structural, on matters related to federalism.

[53] Wolfe, "Interpreting the Bill of Rights: What? Who? Why?" in G. Bryner and A. Sorensen ed., *In Celebration of the Bill of Rights* (Provo, Utah: Brigham University Press, 1995), especially pp. 67–75.

[54] Edwin Meese, "The Law of the Constitution," *Tulane Law Review* 979 (1987).

[55] *Washington* v. *Glucksberg* 138 L.Ed.2d 772 (1997).

to overturn abortion laws on equal protection grounds.[56] Nonetheless, this asymmetry does place cultural conservatives at a great disadvantage, since the educative effects of Supreme Court opinions work in favor of culturally liberal opinions. For example, if all the Court can offer in *Bowers* v. *Hardwick* as a reason sustaining sodomy laws is something along the lines of "if the people of Georgia want to do it, the Constitution doesn't tell them they can't," then should we be surprised if *Bowers* is followed by *Romer* v. *Evans*, which (wrongly) treats the position opposed to sexual orientation nondiscrimination laws as if it were based on a mere irrational animus?[57]

Cultural conservatives thus continuously labor under the burden of never knowing whether their laborious efforts in the political process to achieve certain goals, even when successful, will survive Court challenge. For example, *Planned Parenthood* v. *Casey* lowered the bar for abortion regulation somewhat, by establishing an undue burden test.[58] Abortion opponents also concentrated their efforts on limited forms of regulation, such as prohibitions of a particularly gruesome kind of late-term abortion (so-called partial-birth abortions). But even these limited prohibitions, evaluated under a less restrictive test, have been struck down by unsympathetic courts.[59] And while the Supreme Court, in recent years, has become more tolerant of certain forms of aid to parochial schools,[60] and while there has been significant movement in some states on school choice programs, it is still an open question whether the Court will uphold the constitutionality of such programs.

[56] That is my own position, as elaborated in "Natural Law and Judicial Review," in D. Forte ed., *Natural Law and Contemporary Public Policy* (Georgetown University Press, 1998). I admit, however, that a powerful case can be made for the contrary position, relying on the meaning of the word person and the interpretive norm (described by John Marshall in *Dartmouth College* v. *Woodward*) that constitutional principles apply to matters that fall within their terms, even when the founders did not have those matters in view.

[57] *Bowers* v. *Hardwick* 478 U.S. 186 (1986); *Romer* v. *Evans* 134 L.Ed.2d 855 (1996). On grounds for law and public policy to view active homosexuality as a problem, see *Homosexuality and American Public Life* (Spence Publishing Company, 1999), especially Part III.

[58] 120 L.Ed.2d 674 (1992).

[59] See, for example, Judge Richard Posner's opinion in *Planned Parenthood of Wisconsin* v. *Doyle* 1998 U.S. App. 27992 (1998).

[60] See, for example, *Agostini* v. *Felton* 138 L.Ed.2d 391 (1997).

CHRISTOPHER WOLFE

# The Marketplace(s) and Centers of Private Power

On both the right and the left, there are frequently suspicions that major decisions with society-wide impact are controlled by unaccountable institutions. This is accomplished either through behind-the-scenes power within political institutions, or through a power to shape public opinion and to manipulate it to obtain private objectives.

On the left, it is typically corporations that are considered to have this power. They use their money to buy political access and influence through campaign financing. Or, alternatively, they use advertising to shape popular desires along the lines that will serve their private interests.

On the right, it is the new class — cultural elites in education (especially the higher education "multiversities" and professional schools), journalism, literature and the arts, the media, entertainment — who are thought to exercise disproportionate influence in American government and society. These elites are not monolithic on all issues, but they are distinctly and consistently more liberal on social issues. For example, one study of the media elite has pointed out that 90 percent favor abortion and gay rights and only a small number are actively religious — a dramatic contrast with ordinary Americans.[61]

These criticisms have an underlying similarity in their dissatisfaction with market decisions. This is partly due to a suspicion that markets do not always work properly, but, more importantly, it reflects an unwillingness to take the preferences that the market responds to as simple givens. Preferences come from somewhere, and their development in individuals is not simply autonomous. Whether it is commercial advertising that shapes preferences — focusing on, appealing to, playing upon, and reinforcing particular human inclinations, at the expense of others — or the prejudices of cultural elites transmitted through institutions of education and communication, the power to shape preferences is said to give disproportionate power to certain segments of our society.

There is little doubt in my mind that there is some truth to these allegations, on both sides of the political spectrum. But the extent of shaping power is not clear. There are substantial differences, for example,

[61] Robert Lerner, Althea K. Nagai, Stanley Rothman, *American Elites* (Yale University Press, 1996).

between creating preferences, modifying them, reinforcing them, appealing to them. It is necessary to balance these effects against the fact of free will and the importance of people having opportunities to make choices, even when others are trying to manipulate them, and sometimes succeeding. Moreover — the great practical question — assuming that human beings are susceptible to various forms of shaping, what are the realistic alternatives to the economic and cultural marketplaces?

The substantial displacement of the marketplace — substituting a planned economy or planned cultural offerings — seems to be a dubious idea, if only because of the intrinsic difficulties in such planning, and — even if such planning were a plausible possibility — because of serious doubts about whether there is any institutional mechanism to guarantee that the planners chosen would be capable of performing the job well.[62] The more realistic alternative would appear to be the maintenance of the marketplace, but subject to some limited, democratic regulation. (An example that cuts across both marketplaces, and the political spectrum, is regulation of pornography.)

At the same time, difficulties concerning the determination of the proper nature and extent of that regulation, as well as the possibility — indeed, the likelihood — that such regulatory power will be abused, caution us not to employ such power too broadly. Those who are unhappy with the marketplace(s) — and there is no doubt that there is often enough reason to be unhappy — ought to be satisfied with rather limited regulation of it, and recognize the necessity of themselves competing within the marketplace to achieve their aims, with more or less success.

## The Roles of Civil Society and Government

How much of our common life as citizens of a particular polity should we coordinate through government and how much of it should exist and be conducted in the non-governmental sphere of civil society, with its great diversity of voluntary associations? Modern America, for all the resonance of cries against big government, is certainly committed to an active

---

[62] Salutary effects might be derived from encouraging partisans on both sides of the spectrum to see the parallels between the economic and cultural marketplaces. The effect of such reflection should be a healthy recognition of the problems of the marketplace, and also a healthy recognition of the problems of regulating it.

government of extensive responsibilities. It is hard even to imagine a general rolling-back of the modern administrative state.[63] And yet it seems clear that Americans have become at least somewhat less inclined to believe that the answers to their problems will come from government programs. At the same time, it also seems clear that Americans do not place unqualified faith in the market, where aggregations of individual preferences (as reflected — imperfectly — in an ability and willingness to sell and to buy goods and services) are the primary determinants in the process of allocating and reallocating resources.

In between the market and government is the world of civil society, in which human beings act together to achieve many of the ends they consider most important in their individual lives and in the lives of the communities of which they are a part. Among these communities, the family is the most important. What government could use its ordinary power of coordination of activity through law to induce parents to have children and love them and sacrifice themselves in raising them? What market analysis can explain the worth of the work done by mothers, in particular, to care for their children? While both government and market obviously can have substantial impacts on family life, the dominant forces and typical modes of analysis in neither are able to account *fully* for, to provide for, the family and its contribution to human happiness and well-being, personal and social.

In similar ways, churches, community associations, charitable and educational associations, *ad hoc* groups to advance a thousand causes, all play important and indispensable roles in our common life.[64]

A public philosophy must grapple with various questions relating to civil society. How many of our social problems can be, or must be, dealt with through civil society? What are the underlying conditions for and

---

[63] This seems clear from the relative lack of success of Republican presidents, and a revolutionary Republican Congress elected in 1994, in cutting back the size of the federal government and its programs. (They have succeeded mostly in slowing its growth.)

[64] Don E. Eberly, *America's Promise: Civil Society and the Renewal of American Culture* (Rowman and Littlefield, 1998). Americans tend to take civil society and its benefits for granted, because we have been blessed with a very rich diversity of associations. The experience of Eastern European nations, in some of which communism had destroyed most of the institutions of civil society, and whose reform depends on developing new institutions, should be a strong reminder of the importance of civil society.

sources of the different groups within civil society, and what causes them to be more or less successful in achieving the purposes for which they are formed? How are they affected — both promoted and inhibited — by government and marketplace?

Civil society should not simply be characterized as an alternative to political society, however. The two reciprocally influence each other. The institutions of civil society promote many of the qualities of democratic citizenship. And the laws of a political community, in turn, provide the conditions under which natural and voluntary associations can flourish in society.[65] It is precisely the balance between these communities, the division of responsibilities for various aspects of the common good, and their reciprocal influence on each other that are an important aspect of social life.

## Federalism and Decentralization

One set of answers to the problem of deep pluralism of beliefs in a modern extended republic is federalism and decentralization.[66] Particularly given intractable differences in cultural beliefs, and the practical impossibility of a society that is genuinely neutral on these issues, allowing diversity from state to state (and perhaps from community to community within states) is one response. For example, in *Miller* v. *California*,[67] the Supreme Court acknowledged a legitimate power of states (within certain limits) to adopt different standards for obscenity. Why, it is asked, should a rural Alabama county and New York City have to operate with a single, unitary, national standard?

There are obviously some advantages and disadvantages to the decentralization solution. Even those who believe that there is an objectively right position on an issue that society ought to adopt can recognize that their political power may be insufficient to achieve this standard for the nation. Under such circumstances, the possibility of living

---

[65] See Gertrude Himmelfarb, "The Trouble With Civil Society" in *Unum Conversation*, Number 4 (Ethics and Public Policy Center, Washington, D.C., based on an Unum Project seminar, January 28, 1997).

[66] Note that many of the arguments of this section apply not only to federalism and decentralization, but to privatization as well.

[67] 413 U.S. 15 (1973).

in a more limited jurisdiction that upholds the standard may be considered better than living under some muddled national compromise, or even the possibility of losing the political battle entirely.

On the other hand, the decentralization approach means that it is more likely that somewhere in the nation, state laws will protect activities that are, not just vaguely undesirable, but evil, and some people may consider that their moral obligations or essential goals extend beyond just not participating in or being subject to this evil — to eradicating it. One of the reasons, after all, for the earlier Supreme Court contraction of federalism and states' rights was the sense that it had been used too much to protect racist legal orders in the South.

More objectionable forms of human behavior that might not be able to obtain legitimacy and legal protection nationally, might do so in states and localities. (Liberals might think of sexism, conservatives of pornography and gay rights.) If paying a fairly steep price is considered worthwhile, relocation may make it possible for individuals to follow a course prohibited elsewhere (e.g., companies moving to places where laws protecting workers or the environment are weaker, homosexuals moving to friendlier sites). Once a behavior is established locally, it might be difficult to prevent its eventual normalization in the wider political community (e.g., gay rights, certain abortion restrictions), and, economically, it might provide a competitive advantage to certain (less socially-conscious) businesses over others, in the national market.

Or, alternatively, even if restrictive laws in some states keep the behavior local or regional, the price of the activity, and its availability, may simply be increased by the cost of a trip to an area where it (e.g., an abortion) is permitted.

How satisfactory a decentralization solution is, then, depends on various factors: the perceived magnitude of the evil sought to be prohibited or the good to be obtained, and how the activity is affected concretely by this kind of solution; whether the national truce and local options are likely to remain stable over time; what is the perceived likelihood of the truce giving way to victory for one side or the other; how willing one is to accept the half cup rather than fighting for the whole one, risking the chance of losing everything.

## Common Core Values?

One final, very important question that flows naturally from the issue of decentralization is: how much does the entire community need common core values, and what should these values be, and how will they be transmitted? For example, advocates of public education (and opponents of school choice) have traditionally stressed the role the public schools play in guaranteeing and transmitting core political values of the nation, as a factor providing some balance to the nation's great diversity.[68] Paradoxically, advocates of private education and school choice often argue that one of the chief problems with contemporary public education is its inability to identify and foster key common moral values on which the community depends, and that private education achieves this goal more successfully.[69]

The debate over substantive issues confronting public philosophy today can, in some ways, be seen as a dispute between two fundamental philosophical/theological perspectives. Life and death issues pit those who have a clear definition of life and definite moral demands regarding it against those who find the question of life much less clear-cut and the moral standards regarding it sufficiently unclear to call for leaving the question up to the individuals involved. Family issues involve contention between groups that have a relatively clear and unitary definition of the family against those who, impressed by historical and cultural diversity, prefer to speak of families and to deny that one set of moral views regarding marriage, family, and sexuality can be imposed on all people. Gender issues often are characterized as debates between those who believe that nature establishes norms that call for the fulfillment of particular gender roles and those who regard these roles as artificial and unjust constraints on opportunity for women. Cultural issues involve an evaluation of the ways in which various people use their leisure time, some people applying objective standards and concluding that various elements of popular (and elite) culture are debased, and others doubtful that there are truly objective standards in light of which such judgments could be made.

[68] See, for example, Justice Frankfurter's Court opinion in *Minersville School District* v. *Gobitis* 310 U.S. 586 (1940).
[69] Charles Glenn, *The Myth of the Common School* (University of Massachusetts Press, 1988), and *Educational Freedom in Eastern Europe* (Cato Institute, 1995).

Race issues — especially insofar as there is general public agreement in principle on racial equality of opportunity — tend to gravitate toward issues of diversity and multiculturalism, which often involve questions of whether canons containing disproportionately the contributions of the "dead, white males" of Western civilization should give way to new or newly discovered voices of "marginalized" groups in society, whose voices are as important as anyone else's. Religious issues find one side believing that there is a core or least common denominator of religious belief in the nation (ranging from various forms of Christianity through a generic Judeo-Christian heritage to a very limited or thin theism), which may legitimately be invoked in the public square, and another side believing that religion — however important personally, and perhaps precisely because so important *personally* — should be completely private, with no place in public life. Citizenship issues may place at odds those who have a more determinate conception of the America that immigrants are joining — a conception that immigrants should be able to and be educated to embrace — and others who are somewhat dubious about what Americanism might be and would confine it (if they define it at all) to accepting basic democratic procedures and rights.

In each of these oppositions, there is one side that is somewhat more optimistic that, as a people, we can identify and act on at least some of the truth about the human person, while the other side is more sceptical about whether such truth (if it even exists) is knowable with any certitude and whether it belongs in the public sphere.

But it is too simple to say that the opposition is between believers and sceptics.[70] For the sceptics — precisely because of their belief in the limits of knowledge regarding human ends — believe strongly that certain principles flow from *that* knowledge (the knowledge of our limits): above all, the priority of (a certain autonomy-centered understanding of) human rights. Sceptics, no less than others, have certain fundamental doctrines, to guide their actions and persuade their fellow citizens. Ultimately, then, these issues involve debate and competition regarding different substantive positions on questions about the nature and goals of human beings. That

---

[70] Believers here is meant to include philosophical and ethical doctrines or opinions as well as theological or religious beliefs.

is why they are unavoidably central to discussions (explicit or implicit) about the public philosophy of a nation.

## The Current Situation: Contenders for the American Public Philosophy

This paper is part of a longer project on liberalism, natural law, and American public philosophy. As I have worked through some of the issues surrounding contemporary liberalism, I have been struck by how it is possible to make basically the same argument in strikingly different ways, with very different tones. To a great extent, these different ways of saying the same thing are possible because of the considerable ambiguity of the term liberalism. Let me lay out here, briefly, two of the different ways in which these issues might be viewed.

## Resisting the Call to a New, Purified Liberalism

One way to join in current debates over liberalism, from a natural law perspective, would be the following. Contemporary liberal democratic theory is currently in crisis, and for good reason: it fails to provide an adequate public philosophy. It is inadequate precisely because it is a more "purified" and consistent form of liberal democracy than an older form of liberalism — the one generally dominant in the American founding — since it has been stripped of certain key pre-liberal elements that were necessary to make sound liberal democratic government possible.

The current debate over liberalism can be traced to John Rawls' *A Theory of Justice* (1971), which resurrected social contract theory and gave it a more egalitarian form, drawing on Kant to provide a stronger foundation for liberal rights than utilitarian moral theory seemed able to. A particularly important element of Rawlsian political theory was the requirement that government be "neutral" on questions about the human good.[71] But Rawls' version of liberalism was subjected to powerful critiques from several different directions, including Michael Sandel, Alasdair MacIntyre, and various members of the critical legal studies

---

[71] For an excellent and concise summary of Rawls, see Michael Pakaluk, "The Liberalism of John Rawls: A Brief Exposition," in Wolfe and J. Hittinger, eds., *Liberalism at the Crossroads* (Rowman and Littlefield, 1994).

movement, who had in common a rejection of Rawls' liberal individualism. They denied the possibility of such neutrality and ascertained in Rawls at least some theory of the human good.[72] Nor did Rawls' revised theory in *Political Liberalism* — which backed off what he conceded to be the "comprehensive liberalism" of *A Theory of Justice* — mollify his critics. Indeed, his new central notion of public reason was thought by many to exacerbate difficulties.[73]

There were various possible responses to the perception that Rawls' project had been unsuccessful. One response was to admit theoretical defeat and defend liberalism on pragmatic grounds (as Richard Rorty did). Another possible response was simply to jettison liberalism altogether, opting for the radical program of "critique is all there is" (e.g., Mark Tushnet). Yet another was to deny that liberalism is essentially hostile to a public notion of the human good and to put forward a form of liberal "perfectionism" (e.g., William Galston).[74]

Another, somewhat different response (though it has much in common with the third response above) is the following. Antiperfectionist liberals such as David A.J. Richards look back on earlier liberal thinkers (such as Locke, Kant, and Rousseau) and see in them the seeds, the "incomplete" forms, of their own more "purified" and consistent liberalism.[75] They are certainly correct to see in classical liberalism certain principles that are not fully compatible with contemporary liberal theory. But one might draw quite different conclusions from these differences. It is possible to argue that liberalism cannot, in fact, flourish without the very principles these contemporary liberals would like to winnow out. Two different examples of these non-liberal elements would be a realist epistemology (the belief that it is possible to attain objective knowledge, including knowledge of

---

[72] Ibid, articles on Sandel (by Terry Hall), MacIntytre (by David Wagner) and Roberto Unger (by Russell Hittinger).

[73] Wolfe, ed., *Natural Law and Public Reason* (forthcoming, Georgetown University Press, 2000).

[74] See *Liberalism at the Crossroads*, articles on Rorty (by Gerard Bradley) and Galston (by Brian Benestad), and Wolfe "Grand Theories and Ambiguous Republican Critique: Tushnet on Constitutional Law" in *Law and Social Inquiry (Journal of the American Bar Foundation)* Vol. 15, Number 4 (Fall, 1990), pp. 831–876.

[75] David A. J. Richards, "Rights and Autonomy," in *Ethics* Vol. 92 (October, 1981), pp. 3–20.

human ends and moral values) and natural intermediary institutions (especially family and church).

Enlightenment epistemologies that classical liberals such as Locke and Kant embraced ended up by cutting modern thinkers off from the real world, i.e., from everything but our perceptions of it. The long evolution of that epistemology leaves us in the twentieth century with theories of interpretation that — if they were carried to their logical conclusions — would make any knowledge of reality or communication about it impossible. But for how long can a system of liberal rights flourish in a world without "truth"? How solid can rights be if they are not rooted in an order that at once transcends human opinion and is open to human comprehension?

Liberalism of its very nature aims to achieve a world of liberty, in which human rights are effectually protected. But another aspect of liberal democracy is its tendency toward individualism, and its understanding of intermediary associations, especially religious communities and families, as "merely" voluntary associations. If churches and families are viewed that way, however, as merely human creations, alterable or revocable at human will, then they may be weakened and their capacity to flourish and provide satisfying human communities may thereby be endangered. Religion does, in fact, appear to be much weaker today, and the decline in the strength of the family would be accepted by all, if we could only agree on what a family is (which we can't).

The decline of strong "natural" communities, besides undercutting simple personal human happiness, creates serious difficulties for the transmission of those qualities that together make up "civic virtue."[76] Along with this, there is the danger, as Tocqueville argued, that liberal democracies may leave an increasingly isolated individual confronting an increasingly powerful state.[77]

Liberalism, in this view, has always needed certain prerequisites that it is not adept at providing itself. If modern liberal polities such as America have been successful, it is because they have been heirs to a

[76] Eberly, ed., *The Content of America's Character* (Madison Books, 1995) and Glendon and Blankenhorn, ed., *Seedbeds of Virtue* (Madison Books, 1995).
[77] Alexis de Tocqueville, *Democracy in America* (Random House, 1945), especially Vol. II, Book IV.

legacy whose influence they undercut. The legacy of classical and medieval thought has helped to provide a framework within which liberal democratic political arrangements could be successful, for reasons described, again, by Tocqueville.[78] The constant flux of liberal politics has occurred within a more constant moral framework, derived especially from the natural right and natural law traditions that were so influential in the formation of Western civilization. It has been precisely this "incompleteness" of liberalism — its willingness to coexist with principles derived from pre-liberal thought — that has made it successful.

In sum, then, the dominant, antiperfectionist form of liberalism is in a state of intellectual disarray. Liberalism may still constitute the center of gravity among intellectual elites, but it is a decidedly embattled orthodoxy that is having difficulty offering compelling responses to its critics. The most effective response to this crisis is to recognize the habitual shortcomings of liberalism, and to remedy them with a healthy dose of pre-liberal thought, drawing especially on the natural right and natural law traditions.

## The Choice Among Various Liberalisms

Another way of characterizing the current situation would start out by suggesting caution in any discussion of liberalism. Rather than concede to contemporary, mainstream, antiperfectionist liberalism the status of legitimate heir and successor to early, classical liberalism, this approach might more hesitantly note that there is a whole range of liberalisms that claim that mantle. Moreover, once the focus is taken off the question of which position has the most right to call itself liberalism, we can focus our quest, not on the right or best liberalism, or indeed on any form of liberalism per se, but simply on the best public philosophy applicable to our own times and circumstances. This approach may have the advantage of conducting the debate under the umbrella of liberalism, which does seem to be a widely shared set of ideas that are at the center of debate about the American public philosophy, without reducing the debate to a semantic struggle as to which theory has the best warrant for claiming the title of liberalism.

[78] Ibid., Vol. I, chap. 2 and 17, and Vol. II, Book I, chap. 2.

The choices available in current discussion of public philosophy seem to be: Antiperfectionist Liberalism, Radical or Post-Modern (Super)liberalism, Communitarian Liberalism, Libertarian Liberalism, Classical Liberalism, and Perfectionist Liberalism. These different forms of liberalism are not always sharply differentiated — indeed, some of them blend into other forms rather substantially. Yet each is distinctive enough, I think, to merit discussion. While I must defer to the future a detailed discussion of these options, I would like to conclude this article by giving a very brief description of them, as a way of lightly outlining the current landscape of thinking about American public philosophy.

*Antiperfectionist Liberalism*: The dominant form of liberalism today, in the academic world, is one that has tried to achieve a peaceful system of social cooperation by bracketing substantive questions of political morality. Government must be neutral on comprehensive philosophical and theological questions, confining itself to matters of the just, as distinguished from the right or the good. The goal of liberal democracy is to guarantee to all individuals the basic liberties and necessary resources for pursuing their own life-plans. Prominent among antiperfectionist liberals are John Rawls, Ronald Dworkin, Bruce Ackerman, David A.J. Richards, and Stephen Macedo (though Macedo and Dworkin, at least, would be willing to grant that they are comprehensive liberals and that there are greater limits to liberal neutrality than Rawls would admit.)[79]

*Libertarianism*: Liberals tend to advocate a broad liberty, and to be suspicious of government intervention, in social and cultural matters, but their commitment to equality leads them to recognize a broader role for government in economic matters. Libertarians believe that liberals should carry over their commitment to neutrality and their suspicion of government into economic matters as well. Government's job is the very limited one of protecting the framework within which individuals can pursue their own good, as they see it. Interpersonal cooperation is necessary for human life, of course, but this can generally be secured most effectively by voluntary contracts, with government's function being the

---

[79] John Rawls, *A Theory of Justice* and *Political Liberalism*; Ronald Dworkin *The Tanner Lectures on Human Values* Vol. 2 (University of Utah Press, 1990); Bruce Ackerman *Social Justice in the Liberal State*; David A.J. Richards *Toleration and the Constitution* (Oxford University Press, 1986); Stephen Macedo *Liberal Virtues* (Oxford University Press, 1990).

even-handed enforcement of commutative justice. Leading libertarians would include Friedrich Hayek, Milton Friedman, Randy Barnett, Douglas Rasmussen and Douglas Van Den Uyl, and Leonard Liggio.[80]

***Radical or Post-Modern (Super)liberalism***: Radical or post-modern liberalism is most obviously a strident critique of liberalism, and is usually not thought of as a variant form of liberalism at all. Liberalism is condemned because its formal guarantees of equality and liberty are held to be masks or covers for a continuation of various forms of domination and oppression. Only by uprooting traditional patterns of hierarchy and privileged forms of thought and speech is it possible to achieve freedom, in the form of continual re-inventing of the self. A Critical Legal Studies exponent, Roberto Unger, has a valuable description of this post-modern viewpoint:

> . . . it represents superliberalism. It pushes the liberal premises about state and society, about freedom from dependence and governance of social relations by the will, to the point at which they merge into a large ambition: the building of a social world less alien to a self that can always violate the generative rules of its own mental or social constructs and put other rules and constructs in their place.[81]

The radical critique of liberalism is generally that liberalism has not been sufficiently true to the implications of its own premises: the inability of the human intellect to grasp an objective reality and the absence of a knowable natural order that constrains human freedom. This group of post-modern thinkers includes, besides the Critical Legal Studies movement, Richard Rorty and radical feminists.[82]

---

[80] Friedrich von Hayek, *The Constitution of Liberty,* (University of Chicago Press, 1960); Milton Friedman, *Capitalism and Freedom*, (University of Chicago Press, 1962); Randy Barnett, *The Structure of Liberty: Justice and the Rule of Law*, (Oxford University Press, 1998); Douglas Rasmussen and Douglas Van Den Uyl, *Liberty And Nature: An Aristotelian Defense Of Liberal Order,* (Open Court Press, 1991).

[81] Unger, *The Critical Legal Studies Movement* (Harvard University Press, 1983), p. 4; cited in Russell Hittinger, Roberto Unger: "Liberalism and Superliberalism," in *Liberalism at the Crossroads*, p. 120.

[82] Richard Rorty, *Achieving Our Country: Leftist Thought in Twentieth-Century America* (Harvard University Press, 1998); see also Peter Berkowitz on Rorty and other radical thinkers [his article, chapter 10, in this volume].

*Communitarian Liberalism*: Another line of criticism of antiperfectionist liberalism comes from communitarians. Indeed, communitarianism is largely defined by its critique of liberalism. Communitarians are liberals who criticize what they regard as the excessive individualism of antiperfectionist liberalism, and its excessive emphasis on rights and attempts to avoid substantive moral questions. At the same time, they also distance themselves from the right, rejecting the individualism of libertarianism and the focus of the market on maximizing individual preferences. Self-consciously centrist, communitarians believe in community—against the individualism of right-wing libertarianism and left-wing liberalism — but are hesitant to spell out the substantive content of this community, tending to emphasize the need for public discussion and deliberation to determine community values. Likewise, they believe in virtue — against the moral neutrality of the (antiperfectionist) liberal and libertarian ideals — but tend to focus on less divisive virtues (e.g., toleration and civility), emphasizing issues that cut across the right/left political divide, and avoiding the hard cases that would divide their ranks (e.g., abortion). Moreover, their emphasis on the voluntary associations of civil society reflects their (liberal?) suspicion of legal efforts to promote morality. They are also somewhat divided over the importance of religion, some recognizing its value in promoting virtue and community, but others worried about its potential for divisiveness and authoritarianism. Prominent among communitarians are Michael Sandel, Mary Ann Glendon, Amitai Etzioni, and Jean Bethke Elshtain.[83]

*Sober Classical Liberalism*: Antiperfectionist liberals tend to see their own theory as a simple working out of the implications of the basic principles of early or classical liberalism, such as that of John Locke, and critics of liberalism often accept their claim. But there are also liberals who deny that classical liberalism contains an inner logic compelling it in the (extreme) direction of contemporary antiperfectionist liberalism, arguing that classical liberalism was self-conscious and reflective in its refusal to push some principles too far. In particular, these liberals are

---

[83] Michael Sandel, *Liberalism and the Limits of Justice* (Cambridge University Press, 1982) and *Democracy's Discontent*, (Harvard University Press, 1996); Mary Ann Glendon, *Rights Talk: The Impoverishment Of Political Discourse* (Free Press, 1991); Amitai Etzioni, *The New Golden Rule: Community And Morality In A Democratic Society* (Basic Books, 1996); Jean Bethke Elshtain [her article, chapter 2, in this volume].

likely to reject what they regard as the excesses of 1960s counter-cultural liberalism.

Various elements of (non-sectarian) religion, morality, and family, for example, are not properly regarded merely as vestiges of pre-liberal political communities that must be sifted out of liberalism, but are considered constituent elements of healthy liberal societies (within proper limits). Important elements of political moderation are thought to flow from the commercial character of modern liberal democracies. And liberal principles such as free speech need not be absolutized, by being extended, for example, to groups that are unwilling to accept basic principles of liberal democracy and that would only use free speech as a tool to undermine liberal democratic freedoms and replace them with some ideology.

What distinguishes this group from perfectionist liberals is their fuller acceptance of the natural rights project of modern political philosophy, and their greater scepticism about the political relevance of the full human good (whether based on reason or revelation). Examples of these sober classical liberals include Walter Berns, Peter Berkowitz, and Catherine and Michael Zuckert.[84]

**Perfectionist Liberalism**: If liberalism is concerned with liberty and limited government, and if it arose historically as an alternative to regimes lacking a strong and clearly delineated separation of church and state, nonetheless, these origins do not rule out a form of liberalism that is perfectionist, that is, a form of liberalism that argues for the political relevance of an intelligible and rather broad human good. Such perfectionist liberals tend to take their orientation from natural right (Plato and Aristotle) and natural law (Augustine and Thomas Aquinas).[85]

Government must be sensitive to a political community's moral ecology, and shaping character is a legitimate function of government. At

[84] Walter Berns [his article in this volume]; Peter Berkowitz [his article, chapter 10, in this volume]; Michael Zuckert, *The Natural Rights Republic* (University of Notre Dame, 1996); Catherine Zuckert [her article, chapter 2, in this volume].

[85] For the record, though, I should note that it can be argued that comprehensive liberals (e.g., Stephen Macedo, and the later Dworkin) — who argue that liberalism is desirable not because it is neutral on the human good, but because it fosters human goods more successfully — represent modern variants of perfectionism (though it is a very formalistic perfectionism).

the same time, perfectionist *liberals* are different from perfectionists *simpliciter* in that they emphasize that the appropriate scope of government is limited to those matters that touch most directly on the common good, and that there are some moral issues that touch the common good only indirectly and do not typically fall under the purview of government. Promoting virtue *as such* may not be the legitimate goal of government, but it may be an important instrumental goal (i.e., instrumental to the protection of life, liberty, and property, or to the attainment of the *common* good). (However, given the fact that natural law theory requires limited government and important human rights — though the language of rights is used explicitly only in more modern formulations of natural law, not in the classic sources — one interesting question is where one might draw the line to say, "beyond this point, a perfectionist, natural law theorist cannot be considered a liberal"?) Among perfectionist liberals one might count (the later) Alasdair MacIntyre, William Galston, and (especially more recently) John Finnis.[86]

As I indicated in the beginning of this section, these six different positions overlap significantly at times. Communitarianism, classical liberalism, and perfectionist liberalism blend into each other in important ways, and particular contemporary theorists might easily be placed in more than one of these groups. (For example, Galston is viewed by some as a communitarian, while I believe that his theoretical work places him in a more liberal perfectionist camp.)

These, then, are two different approaches to formulating the current state of American public philosophy from a natural law perspective. We can view recent liberal political theory as a move toward a more consistent liberalism, purified of the vestiges of pre-liberal thought the earliest exponents of liberalism had neglected to purge — and this more consistent liberalism can be viewed as being damaged by the loss of certain essential preconditions that it inherited from classical political thought. According to this view, what we need is a form of mixed government — not a mixture of the one, the few, and the many, but a mixture of liberalism, with its

---

[86] Alasdair MacIntyre, *Three Rival Versions Of Moral Enquiry: Encyclopaedia, Genealogy, And Tradition* (University of Notre Dame Press, 1990); William Galston, *Liberal Purposes: Goods, Virtues, and Diversity In The Liberal State* (Cambridge University Press, 1991); John Finnis, "Is Natural Law Theory Compatible with Limited Government?" George, ed., in *Natural Law, Liberalism, and Morality* (Oxford University Press, 1996).

focus on liberty and rights, and classical and medieval political philosophy, with their emphasis on the human good and duties.[87] Liberal democracy can be a good form of government, according to this view, as long as it is moderately liberal and moderately democratic.

Or, on the other hand, we can view liberal political theory today as offering us a range of possible liberalisms to choose from. These would include: the form of liberalism that has been dominant in late twentieth century Anglo-American academic circles, the antiperfectionist liberalism especially associated with John Rawls; libertarianism, liberalism with a deeper distrust of government, a greater emphasis on property rights, and a less egalitarian cast; the radical critique of liberalism, or superliberalism, with its focus on overturning oppression masked by formalistic liberal equality and on pursuing the radical freedom of self-creation; a more centrist critique, communitarianism, that seeks to balance the liberal focus on the individual and rights with an emphasis on various human communities and responsibilities (tempered by typical liberal concerns about abuses of authority); the sober classical liberalism of Locke and his modern followers, who reject perfectionism, but recognize the need for a certain moderation and certain civic virtues that they see as flowing from within liberalism itself (perhaps especially from the enlightened self-interest of a commercial society); and perfectionist liberalism, with its focus on the achievement on a rich and varied common good, which includes important aspects of limited government and the protection of human rights. From the perspective of perfectionist liberals especially (though also from communitarianism and sober classical liberalism), liberal democracy can be a good form of government, as long as it is moderately liberal and moderately democratic.

---

[87] It could be argued, however, that this modern mixed government really is a variation of the more traditional mixed government, since liberty and rights tend to be associated especially with the rule of the many, democracy, and the human good and duties tend to be associated especially with aristocratic or oligarchic rule.

# About the Contributors

**Peter Berkowitz** is a Professor of Law at George Mason University. Prior to joining the faculty of George Mason University, he was an Assistant Professor of Government at Harvard University. In 1994, Harvard awarded him the Hoopes Prize for excellence in teaching. Books written by Dr. Berkowitz include *Virtue and the Making of Modern Liberalism* and *Nietzsche: The Ethics of an Immoralist*. He has also written articles for numerous journals including *Commentary*, *The New Republic*, *Yale Law Journal*, and *Review of Politics*. A former John M. Olin Faculty Fellow, Dr. Berkowitz serves on the Advisory Committee of the Shalom Hartman Institute's Center for Jewish Political Thought. He earned his Ph.D. in Political Science from Yale University.

**Walter Berns** is a Resident Scholar at the American Enterprise Institute and the John M. Olin University Professor Emeritus at Georgetown University. He has been the recipient of a Carnegie Teaching Fellowship, Fulbright Fellowship, Guggenheim Fellowship, and Rockefeller Fellowship. A former U.S. Navy Lieutenant, Dr. Berns has served as a member of the Judicial Fellows Commission and the National Council on the Humanities. He has written eight books including *Freedom, Virtue, and the First Amendment*, and *In Defense of Liberal Democracy*. Dr. Berns has contributed to numerous journals and newspapers including *The American Political Science Review*, *Commentary*, *The Washington Post*, and *The Wall Street Journal*. He received his Ph.D. from the University of Chicago.

# ABOUT THE CONTRIBUTORS

**Mark Blitz** is the Fletcher Jones Professor of Political Philosophy at Claremont McKenna College. He has written one book entitled *Heidegger's 'Being and Time' and the Possibility of Political Philosophy*. Dr. Blitz has served as senior research fellow of the Hudson Institute and as associate director of the United States Information Agency. He is a member of the advisory boards of *Political Science Reviewer* and *Interpretation* and has published articles in both journals. Dr. Blitz has also written articles for *Perspectives on Political Science*, *The Public Interest*, and *The Weekly Standard*. He completed his Ph.D. in Political Science at Harvard University.

**Douglas J. Den Uyl** is a Professor of Philosophy at Bellarmine College. He has written several books including *Liberalism Defended* and *The Virtue of Prudence*. Articles written by Dr. Den Uyl have appeared in numerous journals including *International Journal for Philosophy of Religion*, *Social Philosophy and Policy*, and *Public Affairs Quarterly*. He is a member of the American Philosophical Association and the American Association for the Philosophic Study of Society. Dr. Den Uyl is also co-founder and executive board member of the Adam Smith Society. He received his Ph.D. in Philosophy from Marquette University.

**Jean Bethke Elshtain** is the Laura Spelman Rockefeller Professor of Social and Political Ethics at the University of Chicago Divinity School. She has been a visiting professor at Harvard University, Oberlin College, and Yale University. Dr. Elshtain has published fifteen books and is the author of more than four-hundred essays which have appeared in scholarly journals and journals of civic opinion. She also writes a regular column for *The New Republic*. Dr. Elshtain has received four honorary degrees. She serves as chair of the Council on Families in America and the Council on Civil Society. She is also a member of the National Commission for Civic Renewal. Dr. Elshtain received her Ph.D. in Political Science from Brandeis University.

**Daniel J. Mahoney** is an Associate Professor of Politics at Assumption College. His areas of specialization include democratic theory and statesmanship and contemporary political thought. Dr. Mahoney has authored or edited numerous books including *Privilege and Liberty:*

*Selected Writings of Aurel Kolnai* and *De Gaulle: Statesmanship, Grandeur and Modern Democracy*. Articles written by Dr. Mahoney have appeared in *The National Interest, Encyclopedia of Democracy*, and *Perspectives on Political Science*. In 1997-1998, he served as an advisory board member to C-SPAN's Alexis de Tocqueville television series. Dr. Mahoney received his Ph.D. in Political Science from the Catholic University of America.

**Wilfred M. McClay** is an Associate Professor of History at Tulane University. In 1997, he was named to the Templeton Honor Rolls for Education in a Free Society. Dr. McClay has served as a Fellow of the Woodrow Wilson International Center for Scholars and the National Endowment for the Humanities. He has authored or edited four books including *The Masterless: Self and Society in Modern America* and *American Intellectual Culture*. Dr. McClay's work has also been published in *The Public Interest, The Encyclopedia of Politics and Religion, Commentary*, and *International Journal of Politics, Culture, and Society*. He earned a Ph.D. in History from Johns Hopkins University.

**Gilbert Meilaender** is the Board of Directors Professor of Christian Ethics at Valparaiso University. He has written eight books including *The Theory and Practice of Virtue* and *Faith and Faithfulness: Basic Themes in Christian Ethics*. Dr. Meilaender's articles have appeared in *Theological Studies, Journal of Religious Ethics*, and *Faith and Philosophy*. He serves on the advisory boards of *Dialog* and *First Things*. Dr. Meilaender is a member of the American Theological Society, the Society of Christian Ethics, and the American Academy of Religion. He is also a Fellow of the Hastings Center. Dr. Meilaender received his Ph.D. from Princeton University.

**David Walsh** is a Professor of Politics at the Catholic University of America. He is the recipient of two University of South Carolina Summer Research Grants, five Earhart Foundation Summer Fellowship Grants, a National Endowment for the Humanities Fellowship, a Bradley Foundation Summer Research Grant, and a Bradley Foundation Fellowship. Dr. Walsh is the author of four books including most recently, *Guarded By Mystery: Meaning in a Postmodern Age*. He has published numerous book reviews and regularly contributes editorial articles to the *Chicago Tribune*, the *Los Angeles Times*, the *Philadelphia Inquirer*, *The Wall Street Journal*, and *The Washington Post*. Dr. Walsh earned his Ph.D. from the University of Virginia.

**Christopher Wolfe** is a Professor of Political Science at Marquette University. He has received fellowships from the Earhart Foundation and the National Endowment for the Humanities. In 1997, Dr. Wolfe was named to the Templeton Honor Rolls for Education in a Free Society. He has authored numerous books including *The Family, Civil Society, and the State*; *Liberalism at the Crossroads: An Introduction to Contemporary Liberal Political Theory and Its Critics*; and *Essays on Faith and Liberal Democracy*. Dr. Wolfe is a member of the American Public Philosophy Institute, the American Political Science Association, and the Federalist Society. He completed his Ph.D. at Boston University.

**Catherine Heldt Zuckert** is a Professor of Political Science at the University of Notre Dame. In 1998, she was named to the Templeton Honor Rolls for Education in a Free Society. Dr. Zuckert has received numerous honors including fellowships from the Earhart Foundation and the National Endowment for the Humanities. Her books include *Natural Right and the American Imagination: Political Philosophy in Novel Form*; *Postmodern Platos: Nietzsche, Heidegger, Gadamer, Strauss and Derrida*; and *Understanding the Political Spirit: Philosophical Reflections from Socrates to Nietzsche*. Dr. Zuckert's articles have appeared in *The Chronicle of Higher Education*, *Journal of Politics*, and *The New Federalist Papers*. She completed her Ph.D. at the University of Chicago.

# *Editors*

**T. William Boxx** is chairman and CEO of the Philip M. McKenna Foundation in Latrobe, Pennsylvania. He is co-founder of the Center for Economic and Policy Education at Saint Vincent College.

**Gary M. Quinlivan** is a Professor of Economics and chairman of the economics, political science, and public policy departments at Saint Vincent College. He is also an adjunct faculty member at Carnegie Mellon University. Dr. Quinlivan is co-founder and executive director of the Center for Economic and Policy Education.

# Index

*References to footnotes are indicated by an* n.

# INDEX

# INDEX

"more perfect structure," 2, 3
movies
  "My Darling Clementine," 22–23
  "Who Shot Liberty Valence?" 23
*Mr. Sammler's Planet*, Bellow, Saul, 180–181
multiculturalism, 41, 47, 188–189. *See also* citizenship; pluralism
"My Darling Clementine," 22–23
*Myth of the Common School, The*, Glenn, Charles, 184n. 24

Nagel, Thomas, *Last Word, The*, 42–43
National Endowment for the Arts, 187–188
Native Americans, 191n. 40
natural law, 134, 135, 212
natural rights, 107–108, 164, 212. *See also* autonomy
nature, 107–108
negative liberty, 164
neutrality of government, 184n. 27, 188, 191–192, 205, 209
*New York Times*, 132–133
*Nicomachean Ethics*, Aristotle, 3n. 4
Nietzsche, Friedrich Wilhelm, 143
  *Beyond Good and Evil*, 156–157
norms, 16–17, 70–72, 74–76, 82, 145–146, 191n. 40. *See also* metanormative principles
*Northwest Indian Cemetery Protection Association, Lyng* v., 191n. 40
nothingness, 26

objects of human desire, 58–61
obligation, 65, 66, 76
*Obligations*, Walzer, Michael, 48
obscenity, 201

O'Connor, Sandra Day, 192n. 48
*Old Regime and the Revolution, The*, Tocqueville, Alexis de, 29
*One Nation After All*, Wolfe, Alan, 18–19, 20, 22
*On Liberty*, Mill, John Stuart, 71, 159, 162
"On Modern Individualism," Manent, Pierre, 26–27
order, 70–71, 72, 82n
"orthodox ecumenicals," 132

Paine, Tom, 11
Panopticon, Bentham's, 163
papal doctrine, 15
  *See also* Paul, Pope John, II
parenting, 4–6, 9, 181, 182–183, 203
partial-birth abortion, 197
particular identity, 44, 46, 47–48, 49–52, 54
patriotism, 10–13
Paul, Pope John, II, 20, 37–38, 39, 171–172
  *Evangelium Vitae*, 38
  *Fides et Ratio*, 38, 147
peace and commodious living, 59–60
peace and order, 82n
People for The American Way, 129
perfectionist liberalism, 212–214
persecution, 141, 145, 146. *See also* justification
Pheidippides (son in *Clouds*), 138–141
philosophy, principles of, xi–xii, 146–147, 150–153, 157, 164–165, 172–173. *See also Clouds*
*Philosophy and the Mirror of Nature*, Rorty, Richard, 164
physical force, 141, 145, 146
*Pico, Board of Education,* v., 184

228